ZION LIBERATED

Former
British
Palestine
Mandate
Boundaries

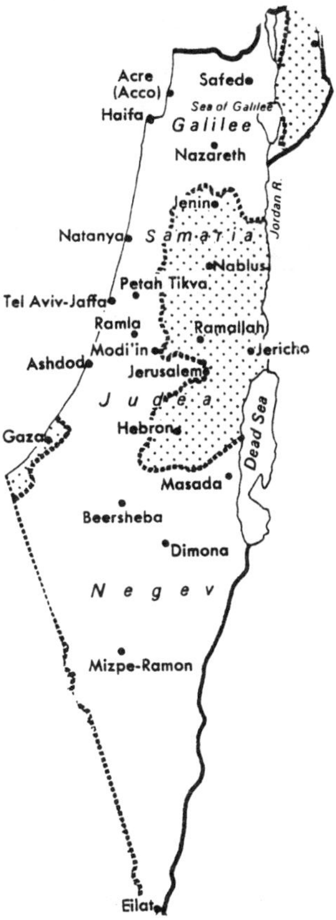

ZION LIBERATED

THE LIFE AND TIMES OF MAX SELIGMAN, C.B.E.; DEFENDER OF JEWISH UNDERGROUND FIGHTERS IN THE BRITISH MILITARY COURTS; JEWISH NATION-BUILDING UNDER THE BRITISH MANDATE IN PALESTINE

by

GIVEON CORNFIELD

Joseph Simon Pangloss Press

Library of Congress Cataloging-in-Publication Data

Cornfield, Giveon, 1926–
Zion liberated : the life and times of Max Seligman / by Giveon Cornfield
p. cm.
Includes bibliographical references and index.
ISBN 0-934710-22-8 : $27.50
1. Seligman, Max, b. 1902. 2. Zionists—Palestine—Biography. 3. Lawyers—Palestine—Biography. 4. Irgun tseva'i le'umi—Trials, litigation, etc. 5. Trials (Political crimes and offenses)—Palestine. I. Title.
DS151.S39C67 1991
320.5'4'095694092—dc20
[B] 90-52877
CIP

ACKNOWLEDGEMENTS

Many friends, colleagues and members of Max Seligman's family helped in gathering the material I needed for telling his story. I assume responsibility for the interpretation of this material, and since I wish it to remain so, have refrained from showing the manuscript to these parties. I hope they will understand and forgive me.

For their cooperation and giving generously of their time, I owe thanks to many individuals, including Menachem Begin, Dr. Sullivan Kaufman, LL.M., M.Phil., Lord and Lady Elwyn-Jones, Max Kritzman, Jack Jacoby, Judge Yehuda Treibisch, Yekhi'el Kadisha'i of the Prime Minister's Office, Jerusalem, Dr. Eli Tavin and Messrs. Pesach Gani and Bezal'el Amitzur of Jabotinsky House in Tel Aviv. For her patience, encouragement, constructive comments and proof-reading, I tender special thanks to my wife Marion.

This book is dedicated to the generations of men and women of the underground movements in Eretz Israel, who gave of themselves so the nation may live.

Hawaii Kai, 1990 — Giveon Cornfield

DEDICATION

IN MEMORY OF A FIGHTER AND DEAR FRIEND

Max Seligman viewed the practice of law as a mission. He devoted his time, energy and talents to save our freedom fighters from the gallows, from concentration camps, and from long incarceration.

His appearances before British courts were marked by his courage, fearlessly confronting the judges, both civilian and military. He handled many historical cases, ably assisted by his partner, Max Kritzman. The heroic saga of Dov Gruner is linked with the names of these two men. They were not able to save this great fighter's life, but their efforts helped him rise to the great spiritual heights that astounded many nations, as we all recall.

We shall remember Max Seligman with gratitude and deep affection, as one of the greatest advocates during the struggle for our national liberation in Eretz Israel.

Menachem Begin
January 1989

Contents

ZION LIBERATED

I will neither conceal anything nor add anything to the facts that have been brought to light.

—Josephus Flavius
The Jewish War

PART I
The British In Palestine

BACKGROUND

The narrow strip of land called Israel on the eastern tip of the Mediterranean is so tiny that its city names are printed on the sea in world atlases. I doubt there is another spot in the world that has been the cause of so much idealism, or over which so much blood has been shed, as the Land of Israel. This is a story about such ideals, and although stranger than fiction at times, it is nevertheless a true story.

Great Britain's mandate in Palestine, granted by the League of Nations in 1920, was barely a year old when Max Seligman, a strapping lad of nineteen and already a veteran Zionist, left his native Cardiff, landing in Jaffa. That was six years before I was born. My mother Lilian Kert was also an ardent Zionist, who had come from Montreal to Jerusalem in 1922 as a *Young Judean*, the movement in which Golda Me'ir was also a member. Young Judea was affiliated with the Scout movement in Eretz Israel, and my father Gaalya Cornfeld, a *Sabra* from Rosh Pina, was a member of the Scouts. There were not that many unorthodox Jews living in Jerusalem at the time, so I suppose it was inevitable that Lilian and Gaalya should meet.

Shortly after Lilian's arrival, she was followed by her younger sister Mildred, who came with their grandmother, Itta Raffaelovitch. The old lady wanted to be in Jerusalem when her time came to depart this earth, and she wished to be laid to rest on the venerated Mount of Olives. Millie was introduced to Max, and it was love at first sight. Max courted Millie ardently, and when she returned to Montreal, he bombarded her with letters, and eventually followed her there. They were married in 1925, and returned to Jerusalem.

Jerusalem in 1926 had no street lighting, and most houses had neither electricity nor running water. Lilian was now pregnant with me, and plainly afraid of having a child in Jerusalem, attended by an Arab midwife. After four years in Palestine, she was anxious to see her family. As for Gaalya, he too was ready to travel beyond the Middle East. And so it happened that on July 22, 1926, I was born at the Royal Victoria Hospital in Montreal.

We did not stay long in Canada. In fact, my parents moved so often during the next seven years, that only the last few in New York are still within my recall. Lilian attended Columbia University, where she majored in nutrition, and worked as dietitian for several institutes. Gaalya taught Hebrew, but did not enjoy his work. These were the Great Depression years, and one could not afford to be choosy about jobs.

My folks had originally planned on a short stay in America, hoping to return to Palestine as soon as convenient. Now they were trapped by the Depression, and it was very hard to save any money for the trip back, a topic which was always being discussed. In fact I remember few other subjects of discussion in our home. Lilian corresponded regularly with her sister in Jerusalem, and Millie says this and Max says that were phrases that constantly rang in my ears. At one point we were all set to leave, when I unfortunately upset the plans. This was in early 1933, shortly after my mother and I had our tonsils removed in tandem. I was playing in the street with my friends, when I suddenly felt faint and feverish, and was barely able to make it up to our apartment, where I must have passed out. My parents were away at work, and by the time they got me to a hospital, the strep infection I had spread up my right arm, and they were advised that unless the arm was amputated, I had only a fifty-fifty chance of surviving. Mother was naturally beside herself, but Father kept a cool head and opted for non-radical surgery—a brave decision for which I shall remain eternally grateful to him.

It took me some four months to recover, though still weak and thin as a reed. By July, I was fit enough to travel, and with (I strongly suspect) some help from my uncle Laddie in Montreal, we boarded the SS *Roma*, bound for Palestine. We arrived in Haifa on my seventh birthday. I was about to meet the man who, more than anyone else during my first years in Palestine and through my adolescence, was to have such a profound influence on my development. As expected, Uncle Max and Aunt Millie were on hand to greet us. Before leaving the boat, I posed for a picture with my cousin Aura.

In writing this book, I felt some background to the British presence in Palestine should be provided. It was certainly never my intention to present an exhaustive survey of the events leading up to the formation of the State of Israel. Many others have done a far better job of it than I could ever hope to do. ("The Siege" by Conor Cruise O'Brien [Simon and Schuster, 1986], for example, cannot be too highly recommended.)

THE PATH TO CONFLICT

The land of Israel (Eretz Israel) has since the dawn of history been a land-bridge between countries and nations. It straddles that narrow strip of land between Eurasia and Africa, the southern tip of the "Fertile Crescent". A short trip south through the "Land of the Philistines" brings one to the edge of inhabited Egypt. Traffic in the region dates back to prehistory, bringing with it first trade and cultural interchange, later a passageway and battlefields for armies, as nations of the Nile Valley to the west and the Euphrates to the east grew and vied for dominance. This conflict, while giving ancient Israel no peace, nevertheless introduced influences important to her development as a nation.

But Israel bridges not only continents: it also links two great oceans, the Atlantic and the Indian. Its western boundary is the eastern shore of the Mediterranean ("The Great Sea" of the scriptures), itself a tributary of the Atlantic, while to the south lies the Gulf of Eilat, which is the northwestern tip of the Indian Ocean.

Historical studies show that even during ancient times of poor technical resources, the Land of Israel was capable of supporting in excess of three million inhabitants. The key elements were absence of war, relatively dense settlement, and a cohesive central government. Yet there was constant danger from the hungry and thirsty nomads to the south and east, who, especially during periods of drought, invaded the country. This required Israel to maintain a strong military presence along its borders, a situation that prevailed even during the Roman occupation. Defenses built by the Romans crumbled with Rome's decline, and the land was invaded by desert dwellers who brought with them their camels and goats, denuding it. The cycle begun by nature was completed by man, and the desert returned.

From the sea came not only invaders and conquerors, but also commerce and western cultural influences. But fear of the return of the Crusaders made the Moslems destroy the coastal port cities, leaving behind a wasteland that has only recently been reclaimed, and not by them.

As a province of the Ottoman empire, the Land of Israel fell into obscurity, a forgotten territory ruled by quarrelsome pashas and plundered by Bedouins. In 1798, Napoleon conquered Egypt, and his campaign took him up the coast as far as Acre. The presence in Palestine of religious and national minorities needing the protection of some outside power was a consideration weighed by those countries interested in the region. Even as Napoleon marched north[1], discussions were underway in Paris concerning the establishment of a Jewish state between Egypt and Acre, although it is not known whether Napoleon supported the idea. What is known is that he planned to set the Druze and Maronite populations of the northern region against each other, dividing and ruling by the old Roman maxim, giving him the benefit of exploiting for his own ends the holy sites.

The opening of the Suez Canal in 1869 brought increasing rivalry between Britain and France, culminating in the former's conquest of Egypt. Now the British were pushing north towards the French strongholds of Syria and Lebanon. In Cairo, Lord Kitchener felt there was danger of a Turkish attack, and more ominously, that Turkey might be aided in such an adventure by a modern power, such as France or Germany. He reasoned there was need for a buffer state (under British rule) between Egypt and Acre. These considerations played an important part in the contest between Britain, France and Germany over the building of railways in the region. A series of agreements on the eve of WWI resulted in the apportionment of rights, whereby Britain got the coastal routes south of Beirut (i.e., Palestine), as well as routes between Amman and Baghdad, and along the Persian Gulf. By the end of WWI, with Russia's collapse and France's attention diverted to European concerns, she was able to take over the Middle East by military force. Agreement was reached with France by which all of Palestine ("From Dan to Beersheba" in Clemenceau's vague terminology) would be ceded, in exchange for support of a French mandate over northeast Syria.

The idea of resettling Jews in Palestine under British auspices was not new. England always had its share of mystics and visionaries, who felt a moral obligation to make amends to the long-suffering Jews. If by restoring these people to their land Britain served her own purposes in the region, so much the better. There had always been great interest in the Holy Land; both Edward VII and Prince George were among the many visitors who came to Palestine. Well before WWI, extensive surveys and mapping expeditions were carried out in Palestine, under the guise of Biblical Exploration, by the Palestine Exploration Fund (1864). These surveys were conducted by British army officers, and the maps printed were naturally used in the campaign against the Turks. Two officers of the P.E.F. were Colonel Claude Conder and Sir Charles Warren. In 1872 they began unearthing Israel's past, and came under the spell of its revival. In 1875 Warren published a book entitled "The Land of Promise", in which he proposed ". . . gradually introducing the Jews . . . who would eventually occupy and govern the country." What he had in mind were the emancipated Jews of east Europe, who were being "Zionized" by the Chovevei Zion[2] movement. He saw little use for the pious Jews who lived in enclaves in Jerusalem and Safed, and who opposed any nationalistic activism. Conder, too, published an account, called "Tent Work in Palestine", with his own illustrations. Conder was a brilliant scholar, fluent in Arabic and Hebrew, a Renaissance Man whose interests covered every related field: architecture, agriculture, archeology, art, geology, linguistics, and theology. It was he who in 1882 guided Prince George (later George V) on his tour of the Holy Land. The list of his published works, nearly a dozen on his favorite subject, show how the land might be restored to its former glory, with even the arid Negev able to support a substantial population. It was the Arab conquest, he showed, that laid waste to the land, "as the locust swarm devastates a corn-field."

In 1840 Lord Ashley (later to become the Earl of Shaftesbury) published a plan "to plant the Jewish People in the land of their fathers." A deeply religious and compassionate man, this aristocrat (credited with enacting the Factory Act limiting the workday to ten hours) sincerely believed *God's Ancient People*, as he called the Jews, were the means for the fulfillment of biblical prophecy. On his finger he wore a ring inscribed "Oh pray for the peace of Jerusalem!" He was instrumental in the appointment of the first British vice-consul to Jerusalem (1838), as a step towards the restoration of the Jewish nation under the aegis of the Anglican Church—his zeal had a distinct evangelical undertone. Ashley's unlikely collaborator in restoring the Jews to their ancient homeland was Sir Moses Montefiore, a deeply religious Jew who concentrated his philanthropic efforts on land purchases and in producing homes to encourage the immigration into Palestine of European Jews. Montefiore enjoyed the support and encouragement of Queen Victoria, who knighted him in recognition of his "unceasing exertion on behalf of his injured and persecuted brethren[3]."

British policy under Lord Palmerston's premiership now openly championed protection of all Jews under Turkish rule. His instructions to Lord Ponsonby, the Ambassador to the *Sublime Porte* (as the seat of Ottoman power was called) were to remind the Sultan how advantageous it would be for the scattered Jews to settle in Palestine "Because the wealth and habits of order and industry which they would bring with them would tend greatly to increase the resources of the Turkish Empire . . . ." Ashley's missionary ambitions were crowned with the appointment of a converted Jew, the Reverend Doctor Alexander, as Bishop of the newly established (1844) Anglican Church in Jerusalem. As Lord Shaftesbury, Ashley became President of the Palestine Exploration Fund, and continued with the promotion of his plans to the end of his days.

Beginning in the mid-1800's and throughout the nineteenth century, there was a steady stream of Englishmen who espoused the return of Israel to its homeland. It seemed as though every traveler returning from the Grand Tour of the east was writing a book about the Holy Land, and these books found a ready audience. Another mystic in the Shaftesbury mold was Laurence Oliphant, M.P., whose book "Land of Gilead" (1880) proposed resettlement of Jews in Palestine under Turkish rule and British protection. His plan was rejected by the Sultan, who feared foreign encroachment on his realm. Benjamin Disraeli is alleged to have proposed a plan to give Palestine to the Jews following the collapse of the Ottoman Empire. In 1876, Disraeli managed the purchase of the Suez Canal [4], and the Cyprus Convention (1878) signed under his administration ceded the Mediterranean island to British protectorship, in exchange for protecting Turkish sovereignty over Syria against Russian aggression [5].

Meanwhile, the early settlers in Palestine[6], completely unqualified for life as farmers, were having a terrible time struggling to survive, and may not have without the largesse of the Baron Edmond de Rothschild of Paris.

*****

Before WWI, then, Britain was the only major power to demonstrate any semblance of sympathy for the Zionist cause. When Arthur James Balfour was Prime Minister (1902–5), pogroms in Russia were at their height, the worst massacre to date (1903) occurring in Kishinev, when thousands of Jewish refugees fled to the United States. In Britain (and other west European countries) there was fear that should American policy turn hostile to Jewish immigration, and pogroms in east Europe continue to worsen, they might be flooded by waves of destitute Jews. This sentiment was fueled also by Jews resident in these countries. While Prime Minister Balfour presided over the Aliens Bill of 1904, the purpose of which was to keep Jews out of Britain, he was, by virtue of his upbringing and beliefs, genuinely sympathetic to the Jewish people and to their resettlement—but elsewhere. He gave consideration to two turn-of-the-century interim plans for saving European Jewry, one for aid in colonizing the Sinai desert at El-Arish, the other, the celebrated Uganda Scheme (1903).

In 1896, Theodor Herzl's "Der Judenstaat" propelled the modern Zionist movement into international orbit. The following year, Herzl convened the first Zionist Congress in Basle. The

Dem wackeren Mitstreiter
Dr S. R. Landau

DER

Th. Herzl

JUDENSTAAT.

VERSUCH

EINER

MODERNEN LÖSUNG DER JUDENFRAGE

VON

THEODOR HERZL

DOCTOR DER RECHTE.

LEIPZIG und WIEN 1896.

M. BREITENSTEIN'S VERLAGS-BUCHHANDLUNG

WIEN, IX., WÄHRINGERSTRASSE 5.

Reproduction of title page of "Der Judenstaat" (1896) with dedication.

main force behind Herzl's brief and meteoric career[7] was the unshakable conviction that statehood was the only solution for the Jews.

Theodor Herzl, at the head of the Zionist Organization, was a tireless worker, one who left no stone unturned in the quest for fulfilling his dream of a Jewish homeland, almost anywhere and under any conceivable conditions, it seemed. He even gave thought, early in his career, to a scheme for mass conversion of the Jews. He had gone to see the King of Italy and the Pope, had traveled to Jerusalem to meet with Kaiser Wilhelm, and held long and fruitless talks with the Czar's ministers. The same was true in his negotiations with Sultan Abdul Hamid. The Sultan was too crafty an Arab to tell Herzl that what he sought the Sultan could never give. Herzl represented a lot of Jewish capital, and as a respected journalist, could help improve Turkey's economy and tarnished image. He failed to see the duplicity behind the lofty rhetoric of the Sultan and his ministers.

As early as 1900, Lord Rothschild, then a director of the Bank of England, suggested to Herzl various schemes put forth by Prime Minister Joseph Chamberlain, for autonomous Jewish settlement in the Sinai, at El-Arish, and in an area near Haifa (the latter requiring approval by the Sultan). Even Cyprus was considered, and finally Uganda. (Barbara Tuchman suggests that what they referred to was not Uganda—which was considered unfit for habitation by Europeans—but rather the cooler and moister Kenya highlands.) The idea for settling Jews in Uganda came to Chamberlain in response to a plea from British settlers there for more Europeans in East Africa, in order to offset the numerical superiority of the natives. The ulterior motive behind the plan to settle Jews in the Sinai was that it would give Britain a foothold and a way into the crumbling Ottoman Empire.

In fairness to Herzl, who pinned such high hopes on the Sinai and El-Arish plans, it must be said that he only began to consider the Uganda option after his hopes for Sinai were dashed. For him, Uganda was meant merely to establish Jewish autonomy, *anywhere*, as *de facto* recognition by Britain of the Jewish nation. That would serve as a stepping-stone to statehood in Palestine later.

Although nothing came of these plans, they are an indication of the favorable climate in which Herzl and later Chaim Weizmann were working. (It is interesting to note that when he was running for re-election in 1906, P.M. Balfour's opponent was Winston Churchill, who, in order to gain Jewish support, found it convenient to oppose Balfour's Aliens Bill. This appears ironic when viewed in the context of Churchill's policies in Palestine during and after WWII.)

When Turkey entered WWI on Germany's side, Cabinet member Herbert Samuel pointed out that the Jews and Britain had a common cause in ousting the Turks from Palestine. Lloyd George and other members of the Asquith government, notably foreign secretary Sir Arthur Grey, also sided with this view.

THE BALFOUR DECLARATION

Dr. Chaim Weizmann was thirty-two years old when he took over leadership of the Zionist movement following Herzl's death. When he first met the newly-deposed P.M. Balfour in 1906, Weizman, who totally rejected Uganda, managed to convince Balfour that Zionists would never be satisfied with anything less than Palestine. Unlike the mercurial Herzl, Weizmann was brilliant, both as a scientist and as a negotiator, possessed of a suave kind of charm that Balfour found irresistible. The two men became fast friends. Weizmann's important wartime contributions and excellent personal and press contacts enabled him to favorably influence British public opinion. A more coherent policy regarding Palestine began taking shape when Lloyd George became P.M. in 1916, with Sir Edward Grey his Foreign Secretary. Grey suggested that the French and Russian governments issue a joint declaration with Britain undertaking the encouragement of Zionist aspirations in postwar Palestine. Sir Herbert Samuel and C. P. Scott, editor of the influential *Manchester Guardian* also joined the circle of supporters. The British government was now committed to the idea of a Jewish National Home (also referred to as a Jewish Commonwealth) in Palestine. Largely through the influence of American Zionist leader Louis Brandeis, who convinced President Woodrow Wilson that support for a national home in Palestine would win him Jewish votes, Wilson also joined the cause in 1917. America had entered the war in April, and relations with Britain were now cordial. President Wilson let Balfour know he would support him in encouraging Zionist aspirations.

On 2 November, 1917, Balfour, now Foreign Secretary in Lloyd George's government, wrote a letter to Lord Rothschild. The letter was made public a week later.

Foreign Office,
November 2nd, 1917

Dear Lord Rothschild,

I have much pleasure in conveying to you, on behalf of His Majesty's Government, the following declaration of sympathy with Jewish Zionist aspirations which has been submitted to, and approved by, the Cabinet

"His Majesty's Government view with favour the establishment in Palestine of a national home for the Jewish people, and will use their best endeavours to facilitate the achievement of this object, it being clearly understood that nothing shall be done which may prejudice the civil and religious rights of existing non-Jewish communities in Palestine, or the rights and political status enjoyed by Jews in any other country"

I should be grateful if you would bring this declaration to the knowledge of the Zionist Federation.

Facsimile of the Balfour Declaration of 2nd November 1917

Support for the Declaration was not late in coming: France and Italy, followed by China, Greece, Japan and Siam. The provisional (pre-revolutionary) government of Russia gave notice of its support to the Zionists. The Declaration helped Britain's war effort by rallying world Jewish opinion in the Allies' favor, especially in America, where Jews had been opposed to entering the war. A year later, almost to the day, a vaguely-worded Anglo-French *Joint Declaration* was made public (6 November, 1918). It countered the Balfour Declaration and amounted to an apology to the Arab world for this indiscretion[8].

The Balfour Declaration (2 November, 1917) was exquisitely timed to lend moral weight to the British military campaign in Palestine, begun in October. General Allenby's forces were now poised to enter the Eternal Capital, Jerusalem. Taking it and the rest of the country as custodians for its biblical owners would amount to a fulfillment of the Prophecies—justifying the conquest in the eyes of the British and world public.

Lords Robert Cecil and Milner enthusiastically supported the Zionists, but for sheer energy, zeal, inventiveness and tenacity, Sir Mark Sykes had no equal. Like T.E. Lawrence (Lawrence of Arabia), Sykes' interest lay primarily in the overall development of the Middle East, through the good offices of the Arabs. In 1916, Sykes negotiated the Sykes-Picot Treaty[9], before developing his enthusiasm for Zionism. Having embraced Zionist philosophy, he declared that the Jews might "be the bridge between Asia and Europe, to bring the spirituality of Asia to Europe and the vitality of Europe to Asia." As the liaison between the War Office, the Foreign Office and the Cabinet, he was able to give inestimable help to the Zionists and clear many of the obstacles that stood in their way.

A PLEDGE BROKEN

The main purpose of the Balfour declaration was to obtain the Allies' consent to British rule in Palestine. This led to the San Remo Conference of 1920, with predictable results. His Majesty's Government was now the Mandatory Power, obligated to exercise its mandate "on behalf of the League of Nations and in conformity with . . . provisions" which specifically bound

Britain to "place the country under such political, administrative and economical conditions as will secure the establishment of the Jewish National Home." Another Provision (No.6) assumes responsibility to "facilitate Jewish immigration and encourage close settlement by Jews on the land." The Arab, Christian and other minorities are referred to only peripherally, as communities whose rights should be protected. In an article he wrote the same year (1920), Winston Churchill is even more specific, foreseeing "the creation of a *Jewish State* (my italics) under the protection of the British Crown[10]. "The Mandate was no more than the inevitable recognition of an accomplished fact" (Tuchman): the British had conquered the land from the Turks and their army was in place, a fact on the ground. Other contenders for the mandate were out of the running: Russia was eliminated due to its revolution. The United States[11] was too far removed, and nobody wanted France. In order to placate the Emir Feisal, who aided the British in the war, it was agreed that his brother Abdulla would rule over a new British protectorate east of the Jordan; Trans-Jordan was thus carved out of the proposed Jewish national homeland[12]. Weizmann held several meetings with Feisal, finally reaching an accord in 1919[13].

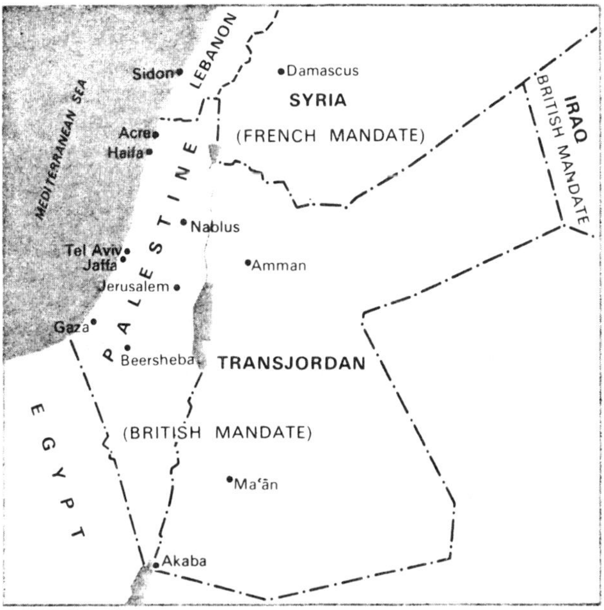

The ruling Arab circles in Palestine, however, fearing that Zionist enterprise would bring about a general improvement in the economy and an end to their domination, opposed these ideas. Highly-placed Arab officials of the Mandate prevailed, and opposition to Zionist efforts became the unannounced policy of the government.

It was not long before Arab extremists took their cue from this state of affairs, and launched a series of bloody attacks on the Jews. In March 1920, Joseph Trumpeldor and six others were killed defending the northern agricultural outpost of Tel-Hai, while in Jerusalem mobs ran rampant for three days, killing six more and wounding two hundred Jews, as the authorities looked the other way. Revisionist leader Ze'ev Jabotinsky, who had been authorized by the military government to organize self-defense for the Jews, was arrested along with Hagana members, and all were sentenced to long prison terms.

This terrorist activity was planned to adversely affect the outcome of the San Remo Conference, but it had the opposite effect. Britain decided to replace the military regime with a civilian one that would govern in the spirit of the Balfour declaration, and Cabinet member Sir Herbert Samuel was appointed the first High Commissioner. Although he meant well, Sir Herbert's appointments were ill-chosen. As leader of the Arab community he accepted Amin al-Husseini, Mufti of Jerusalem and an instigator of the earlier riots, while his administration was peopled with British officials known for their anti-Zionist views. Immigration was soon limited to 16,500 in 1920, and a year later, following new massacres in Jaffa and elsewhere, it was temporarily suspended altogether. Attempts to introduce an elected legislative assembly failed in the face of Arab intransigence, and government policy became one of open support for the Arab population, leaving the Jewish organizations (The Jewish Agency) to look after the welfare of the Jewish community in Palestine (the Yishuv).

THE UNDERGROUND

In the face of government indifference to Jewish security, it became necessary to improve self-defense. Aware of this, the authorities gave tacit agreement to the Hagana, it being the easy way out for them. Hagana had a loosely organized central command, charged mainly with the supply of arms to local outposts manned by volunteers.

The circumvention of restrictions on immigration took many forms: people arriving on tourist visas remained in the country; fictitious marriages were arranged, enabling two persons to enter on one certificate, and non-existent funds were ascribed to penniless immigrants, granting them capitalist entry permits. The smuggling in of people through Lebanon, Syria and Trans-Jordan increased, and in 1934 the first shipload of immigrants managed to slip through. The newcomers were dispersed to kibbutzim and local communities. Additionally, Jewish policemen in the British service helped, but in many cases, Arabs on both sides of the border as well as Arab and British policemen had to be bribed. Some fifty thousand Jews entered Eretz Israel "illegally" between 1920 and 1937 (in addition to the limited number that were allowed to enter legally).*During the same period, some* 100,000 *Arabs from neighboring countries entered the land unopposed*, attracted by improved economic and labor conditions brought about by Jewish development. Increasing support for Arab nationalism was coming from the totalitarian regimes of Germany, Italy and Japan, and was further agitated by the dynamism of Soviet foreign policy. The Palestine Government's policies were an encouragement for the troublemakers, aided and abetted by a general lack of direction from London. Tensions finally erupted in 1936 when a series of bloody attacks heralded the beginning of the "Arab Rebellion", which failed for several reasons: Palestinian Arabs were reluctant to support the imported mercenaries who comprised the bulk of the 2,000 marauders, who had to resort to assassination of local leaders to get compliance. Outside support was mostly lip-service, and the leaders of the revolt eventually got so carried away with their mission that they began attacking British forces and installations, forcing an official reaction.

Following the 1929 Hebron massacre, the Hagana consolidated its command structure and expanded the scope of its operations. It was now not a purely defensive organization, but a force able to deploy mobile strike units and operate with military precision. Still, Revisionists in the ranks did not feel this was enough.

THE PARTITION PLAN

Soon after the outbreak of the 1936 disturbances, a committee headed by Lord Peel was appointed. Following three months of investigation, the committee recommended that in view of Britain's failure to live up to the spirit of the Balfour Declaration, it would be best for her to give up the Mandate in favor of partitioning the land. A tiny Jewish state would be surrounded by a much larger Arab one, with the safety of the holy sites ensured by British-controlled areas. In addition, it was recommended an exchange of populations take place, a ban on land purchases imposed, and immigration be further restricted. The Jewish state was to pay the Arabs annual compensatory fees, and there was even talk of handing over the government of Palestine to Trans-Jordan.

Controversy raged over the plan. Weizmann felt the prospect of a state, however small, was too good to turn down, while Jabotinsky maintained that after granting the Arabs sovereignty, the British would remain in control of the Jewish state in one guise or another. Opposition to the plan in Britain resulted in its being watered down, with only the restrictions on immigration and land purchases remaining. Small wonder, then, that when the 20th Zionist Congress convened in 1937, Partition was rejected.

The Arab leadership did not react openly, but instructed its bands of marauders to renew their attacks on Jewish as well as British targets. Government patience finally snapped: Arab leaders were arrested, some exiled, and the Mufti escaped to Germany, where he was received by Hitler. In order to control the Arab rebellion, it became necessary for the British to enlist the aid of the Yishuv. In addition to toleration of the Hagana, the government now recruited thousands of Auxiliary Policemen (Notrim), and an English mystic and guerrilla war expert, Captain Orde Wingate, trained special night squads (S.N.S.) in unorthodox, highly efficient tactics. Still, the Palestine Government continued in its antagonistic attitude towards the Jews, and in 1939 published a "White Paper", outlawing land purchases and restricting immigration even further.

THE JEWISH REBELLION

Hagana activities were no longer confined to matters of defense. Beginning in 1936, punitive actions were carried out against known offenders, though the official policy remained one of restraint. Such actions were prompted by dissatisfaction in the ranks, especially among the Revisionist members. In 1937, a new organization made its appearance: Irgun Zeva'i Le'umi, or National Military Organization (I.Z.L., or Etzel, as it became known), an offshoot of the National Defense Organization, founded in 1931.

The fledgling Irgun immediately ran into extremely stiff opposition. The Jewish Agency and Hagana saw it as undermining central authority and its tactics not in keeping with Jewish morals(!) The British reacted violently, hundreds of Revisionists and Irgun members were thrown into stockades, and sentences were handed down which were out of all proportion to those given Arabs for similar offenses. In June of 1938, the first death sentence was carried out when Irgun member Shlomo Ben Yosef was hanged.

While Hagana and Irgun occasionally collaborated in matters of immigration, they differed widely in their response to Arab attacks. The greater part of the youth was in the Hagana, and in order to augment its purely voluntary activities it formed special strike units (Plugot Machatz, or Palmach), made up of full-time personnel. These benefitted from larger-scale training, made possible by the Jewish Auxiliary Police and Capt. Wingate's Special Night Squads. Hagana activities, however, remained essentially defensive, its leadership convinced that the future of the Jewish state lay in cooperation with the British. The Irgun on the other hand operated on the premise that Britain's policy was irrevocably opposed to Zionist aspirations, and that Britain must be fought for freedom to be achieved. There were also some Hagana leaders who considered this possibility.

With the approach of WWII, immigration activity was

stepped up, and Britain's war on it intensified. Countries from which the ships disembarked were subjected to heavy diplomatic pressure, the ships' crews prosecuted. The vessels were shadowed by aircraft and chased by battleships in international waters, and their occupants, once in Palestinian territory, forcibly removed and thrown into concentration camps. The British began massive searches and imposed collective punishment on communities guilty of aiding refugees. This repression only increased the numbers of members in the underground. About this time, Max Seligman, the foremost criminal lawyer in Palestine, made a commitment to devote all his time and energy to the defense of underground members. With the onset of WWII, matters eased off somewhat, 130,000 members of the Yishuv joining the British armed forces in the common effort to defeat Nazi Germany.

NOTES TO THE BRITISH IN PALESTINE

1. Unable to breach the walls of Acre, Napoleon marched north to Beirut, only to be driven out of Syria by fire from a squadron of British gunboats.

2. Chovevei Zion (also known as Chibat Zion), Lovers of Zion, the movement for recruiting and encouraging, mostly in Russia, emigration and settlement of Jews in Palestine. It was headed by Nachum Sokolov.

3. Montefiore accomplished the release of fourteen Jewish prisoners in Damascus, accused in a French-inspired blood libel in 1839 that resulted in a pogrom. In addition to full acquittal of the prisoners, he obtained from the Sultan a *firman* (decree) granting Jews equality under Ottoman law.

4. The price paid to the bankrupt Khedive Ismail was 4,000,000 Pounds Sterling. The funds were raised on very short notice by Lord Rothschild.

5. Cyprus was annexed by Britain at the outbreak of WWI. When Turkey realized it got the short end of the deal, it began treating Britain with suspicion, and gradually drifted into Germany's sphere of influence.

6. Including my paternal grandfather , Reb Aryeh Cornfeld, who settled in Rosh Pina in 1882, and was the first Hebrew teacher there.

7. Herzl's reign as leader of the Zionist movement lasted only eight years. He died in 1904, at the age of forty-four.

8. As a schoolboy in 1930's Tel Aviv—the school appropriately enough named the Balfour Elementary—I learned that British officials who were even slightly inclined towards the Jews were all painted white with the same wide brush. Teachers and textbooks alike extolled the virtues of those after whom streets, institutions, bridges and forests were named.

9. The Sykes-Picot Treaty was a secret agreement between Britain, France

and Russia (and incidentally Italy) signed in 1916. Its purpose was to partition the Middle East along lines that virtually ignored Zionist aspirations. Details of the plan became public after the Russian revolution in 1917.

10. All of this is alluded to in the 1937 report of the Peel Commission, which concluded that the primary purpose of (the drafters of) the Mandate "is to promote the establishment of the Jewish National Home." The problems arose from the British interpretation of their commitment.

11. President Woodrow Wilson was adamant about self-determination by the local inhabitants. He went so far as to send a mission of inquiry to Palestine.

12. Winston Churchill as Colonial Secretary presided over the separation from Palestine in 1922 of the entire area east of the Jordan River, henceforth known as Trans-Jordan.

13. An agreement with Sherif Hussein of Mecca and his son Emir Feisal was formalized in Amman in a meeting with Weizmann, also attended by T.E. Lawrence. It guaranteed ". . . carrying into effect . . . the Declaration (Balfour) of November 2, 1917 . . . to encourage and stimulate immigration of Jews into Palestine on a large scale." In a letter addressed to American Zionist delegates to the Paris Peace Conference in 1918, he stated that the Arabs wished Jews "a most hearty welcome . . . there is room in Syria for both of us . . . indeed, I think that neither can be a real success without the other." If all this sounds too good to be true, events proved so: the Hashemites were unable to unify the Arabs, and elements hostile to Zionism took control.

Setting Down Roots

OUR STORY BEGINS in 1921, when young Max Seligman, in what has become the accepted term, "made Aliya". Max was then nineteen years old, and already a veteran Zionist.

According to Max's research, his grandfather Aryeh Leib Zeligman came from the great Jewish center of Vilna in Lithuania. Aryeh Leib had three sons: Raphael David, Shimon and Chaim, Max's father. Shimon, in the time-honored tradition of evading compulsory military service in the Tsar's army, changed his name to Zloty Yapke, and as part of the Bilu revival movement, moved from Lodz in Poland (Russia) to Palestine in 1880, settling in Rishon le Zion. Once in Palestine, he changed his name again, this time to Zahavi (Hebrew for Zloty), and toiled in the Baron Edmund de Rothschild's vineyards. (About this time, my own grandfather Aryeh Cornfeld settled in Rosh Pina). In 1882, Shimon Zahavi became one of the founding fathers of the colony of Petach Tikvah, in the Jaffa district (Tel Aviv was yet to be built).

Two of Aryeh Leib Zeligman's sons left Lodz around the turn of the century and settled in England. Raphael David went to Manchester, where his son Ephraim was born in 1897. Chaim settled in Swansea, Wales, where Max was born on 12 October, 1902.

Max's family moved to Cardiff when he was eight. Chaim and Rebecca Zeligman were Herzlian Zionists, and the leader's familiar portrait hung in their home. Max's father was also active in the *Ancient Order of the Maccabeans*. In addition to the usual elementary schools, Max also attended *Talmud Torah*, and was boy soprano in Cardiff's Cathedral Road Synagogue choir.

If Max Seligman's youth was unremarkable, this changed rapidly as he began to mature. He was fifteen years old when in 1917 the Balfour Declaration changed the history of Zionism, and with it the course his life was to take. A boyhood friend, Joseph Danovitch, relates:

The Balfour Declaration and the October Revolution (in Russia) almost coinciding, we thought in our youthful euphoria that the millennium had come for the Jews, and social justice predominant in our minds, we carried red banners in demonstrations and sang "Then raise the scarlet standard high, etc." Disillusionment came later. When merely sixteen years old, Max founded the Junior Zionist Society in Cardiff in 1918 and was its chairman until he left for Palestine in 1921. (A leading light in the Society was Maurice Rosetti, later First Clerk to the Knesset, Israel's first Parliament in 1948.)

While still a student at the Technical College in Cardiff, Max heard a speech given by Ze'ev Jabotinsky during his campaign for the establishment of the Jewish Battalion in WWI. Jabotinsky's magnetic personality captivated the boy's imagination, and he closely followed his exploits in the defense of Jerusalem and his arrest by the British. At the age of nineteen, Max decided to go to Palestine. He was an ardent philatelist, but to help finance his trip he did not hestitate to sell his beloved stamp collection.

He boarded the *Sphinx* in Marseilles, bound for Jaffa. Enroute, the ship put in at Port-Said, and Max was dismayed to see anchored alongside the *Sphinx* another boat full of Jewish immigrants who had arrived in Jaffa during the Arab riots. In an attempt to appease the Arabs, High Commissioner for Palestine Herbert Samuel had ordered their removal to an Egyptian port.

On 21 August, 1921, Max arrived at the port of Jaffa. As the port had no pier, passengers were offloaded onto small fishing boats and rowed ashore. The Arab dock workers refused to unload the Jewish immigrants, and the District Commissioner, instead of hiring Jewish workers to break the Arab strike, decided to treat the passengers as tourists. Their passports were stamped accordingly, but the Arabs still refused to row the boats. The Commissioner then ordered British troops to do the work, and the *Sphinx* passengers, all American Jews with the exception of briton Max, were put ashore.

Max's nephew and fellow-Mason Ephraim (Ralph) Seligman reports that upon his arrival in Palestine, Max enlisted in a force created by General Allenby and became a Supernumerary Constable. He was obviously not cut out for a career in the police force, and sought other employment.

The only work Max could get was at his uncle Shimon Zahavi's orange-grove in the town of Petach Tikva, not far from Jaffa. He worked hard for many months, earning wages that were barely sufficient for keeping body and soul together, but he was happy and enthusiastic to be working in the land of his dreams. The disturbances of 1921 were not confined to Jaffa alone—they affected all Jewish settlements, and in Petach-Tikva, four people were killed by Arabs. When community leaders appealed to the government for help, the British sent a locked case with twenty rifles and ammunition, with strict orders that the case was not to be unlocked unless the town was attacked. The police officer who brought this arsenal further stated that the community leaders were to be held personally responsible for each rifle and round of ammunition. To make sure that he was perfectly understood, he insisted on his instructions being translated by an English-speaking individual, and Max was sent for. He arrived from the orange-grove, heard with astonishment the officer's message, and relayed it to his people. He then turned on the officer and sternly lectured him on the unfair treatment given Jews who were attacked by Arab hoodlums. Word of his proud address spread in Petach-Tikva and beyond. One person who heard about Max was the English-Jewish lawyer Harry Sacher, who had been chairman in Britain of the *Ancient Order of the Maccabeans.* In addition, Sacher was a regular contibutor to the *Manchester Guardian*, and had come to Palestine to launch the English language *Palestine Weekly.* He needed English-speaking people for his staff, and offered Max a job at the then handsome wage of ten Pounds a month.

The Jewish community in Palestine (the Yishuv) now numbered some 120,000, a third of them in Jerusalem, where Max moved. He settled easily in the Holy City, and together with some other Jerusalemites founded the Yeshurun Synagogue, which had a style of its own in the traditional prayer services. The *Alliance* school put at their disposal their main hall for Shabbat and holiday services. Its first *chazanim* (cantors) were Max and his friend Joseph Rivlin, a son of one of the greatest of Jerusalem's chazanim. The congregation increased in size,

Members of Hashomer, ca 1909.

Soldiers of the Jewish Legion, 1917.

General Allenby entering Jerusalem, December 8, 1917.

Zionist leaders meeting in Jerusalem with friendly sheiks from Trans-Jordan. Seated are Dr. Chaim Weizmann and Dr. Chaim Arlosoroff, who was one of the strongest proponents of Arab-Jewish friendship, but who was killed by an Arab assassin.

Max Seligman, on the eve of his departure for Palestine in 1919.

Lord Balfour, left, *and Dr. Weizmann in Palestine*, ca 1923.

1922 *Photo of Max Seligman; Gaalya Cornfeld is on the left.*

Max Seligman, Correspondent in Palestine.

Auxiliary Policeman Moshe Dayan, 1938.

The author (left) *with Aura Seligman Haifa*, 1933.

Jewish Auxiliary Policemen Drilling, ca 1940.

"Illegal" immigrants disembarking from the S.S. Shabbetai Luzinski *at Ashdod*, 1947.

Max Seligman in full Masonic Regalia.

and so did the number of factions within. As is so often the case, bickering and infighting began and would not stop in spite of Max's efforts to mediate the disputes. Discouraged, Max left.

As I mentioned, he fell in love with Mildred (Malka) Kert, who came from Montreal to Jerusalem with her aged grandmother. Like all pious Jews, Itta Raffaelovitch wanted to die in the Holy Land and be buried on the Mount of Olives. Mildred's sister Lilian had preceded her and was married to a *Sabra*, Gaalya Cornfeld, and they lived in Jerusalem. Mildred worked as secretary to Gershon Agronsky, founder and editor of the *Palestine* (later *Jerusalem) Post*. The pretty, vivacious Millie was a definite asset in the English-speaking colony, and since secretaries who knew the language were very scarce in those days, she was loaned on occasion to Colonel Kisch[1] to help in his work. Max and Millie loved riding and tennis, and made a very handsome couple. They were married on 18 June 1925 in Montreal. Their daughter Aura was born 11 November 1926, and another daughter, Sheila, was born 11 July, 1932, both in Jerusalem.

Max was working in a law-oriented environment, and was encouraged to study law at the school opened by the Mandate Government for the few lawyers left over from the Ottoman period and for above-average youngsters from the various communities, in order that they should accustom themselves to English law. He passed the Bar examination in 1930, the first English-speaking Jew in Palestine to receive this distinction.

Another British lawyer in Jerusalem at the time was Horace Samuel, who had come to Palestine with General Allenby. He served as a senior military judge until the administration was changed and Herbert Samuel (unrelated) was appointed High Commissioner. He then left the military and started a law practise in cooperation with his old friend Harry Sacher. They were members of a circle of highly-placed English Jews and gentiles friendly to Zionism. Some members of this group were Norman Bentwich, Victor Levy, Julius Jacobs and Julian Meltzer. Max was drawn into this circle, and his lively personality made him the life of the party. The club soon became the social and cultural center of Jerusalem, and Max was elected club president. British members of the civilian and military administration, far from being pro-Zionist by inclination, nevertheless felt a closer affinity to the European-bred Jewish society than to the Levantine Arab circles. They were frequent guests at the club and dinner parties in Jewish homes, and it was here that Max made his initial contacts with the higher echelons of the Mandate Administration. To augment his income, Max became secretary of the Rutenberg Electric Corporation, which was privately owned at the time. In 1925 while still attending evening classes at Law School, Max was invited to join the newly-formed Potash Company as secretary. The company was having difficulties in obtaining rights to mine the Dead Sea potash. High Commissioner Herbert Samuel, though himself a Jew, went out of his way to make matters difficult for the Yishuv, thus showing his "lack of bias". It was only after he resigned that the new High Commissioner, General Plumer saw fit to give the concession to the Potash Company.

MAX SELIGMAN, CORRESPONDENT

The series of newsletter/articles which follow were written by Max Seligman for the English-Jewish publication IVRI ANOCHI and the JEWISH CHRONICLE in 1925/6. They afford an opportunity to read the brilliant young writer's impressions and views on a wide range of subjects, and offer a fascinating glimpse of Palestine at that time. Seligman was in his early twenties when he wrote these pieces, yet his language is rich and clear, and the style mature and engaging.

OUR PALESTINE LETTER
(Special to "Ivri Anochi")

Jerusalem, October 1925

The decision of the Zionist Congress at Vienna, to transfer the remains of the late Theodor Herzl to Palestine has been received with much favour by Palestine Jewry. There is no doubt, after the reception accorded to the Zionist delegates at Vienna, that Vienna is not a fitting place for the resting of the mortal remains of our great leader. But the second part of the decision, viz., that the bones of Theodor Herzl should be buried on Mount Carmel has aroused a great deal of indignation, with which even those living in the galuth must feel some sympathy. The objection is that the resting place should be in Jerusalem and not in Haifa. Jerusalem is regarded with respect and affection by almost all religions and by all nations, and to the Jews Jerusalem means much more than any other part of Palestine. Haifa is a business city and with the promise of a port is probably destined to be the great commercial city of the future in Palestine. That was also part of Herzl's great scheme. But Jerusalem is the capital of Palestine and will always remain the capital of Palestine. It will always be the centre of cultural and religious efforts and the greatest part of Herzl's noble idea was directed towards the building of a new Jerusalem. Here the Hebrew University stands, or will stand. Here is the seat of Government and the Zionist Executive or Jewish Agency, and there is a great deal to be said for the argument that the Mount of Olives will be the best spot for the resting place of our leader.

A committee has been appointed by the Congress to deal with the matter, and though the completion of the arrangements will take some time, it would be well for Zionists to stress the demand for Jerusalem and no other place.

The Day of Atonenment (Yom Kippur) did not pass without incident. You are probably aware that some time ago a harsh decree was issued by the authorities of Jerusalem forbidding the placing of chairs or benches before the Wailing Wall. This step was taken in order to prevent the non-Jewish neighbours who pass the Wailing Wall with their donkeys laden with manure from being disturbed. As a result the old people were obliged to pray before the Wall standing. On the Day of Atonement a number of old people dared to bring with them chairs in order to ease their lot during the long fast. The action was immediately noticed by the neighbours, who hastened to the police to complain about the matter, whereupon the police ordered the removal of the offensive articles. A great tumult arose but the pleas of the old people were of no avail. A delegation waited upon the Governor of Jerusalem, who instructed his assistant to proceed to the Wailing Wall to effect a temporary settlement of the matter, and the assistant ordered that the chairs must be taken away but that the people may sit upon old tins.

The matter has been brought before the High Commissioner who has expressed his sympathy but declared that the law must be obeyed. The Wailing Wall is one of the few sites in Palestine which is admitted to be a relic genuinely belonging to the Jews and the affair has aroused the ire of the whole Jewish population, and the Jewish press is demanding the cancellation of this harsh and unconscionable order.

In Tel Aviv the Day of Atonement created a very profound impression upon visitors. The whole city appeared to be engaged in prayer and thorough quiet prevailed in all the business sections. All the synagogues were filled to the doors, particularly so on the evening of Kol Nidreh. There were synagogues everywhere; Ashkenazic, Sephardic, Yemenite, American, Russian, Polish and private synagogues, and everybody seemed to be either going to or coming from a synagogue. The one exception was the Workers' Kitchen where the Chalutzim were busy discussing various phases of socialism and atheism.

Tel Aviv has been growing at more than its usual speed during the last year. The Tel Aviv municipality has begun the issue of its own bulletin, which is a very interesting record of achievements. A sign of the increase of the population of Tel Aviv may be obtained from the report on education. At the present moment there exist in Tel Aviv forty-nine educational establishments including schools of all kinds. Attending these schools there are seven thousand pupils, almost equally divided as between boys and girls. There are over three hundred teachers and the taxable capacity of these institutions amounts to over 50,000 Pounds a year.

The Mizrachi Party announces that its organ the "Hator" will soon be issued as a daily, in which case there will be four Hebrew dailies printed in Palestine. The other dailies are the "Do'ar Hayom", which is the organ of the Benai Benyamin (Mrs. Fels Group), the "Ha'aretz", the middle-class paper, and the "Davar", the organ of the Labour Party.

The Jewish Chronicle Supplement
December, 1925 (Kislev, 5686)
FROM JERUSALEM TO METULLA

A long-ungratified desire to see with our own eyes the Zionist achievements in the much-spoken-of Emek, Galilee and other parts of Palestine was at last about to be realised, so that we felt rather excited as we took our seats in the car.

We soon left Jerusalem, the city of rugged beauties, and its outlying Arab villages behind us, and were racing along the high road in the cool breeze of a September afternoon. We have very vivid recollections of pink and blue skies, a vast expanse of brown, rocky territory, and a setting sun which looked like a huge golden ball falling into the brink of the Universe. The first place we reached was Kalendia, a little Jewish colony, part of whose lands had been expropriated by the Royal Air Force for use as a landing-ground. From Kalendia a half-hour's ride brought us to Ramalleh, a very old Arab city with an old and a new section. The old section consists of the usual style of Arab mud huts, while the new section contains some very beautiful houses, built of stone and erected by wealthy Arabs retired after successful business careers in America. From the top of Ramalleh there is a view commanding a great deal of south-western Palestine, and even a glimpse of the Mediterranean. There is a very nice hotel here owned by an ex-American Arab where many people come to spend the summer months. According to the proprietor of the hotel, Ramalleh is situated even higher than the Lebanon Mountains in Syria.

In a couple of hours we reached Nablus, the old Shechem of the Bible. This is one of the largest Arab towns in Palestine, and inhabited almost entirely by Moslems. It is a hotbed of politics, meaning anti-Zionism, and there is not one Jew living there. There are one or two soap factories and tobacco factories, and for the rest the people seem to be mainly cafe proprietors smoking nargilehs and listening to weird tunes on the gramophone all day long.

Our next stop was Nazareth, as we had decided to visit the Emek colonies on our way back from Metulla. At Nazareth we dined at a very nicely-appointed German hotel, and then left immediately for Tiberias. Tiberias was most disappointing. We knew that it was an ancient city, but we did not expect to find it so small, so filthy, and so neglected. The ancient city wall exists only in parts, and its remains are crumbling to nothing. It would appear to have two redeeming features. One, the Rutenberg Power Station, is a very recent addition; the other is the famous Lake of Galilee, upon which Jesus is said to have walked. The lake stands out in refreshing relief from the sordid dilapidation and decay along its banks. In the evening we went for a trip round the lake on one of the Arab fishing-vessels, and though there was not a breath of wind it was a very pleasant experience. There is a great fishing industry on this lake in which most of the local Arabs are engaged. On the following morning the writer attended a business meeting at the municipality, a two-roomed building. Here we met the Mayor, a native Jew, whom it was difficult to distinguish from his Arab colleagues. Most of the time of the meeting seemed to be taken up by his Arabic gesticulations and quibbles over items of a few piastres. We stayed at an excellent German hotel (there would appear to be a chain of good German hotels throughout the country). The heat at Tiberias was intense, and for Europeans it is only tolerable as a winter resort. It is during the winter months that thousands of people repair here to enjoy the natural hot sulphur baths, which are situated a little way out of the town. We were conducted through the bath houses by the Superintendent, and found it very interesting. There are three sections, ranging in price from one piastre to ten piastres a bath. The baths are guaranteed to cure rheumatism and like ills. A little way from the town a new settlement is springing up called "Kiryat Samuel", named in honour of the late High Commissioner.

In the afternoon we proceeded to Rosh Pinah (Head of the Corner). Most of the road between Tiberias and Rosh Pinah runs along the lake shore and makes very pleasant driving. On our way we passed through Migdal, a beautiful little settlement noted for its intensive plantations of eucalyptus trees, and containing a street of neat little cottages built by an American investor. Sir Alfred Mond is building a residence here. Rosh Pinah is a Jewish colony of the old type. It is situated at the foot of the mountains, and is very well kept. It is the last post on the mail route, and representatives of the settlements all the way up to Metulla come here periodically to collect their mail. After tea, at a colonist's humble hotel, we again started off for Metulla. It grew dark early and our driver was a little concerned at the task ahead of him. For the most part, there is no road, only a rough track. However, we seemed to be travelling at a great speed, though it was obviously difficult to follow the track, and we jumped innumerable ditches, rocks and shrubs. The going in these parts is very dangerous at night, as attacks are not unknown from marauding Bedouins. In the darkness we passed the numerous co-operative settlements which we were to see on our return in the morning. About half an hour before we reached Metulla the car was held up, and we were examined by two Palestinian gendarmes—one Jew and one Arab. There is a very careful watch kept here upon smugglers into and from Syria.

At last we reached Metulla, and as the car stopped outside the one small hotel of the colony, we were met by the entire settlement of Chalutzim in one body with the heart-rending request: "Hayesh lachem itonut?" ("Have you newspapers?") Visitors are not so numerous here, and the colony had not seen a newspaper for several days. They were particularly anxious for news of the Congress, which had only just concluded. The news we brought was received with great interest. The hotel was very barely furnished but clean, and the food good. The air was delightful, and we slept very well. There are no mosquitoes in Metulla, but these were amply made up for by the number of flies served with our breakfast in the morning! The scenery around Metulla is the most wonderful in Palestine, and we spent a very pleasant time touring the colony. It is situated on the highest point of a steep mountain with many hills and valleys beneath it. The mountains of Lebanon can be clearly seen from the colony, as also snow-capped Mount Hermon. Across the Valley of the Jordan is the Druse territory, and the colonists told us that very often they can hear sounds of war. There is a pretty little waterfall near the town, but we had to imagine the water, because it dries up towards the end of the summer. Metulla is an old colony, although it has only been officially included in Palestinian territory for little more than two years. There has been very little progress here during that time, the only change probably being the introduction of Chalutzim in place of Arab labour. There are some forty colonists with their families, who are all engaged in farming. Tobacco has of recent months become an important product, and is to be seen strung up to dry in the gardens attached to every house. Of public institutions there are the schoolhouse, the library, a synagogue, and a small clubroom attached to the school, mainly utilised by the Chalutzim. The only means of communication Metulla has with the rest of the country is the wireless installation attached to the gendarmerie camp, which lies just outside the colony. In the days before the wireless was set up (it was installed only a few months ago), rockets were sent up in case of sudden attack.

On our return trip we marvelled how we had ever reached Metulla the night before. Whatever track there was was badly torn up, and seemed to be fit only for camels, of which we passed many carrying imports from Syria. It was very difficult travelling even by daylight. We were now enabled to see the co-operative settlements which we had passed in the night. The first of these was Kfar Gil'adi and Tel Hai, the latter famous as the place where Trumpeldor and his brave comrades fell in withstanding a raid by Bedouins from across the border. A tomb has been erected here in Trumpeldor's memory, and also a statue of the two brave girls who were killed at the same time. These are an inspiration to the workers at present in the colony. Other workmen's settlements which we went through were Machnayim, Ayelet Hashachar, and Yessod Hama'ala. These have all been recently rebuilt by the *Keren Hayessod* in partnership with the Jewish Colonisation Association, on whose lands the settlements stand. They are all situated very near to Lake Huleh, the district of which is infested with malaria. The marshes of Lake Huleh will, it is hoped, shortly be drained. A concession for this work has already been granted by the Colonial Office.

Arriving back at Rosh Pinah, we ascended the lofty heights to Safed. The road winding up and through the hills is a very good one, and was built during the British occupation. Safed is a small city, almost clearly divided into Arab and Jewish sections. The majority of the population is Jewish, who are for the most part very poor. Safed is recommended as a health resort, and is reckoned to cure consumption. The Hadassa Medical Organisation conducts a hospital here. At the entrance to the town there are several very imposing structures, including the municipal building, a Scots' Girl College and a Scots' Boy College. Inside the town the streets are narrow, stony, and dirty, and one has to walk. The living quarters are badly huddled together and most insanitary. There are a number of old synagogues, each making claim to being the original synagogue of one or other of the famous sages. A road is now being built from Safed to Meron, which latter place can be seen quite easily from the Jewish section of Safed. At Meron are reputed to exist the graves of the great Rabbis, Me'ir Ba'al Haness, Hillel, and Shamai, and here many thousands of Jews from all over the country gather from the early days of Passover until Lag b'Omer to pay honour to the great Tzadickim, who died rather than submit to the demands of the Romans and sacrifice their religion. The only building in Meron is a synagogue, which is deserted almost all the year round except for a Shamash. So that the crowds that gather there before Lag b'Omer are compelled to sleep on the mountain-sides.

Downward again, via Rosh Pinah, Migdal, and Tiberias, until we reached Kinnereth, a flourishing colony a few miles west of Tiberias. Kinnereth and Degania Aleph, which we next visited, are both situated on the bank of Lake Tiberias. At Degania Aleph, which is a Jewish National Fund Settlement, we were shown some very fine dairies, excellently managed and well-kept by Chalutzim.

Not at all sorry to leave the heat of lower Galilee (which is some three hundred feet below sea level), we proceeded to the Emek. This is the most wonderful tract of land in Palestine, being now thoroughly drained of the swamps which previously made it malarially infested. Several hundred thousand dunams of land have been bought up here by the Palestine Land Development Company and the American Zion Commonwealth, and numerous colonies are being rapidly developed here by the *Keren Hayessod*, the *Keren Kayemeth* and the American Zion Commonwealth. The Centre of these is Afuleh, where there is a railway station, and which it is hoped to develop into an industrial town. We did not visit every one of the colonies, but selected typical ones. The first was Balfouria, the proud possession of the American Zion Commonwealth, where about half the colonists are American settlers. The rest are Russian and Polish families who have been settled there by the American organisation. One of the American settlers has established a hotel here so that tourists can spend a night in the Emek instead of rushing off to either Haifa or Jerusalem. The houses are neatly built, and the whole colony presents a pretty and effective appearance. Of communal institutions there are a school and a synagogue. It may be observed that every colony has its own little school and its own synagogue.

At Balfouria there is an orphan institution under the auspices of the Palestine Relief Committee assisted by the funds of the Joint Distribution Committee. We saw Merchavia and Tel Adashim which are close at hand, and are excellent proof of the adaptation of our Jewish pioneers to the soil. There are flourishing plantations, presentable dwellings, and excellent roads. The children who were romping about were the picture of health, for they are given the very best, morally and physically, even if their parents have to forgo the luxury of milk and butter.

Nahalal, our next point on the way to Haifa, was a very pleasant experience. The colony which is built in circular form, was much larger than any we had seen. On the outer edge of the road around the colony are the farmyards of the colonists. The centre of the colony is on the top of a hillock, where are situated a number of communal buildings, including a school, a synagogue, communal office, and co-operative stores. There is also a school here for the agricultural training of young women under the auspices of the International Women's Zionist Organisation. The colony is run on a communistic basis, each inhabitant having his portion of work allotted to him and the produce being equally divided. I understand that the experiment has so far proved successful.

From Nahalal it is but an hour's ride to Haifa—the future commercial capital of Palestine. We neared Haifa in the evening, and on approaching it seemed as if the whole city was alight. But the nearer we got the more concentrated appeared the blaze. However, on arrival it proved to be merely the new Power House of the Rutenberg Electric Corporation all lit up. The erection of the building had only recently been completed, and as yet the city was not being supplied by electricity. We were informed that there had been continual hitches in the settlement of the contract with the municipality, but were unable to discover the real causes. The Power House is a building in which beauty of architecture is displayed everywhere, from the watchman's house at the entrance to the surrounding grounds. There is a lovely garden in front of the building, with graceful fountains—a rare sight in Palestine—playing upon it. In the whole, it is an edifice of which any European city might be proud.

We made our way up to the Carmel, where we were to stay the night. At every turn on the long winding ascent up the mountain we could plainly see the Mediterranean lying calmly beneath us, and the air became ever more invigorating as we reached the top. The bright moon shed a soft radiance upon the thick afforestation on the mountain, and we enjoyed immensely our walks around the hotel. In the evening there was a dance on the large open verandah outside the hotel.

The town of Haifa itself, by reason of its being a seaport, is dirty and very busy. There is a fine natural bay, and it is easy to understand why preference should be given Haifa rather than Jaffa for the building of the harbour. There are some Jewish suburbs, including Bat Galim (Daughter of the Waves), situated right on the seashore, a pretty little settlement with several Anglo-Jewish inhabitants. In Haifa as in the other large towns, the German Templars have their own colony, with good roads and buildings. We visited the Nesher factory, which is practically completed and will shortly be producing Portland cement for local consumption and for export. It is an enormous building containing the most up-to-date machinery, its own railway siding and reserve workshops. The company owns a large tract of land on the mountain hard by from which it will obtain its raw material. In the daytime we were enabled to observe the extraordinary building activity on the slopes of Mount Carmel, where a large Jewish settlement has developed. From Haifa a few miles run in the sand right on the sea edge brought us to Acre—the ancient seaport town and scene of many battles. Upon a broken-down table in the open air, behind guarded gates, there lay pieces of ancient French siege guns, relics of Napoleon's unsuccessful attack in 1799, in his attempt to establish an Eastern French Empire. There is a very important prison in Acre, where prisoners are sent from Haifa and Tiberias. There are very few Jews living in Acre, but the Arabs are very friendly disposed, and are anxious to attract a Jewish population in the sensible hope that they may assist the town to recover its ancient prosperity and importance. At present fishing is the chief industry of the town.

On our return trip we visited the salt basins at Athlit. The Athlit Salt Company has already begun the sale of salt in Palestine, for which it has a concession from the Government. Formerly one of the worst malarial districts in Palestine, Athlit is now a thriving little colony.

Dusk was fast gathering as we passed under the shadows of Mount Gerizim, the historic site on which the Samaritans annually make their gruesome sacrifice of the Paschal lamb, and we hurried on to Jerusalem.

Jerusalem, March 12, 1926

We have just finished celebrating Purim in the real Palestinian style. A Yiddish saying in the Galuth has it that "Purim is nisht kein Yomtov und Kadoches is nisht kein krenk" ("Purim is not a Holiday and fever is not a disease"). The very reverse is, however, the case in Palestine. Or, it would be more correct to say, the very reverse is the case in regard to Purim. As you know, fever was a terrible scourge in Palestine until very recent days, and has now been practically wiped out as a result of the great labour and devotion of our heroic chalutzim. It is rarely indeed that one hears nowadays of cases of malaria or other tropical diseases breaking out in Palestine. But to revert to Purim, which is a real holiday in Palestine. Im am sure that the younger element look forward to no "Yomtov" so much as to Purim with its many festivities, carnivals, fancy-dress balls, etc. These Purim celebrations are mainly conducted by the National Fund and the ex-soldiers organisations, such as the "Menorah" clubs, and there is quite a military touch to the festivities. The "big" affairs take place in Jerusalem and Tel Aviv. Curiously enough, they celebrate on different days, Jerusalem on Monday, a day later than Tel Aviv. According to custom, various holidays are observed a day later in the walled towns, such as Jerusalem and Tiberias, the reason being that it took a day longer for news to reach the communities in the walled towns. Although the new Jerusalem was not and is not within the walls, yet it also follows the rule of a day later. And so it is that Motza, the little Jewish colony which is less than fifteen minutes ride from Jerusalem, celebrates a day earlier than Jerusalem. The custom, however, has its advantages, for there is a regular large migration from Jerusalem to Tel Aviv for the first day's festivities and a return with hosts to Jerusalem for the second day's celebrations. All Jewish banks, shops and offices close on Purim, although it is not an official Government holiday, and from a very early hour until late in the night the streets present a very festive air with schoolchildren, ex-soldiers en masse and others parading the streets in every conceivable mask and fancy dress.

This year's Purim festivities were a little overclouded by the many meetings of protest against that latest "military" scheme of the Government. The force of British Gendarmerie, which has done nothing since its inception except incur a very heavy item in the Palestine budget, is to be disbanded, the majority of the force to be sent home and a small number to be drafted into the local Police and Gendarmerie. This step meets with universal approval. But it has been decided to make certain changes in the Palestine Gendarmerie by increasing its number with the addition of some of the British Gendarmerie and new recruits. At the same time an order has gone forth that the Jewish members of the Gendarmerie (which is to act in future as the Palestine Frontiers Defence Forces) are to be transferred to the Palestine Police Force and no Jews at all will be admitted to the Defence Force. No one knows what is at the bottom of this new policy, but it must be exceedingly difficult to justify because one of the primary rights of the Jew must be to share in the defence of his National Home. The order in writing forbidding the recruiting of Jews in the force has been withdrawn, which constitutes a frank admission of an unfortunate error. But the instructions remain and have not been changed to time of writing. It is a very difficult position for the Zionist Executive, who carry on the negotiations with the High Commissioner, because if there is one field upon which Field Marshal Lord Plumer is considered supreme it is the military field, and he does not like to be questioned on military matters. The matter has already been raised in Parliament by our old good friend, Colonel Josiah Wedgwood, and no doubt some solution will be found. It is regrettable because up to now no fault has been found with Lord Plumer, who has commanded the respect and almost affection of every class of the population, in particular the Jews. He has made it evident that during the two years of office his sole aim is progress and much has been done since he took office, the amount of work being achieved in a year being in distinct contrast to that accomplished by the previous High Commissioner during his five years of office.

Jerusalem, June 28, 1926

The latest political advices are a little encouraging. The Delegation of the National Council of Palestine Jews (better known as the Va'ad Le'umi) has completed its work at Geneva and a telegram to hand today states that it is very satisfied with the results of its labours. When the Delegation got to Geneva, it discovered there was no provision in the regulations of the Mandates Commission for representatives of local communities in Mandated territories to be officially heard. The Delegation, however, was fortunate enough to be able to secure private interviews with members and attaches of the Mandates Commission. The Delegation reports that the members were all friendly disposed towards the desires of Palestinian Jewry as represented in the Memorandum submitted by the Va'ad Le'umi. By the time this reaches you, you will probably have received telegraphic news that the Mandates Commission closely cross-examined Colonel Symes, Chief Secretary to the Palestine Government, who appeared as the accredited representative of the Mandatory Government. The cross-examination dealt practically exclusively with the Jewish questions, and as a result the Mandates Commission held officially that certain of the demands put forward by the Zionist Organisation and the Va'ad Le'umi must receive more favourable attention from the Mandatory Government. In particular, the Mandates Commission requested the Government to take steps to provide land for Jewish colonisation, a matter which has been deliberately and shamefully neglected up till now by the Mandatory Government on the thin excuse that it was necessary to wait for a satisfactory survey of the country to be made first. The Mandates Commission also took particular note of the fact that the Palestine Government was going to substantially increase during the coming year its subvention to the Jewish schools. At a crowded meeting of the Va'ad Le'umi held here today the above news was received with great enthusiasm and a cable of congratulations from the Yishuv is being sent to the Delegation which has now proceeded to London. The general feeling here is that while we have absolutely no confidence in the Palestine Government and are rather skeptical of the attitude of the Colonial Office in London, the Mandates Commission of the League of Nations is a body to which we can always turn with confident anticipation.

Speaking of our confidence, or rather lack of confidence, in the local Government, I might say that the changes in the personnel of the administration have far from justified the hopes which they aroused in the beginning. Of Plumer there is very little, if any, complaint to be made. He does not exhibit any bias or prejudice and carries out his duties in a manner which commands respect. But the advisers of His Excellency would appear to be very ill-disposed in regard to Jewish matters, and time and again facts have shown that whenever there is an opportunity to block Jewish progress they quickly seize it. The programmes of various Zionist institutions and other bodies are pregnant with practical propositions for the development of the country in the interests of all sections of the population and of the Government itself, and they are almost all held up by the Government. In most cases the propositions are such as should receive moral and material assistance from a Government in any country. Yet here, the schemes are put forward practically with the condition that the entire cost and labour of putting them into fruition shall be borne by the Jewish institutions. There are schemes for building harbours and jetties and roads which are of prime importance to the development of the country, but all these are put on the shelf or are definitely refused. Perhaps the attitude of the Mandates Commission as evinced at its last session will work a few miracles.

The economic situation here is bad. The scarcity of money, to which I referred in a recent letter, continues. The situation in Poland has not materially improved so far as it reflects on Palestine, and the campaign in America for Palestine funds, which we understand has been successful, has not yet noticeably affected matters here. The Jewish unemployed number several thousand, and with the negative attitude of the Government in the matter of practical schemes for work, there appears to be little hope of ameliorating their position until the arrival of the funds from America. Cables to hand during the last few days announce that the campaign which is being conducted in South Africa by Mr. Sokolov is proving very successful. No time should be lost in getting the money itself delivered at Jerusalem; it was never more urgently needed.

This is a period of new ordinances and laws for us. We hardly finish reading one issue of the "Official Gazette" with half-a-dozen ordinances than, without allowing us time to digest and understand them (and believe me, they take some understanding), we are flooded with another paltry dozen or so. It hardly goes without saying that it is a rare ordinance indeed which does not merit bitter opposition from our ranks. Every ordinance is carefully worded so as to give Jews the minimum of benefit and the maximum of difficulty. The recent Palestinian Citizenship Ordinance which was intended to give Jews the opportunity of becoming citizens of the country with every facility to do so (as provided for in the Mandate) only succeeded in raising a storm of protest. The authorities set up offices all over the country to provide for about a hundred thousand applications, but in spite of all the elaborate preparations Palestinian Jewry held back and demanded immediate changes in the legislation. During the several months that the Ordinance has been in force the total number of applications for citizenship has not exceeded more than a few thousand. However, it is realised that the acquisition of Palestinian citizenship by as many Jews as possible is of great importance. Therefore, although the Government makes no move to improve the law, the Va'ad Le'umi has appealed to Palestine Jewry to accept the citizenship even under the present circumstances. In order to set a stimulating example Colonel Kisch, the Political Officer of the Palestine Zionist Executive, has surrendered his British citizenship and applied for Palestinian nationality. It is said that he is the first British Jew to have taken this step.

Some interesting figures have been issued by the Department of Labour of the Palestine Zionist Executive regarding the classes of recent immigration into the country. During the last nine months something over 20,000 Jewish immigrants have entered the country. Of these, less than ten percent belong to the category of persons of independent means, that is to say, people who were in possession of at least 500 Pounds. The whole of the remainder consist of the Chalutz type of people dependent on relatives in the country. In April the percentage of capitalists was only 4%, while that of Chalutzim was 72.5%. In May the percentage of capitalists was 5.2%, while that of Chalutzim was 83.7%. The diminution in the immigration of people of independent means is due to the economic position in Poland and other East European countries, and to a great extent to the financial stringency in Palestine. It means that there was during the period under review a very unappreciable increase in private investments or initiative. The workers were thus left to be absorbed in existing enterprises, mainly in agriculture.

AT JABOTINSKY'S SIDE

A new wave of Arab violence erupted in 1929, culminating in the massacre of the Jewish community in Hebron. The lives of the workers of the Potash Co. facilities at the Dead Sea were in danger, as was the property. By now Max was General Secretary of the firm, and in this capacity he tried in vain to secure added protection from the police and military. Eventually he had to threaten to close down the operation unless adequate security were provided. He pointed out to the officials he was dealing with that inasmuch as the Government[2] was a partner in this venture, closing the operation would be *their* loss. A committee was sent to investigate, and the result was that a police post was opened at the Dead Sea, and the workers' council was given some arms for self-defense.

Max leaned towards the views of Jabotinsky and openly spoke about them. When Jabotinsky was appointed Managing Director of the Judea Insurance Company, he chose Max as his secretary. If until then Max was charmed by his teacher and mentor, now working close to him he became his ardent admirer. When in 1929 Jabotinsky had to leave the country on a mission for Keren Hayesod ("The Foundation Fund"), he asked Max to take over for him. Max warned him not to leave, as he felt the British would not allow him to return. But Jabotinsky believed that since he was head of a large insurance firm and had a return visa, he should have no problem returning. But

Max was right: as soon as Jabotinsky left, the Government canceled his return visa and he was never allowed to return to Palestine until his body was brought back for reburial in Israel in 1964. Max was convinced even then that Jabotinsky's exile was not entirely the idea of the British, but that important elements in the Zionist leadership were behind the move to keep him out of the country.

At this time, Max passed the Bar and was appointed General Manager of the Judea Insurance Company, a post he held for four years. He then decided to go into law practice, and joined the firm of Asher Levitzky in Jerusalem. Although he was not a member of the Zionist Revisionist Party, he was sent (at Jabotinsky's request) as a delegate to the Zionist Congress in Basle in 1931. Upon his return from Basle, he became Chairman of the committee formed by Jabotinsky called "Zechutenu" (Our Right), the aims of which were to preserve the rights given to the Jews under the Mandate and by virtue of the Balfour Declaration.

By 1933 Max decided to open his own law office and move to Tel-Aviv, which had become the largest city in Palestine, with a population approaching 100,000. He soon added a branch office in the port city of Haifa. His professional and public work brought him not only into the most influential circles of the Yishuv, but also into the homes of leading civil servants of the Mandate Government, who, although fully aware of his ardent Zionism, still counted him as one of their own. He thus became the confidential advisor and defender of Administration police officers and of British army officers who in the course of their service were prosecuted before the civil courts as well as Army and Police courts-martial (He was made an honorary member of the Association of Former Police Officers of Palestine, and regularly attended their reunions).

NOTES TO SETTING DOWN ROOTS

1. Frederick Hermann Kisch (1888–1943) was the Indian-born son of a civil servant. He attended the Royal Military Academy, following which he joined the Indian Army, rising to the rank of Colonel, and suffered injuries severe enough to force his resignation from the army. He accepted Chaim Weizmann's invitation to head the Political Department of the Zionist Executive in Jerusalem. His main task was to interpret the Jews to the government and vice-versa. An Englishman to the core, Kisch had one problem: while he and the British understood but did not agree with each other, he and the Jews agreed but did not understand one another. He later acted as an advisor to the Yishuv on security matters, and wrote a book: *Palestine Diary*(1938). In WWII he rejoined the army, and served with distinction in North Africa, where he was killed in 1943. A settlement and forest in the Galilee are named after him.

2. The potash was marketed by Imperial Chemical Industries (I.C.I.), a British firm.

Uncle Max

A BOY'S VIEW

In July of 1933, I left New York with my parents on board the *SS Roma*, arriving in Haifa on my seventh birthday. We stayed with the Seligmans for a few days, then moved to a *pension* on Allenby Street, run by a German couple. I was farmed out to a summer camp in a place called Tel-Litwinsky, not far from Tel Aviv, while my parents went about finding work and a place to live—neither task a simple matter. Max and Millie lived at 59 Rothschild, the broadest boulevard in Tel Aviv at the time. Named in honor of the great benefactor Baron Edmond de Rothschild, it was planted with splendid poincianas and had benches for strollers to rest upon. It ran the breadth of the city, south to north, and was *the* address of choice, although 59 was an older house. (The Seligmans were soon to move to the top floor of an elegant new building at No. 87—an address they were to keep for many years[1].)

My uncle Max (Aunt Millie called him Mordie, after his Hebrew name Mordechai) was an impressive man. He towered over me, and his square, broad physique and deep, rich voice made him appear even larger, though he was only slightly above average height. He had a kind and pleasant face, and behind rimless glasses, a merry twinkle in his eyes. I was not familiar with the Oxford accent; it sounded very classy to me compared to the squeaky Canadian-American chatter of my aunt, mother and cousins. Max made a great show of *bonhomie* in welcoming us, and was very kind to me, the newcomer.

Camp, of course, was a terrible place. Although Father taught Hebrew in America, he somehow neglected to impart much of it to me, so I spoke not a word of the new language into which I was plunged. Children are nothing but little animals, possessed of all the delightful qualities of their elders but lacking in society-imposed restraints. My fellow-inmates set upon me with glee: here was this fat (there was an abundance of good pasta on the Roma), freckled, goddam *American* who couldn't even speak Hebrew! My numerous tormentors were suntanned, lean and mean. Given the spiteful nature of this first exposure to my peers, I am surprised not that I became a Jewish misanthrope, but that there are many otherwise apparently normal people in the world, even some in Israel, who genuinely enjoy the company of others. Getting acquainted with the local flora and fauna was pretty interesting, but the flies! We were given an afternoon snack *al fresco*, in the shade of an ancient fig tree, and the flies were so thick the table was black with them; if I brought my hand down fast enough, I could kill about fifty in one swipe. When I was ready to leave camp at the end of summer, I spoke Hebrew freely. I was enrolled at the Balfour public school across the street from our home; cousins Aura and Sheila attended the private Balfour Gymnasium near Rothschild Boulevard. I discovered Max was an avid stamp collector, and he invited me to come over and look at his albums. Now stamp collecting is an excellent hobby which should be encouraged in every child, as it helps in acquiring extracurricular knowledge of geography, history, languages and not less important, tidiness and organization. I was launched on my philatelic journey by Father, and helped along by Max.

Other boys at school also collected stamps, and we would bring our extras and trade during intermissions. I made the mistake of bragging about my album, and one afternoon, a couple of older boys dropped by the house and asked to see it. Foolishly, I let them in. They took the album, and beat me up in the bargain, later denying they had ever visited me. I was beside my self with powerless rage, but had learned a valuable lesson: real life was a far cry from the moralistic fairy-tales I had been reading. Father's reaction to my tragedy was typically Middle-Eastern: I should have known better. Max was more sympathetic, though, and with his generous help I was able to start a new collection.

About that time, the spring of 1935, my grandmother along with my uncle Laddie and Aunt Violet arrived for a visit from Montreal. There were many family get-togethers, and I was given for my birthday my first pair of roller skates. I now had wheels! I roamed the streets of Tel Aviv, pretending to be a detective following dangerous criminals.

After overcoming the horrible sores and stomach disorders brought on by the change of diet and climate, I started gaining weight and was becoming a fatso. This did not sit well with Father, who in his youth had been a long-distance runner and enthusiastic soccer-player. I too was anxious to develop some skills that would help me lose the status of punching-bag I held for the mean kids at school and on the street. We began going to the beach before sunrise for a preprandial run. Father had a bad knee, and I was soon outrunning him. One morning, I almost stumbled on the body of a drowned man washed ashore. This was the first time I had seen a dead man up close, and my appetite that morning was not great. Yet I was destined to discover more corpses, as I developed a liking for running on the beach: sailors falling off ships, suicides and other drownings were fairly common.

A couple of years later, the Seligmans and my parents took a trip to Beirut. The Canadian sisters were of course accomplished skiers, while the men contented themselves with sightseeing. I was left at home in the care of my Aunt Violet, who was staying with us during her visit from Montreal. Rather than get up to prepare a sandwich for me to take to school, she preferred to sleep in, and gave me some money. This was fine with me, since I could indulge in my favorite snack of *falafel*[2].

One day—I must have been about ten at the time—I went up on the roof of our house where I would fly little paper kites I learned to make—and noticed on the roof of the next building a cage with colorful birds in it. I decided to take a closer look. I went there and was looking at the parrots in the cage when I was suddenly attacked by the owner, who must have been some sort of maniac. Not content with bloodying my nose and tearing my shirt, he dragged me to the police station, where I was accused of attempted theft, and was booked and *fingerprinted*! Thus I joined the ranks of dangerous criminals with police records. While all this was happening, my parents were not at home.

I knew instinctively that I had to turn to Uncle Max in my hour of need. The officer taking the report had the unusual name of Avatichi (watermelonish); I told him that "my uncle is Lawyer Max Seligman". He said nothing, but I could tell he was impressed: everyone in town knew Lawyer Max Seligman. And it was indeed through Max's intervention that the ridiculous charge was dropped. Nor was this the only time Max was to help me when I got into trouble—and when this happened, he never lectured me or was in any way unpleasant, always acting in the most natural and friendly manner. (Years later, when my girlfriend—later my wife—Marion was on the run as a member of the Irgun, we knew we could turn to Max for help if she were caught. She wasn't.)

Religion played no part in my upbringing. On the contrary, my father was a freethinker who was always deriding orthodox Jews for their ridiculous, ghettoish appearance and would mimic their Yiddish. For my part, I had never seen these hangovers from the shtettls before coming to Palestine. My father dismissed all ultra-orthodox types as parasites, who didn't work and contributed nothing to society. Business dealings he had had with some religious types only increased his dislike.

My own distaste was reinforced by a traumatic experience I had when I was studying for my Bar-Mitzvah *Drasha* (reading of the Torah). The scholar chosen to teach me worked in a shabby synagogue downtown. I was not pleased at having to spend so much time on this distasteful duty, and besides, the fellow smelled bad and kept spraying me with saliva as he spoke. One day on the way home, a man boarded the half-empty bus I was on and sat beside me. I was annoyed that this seedy looking type, (who wore a skullcap) should sit beside and start questioning me. I was carrying the bag with my phylacteries, so it was obvious I was studying for Bar-Mitzvah; why then was he pestering me? Then he started to unbutton my trousers, and I was so horrified that I jumped off the bus before it stopped. I decided not to mention this disgusting incident to anyone.

I was once approached by a drunk British police sergeant, and another time, by an Arab ice-cream vendor who pretended to be interested in my dog. I remember "couples", Arab men from Jaffa walking along the promenade, their little fingers intertwined. In Hebrew, they were called *Nablussim*; the streets of the town of Nablus, it was said, were littered with gold, but no one dared bend over to pick it up. It is not surprising that homosexuality should be widespread in Arab populations whose majority was grindingly poor, and where the only way a man could have a woman was by buying her from her father, or going to a prostitute. Common street knowledge was that "they did it with sheep and donkeys". Another expression prompted by Arab visitors to Tel-Aviv was *dislocated eyeballs*, referring to the hot, hungry looks with which they would devour Jewish women, who by their standards were scantily dressed.

I know now that Max had deep religious convictions, but that is not how I perceived him as a child. In my eyes he was just another member of my parents' circle of intellectual, non-practicing Jews. He was such a suave, worldly type, who told what would now be considered racial-slur jokes in a heavy accent—I simply never associated him with anything remotely connected with "those people", the ultra-orthodox. The growing German-Jewish community had their own synagogues, where services were a lot more dignified than the East-European orthodox or wilder-still oriental styles. I would venture to guess that services at the Yeshurun Synagogue, founded and presided over by Max in Jerusalem, were on a high aesthetic level. Max often spoke about religious coercion, which was increasing as orthodox elements were strengthening their control over the Yishuv, a control to which he was adamantly opposed.

There were those in the Yishuv who were for having "an understanding" with our Arab neighbors. Father, who was born in Rosh Pina near the border with Lebanon and grew up among Arabs, could speak, read and write their language like an Arab. In some ways he also thought and acted like one. (With a little tuition, I could have had a far better command of the language.) He often criticized David Ben Gurion and the left-wing leadership in general for pretending the Arabs did not exist. He had some Arab friends who in peaceful times visited our home (openly ogling Mother), and he took me occasionally into Jaffa, where I was introduced to the finer points of Middle-Eastern cuisine. Max had some bad personal experiences with Arab colleagues, and while his attitude was not as unrealistic as those who thought like Ben Gurion, he nevertheless recognized the duplicity, evil and implacable hostility that characterized the Arab mind-set, and did what he could to avoid them[3].

There was a time during the 1936 "disturbances" when deaths

were reported in the newspapers almost daily, the outcome of Arab attacks on Jews. I recall reading with horror the description of a man named Belkind, one of several victims of an ambush on a northern road. He lay with his brains half-spilled out, but was still conscious when found. About this time, the right-wing underground stepped up its activities, and some of the boys were caught and prosecuted under special laws enacted by the Mandate government. Max co-ordinated a campaign with Jabotinsky, who was in London and not allowed to return to Palestine. The draconian laws imposed on the Yishuv, they pointed out, could have never been passed in England. Max attempted to get the Jewish Agency and National Council involved in his campaign, but they refused to co-operate, preferring to believe the Emergency Regulations were only aimed at curbing the rioting Arabs. Little did they realize that these measures would soon be used as an excuse for arresting the very same leaders. Max and his partner in Jerusalem, Asher Levitzky, were involved in the defense in most of the cases against the underground. At times even meeting with clients involved risky trips into hostile territory, such as the Jaffa and Acre prisons where they were held, and travel between Tel-Aviv and Jerusalem was also fraught with peril.

I earned pocket money by translating Mother's newspaper columns and radio program scripts on nutrition and cookery into Hebrew, as she never mastered the language. (She published a dozen or so cookbooks over the years, with Marion serving as editor/translator and even modeling in some of the photos occasionally. On her 80th birthday, an admiring journalist wrote about her as "Israel's First Lady of Cuisine.")

We had a cleaning woman, a buxom Yemenite girl called Shoshana, who came once a week. As she would be washing the floor on all fours, I became interested in her cleavage. When her skirt hiked up to reveal an expanse of thigh, I felt a strange, warm feeling come over me. I began to look forward to cleaning day, and when she saw me staring ("dislocated eyeballs"), she'd giggle in embarrassment. One day I got up my courage and asked to see more, only to be dismissed with an "Oh, it's only flesh". This of course hurt my manly feelings (I was about twelve then). I proposed to my parents that I take over the house-cleaning, and at a quarter the price Shoshana charged. Wouldn't this affect my homework, considering I already had Mother's weekly columns to do? Of course not, I stated. (My grades at school left a lot to be desired—not that I was particularly slow—it was simply a matter of not caring for subjects that bored me, and most did.) At any rate, I got the job, and with this double income I became, to use a rather impressive term, financially independent. From the age of twelve on, I purchased all of my clothes (they were not that many), thus gaining autonomy in yet another area. Children try to be the opposite of their parents, which makes rearing them such a wearisome task. Mine, bohemians at heart, cared little for tidiness, and as I was developing into a compulsive neatnik, we often came onto a collision course. The problem was eventually resolved when I left home to join the R.A.F.

In matters of sex, swimming and other basic skills I received precious little instruction, though this did not prevent me from developing normally in these areas. As a pre-pubescent child I was aware of a mysterious yearning, amorphous though distinctly female-oriented. I could not pinpoint what I desired, though I was fully aware of what pleased me aesthetically. In those days, the few cinema houses in Tel Aviv had contracts with certain film companies (or were perhaps owned by them) and showed their films exclusively. The *Ophir* in the heart of town was MGM; the *Migdalor* on Ben Yehuda Street (which was near us) had a contract with Columbia Pictures. Each Columbia film was preceded by the vision of a demure, dark-haired beauty dressed in a clinging toga whose folds emphasized her lovely form, a torch held aloft in her hand. I was quite taken by this exemplar of female loveliness. It is probably no coincidence that when I married, my wife Marion closely approximated the Columbia-inspired specifications. (I recently saw a television interview with the model, still lovely after all these years. She related how they stood her on a soap box, her long gown draped to cover it, in order to make her appear taller.)

Tel Aviv then had only one designated beach, near the foot of the still-unpaved Allenby Road. Raw sewage flowed into the ocean, and one always had to look out for "mines", in the water and on the sand. It irked me that the city fathers, who obviously never went to the beach, should be so indifferent to the problem.

There was one lifeguards post, and few people dared go in the water without their reassuring protection, so it was always pretty crowded, especially on weekends and holidays. The lifeguards used a rescue craft called *Hassakeh*: it resembled an oversize surfboard, and one stood on it to paddle. It was hollow, and drew a lot of water, which made it extremely heavy and hard to maneuver. A corncob wrapped in cloth was used for stopping the drain-hole. The lifeguards would go careening on the surf right into the crowd of swimmers, who had to scatter in all directions to avoid the 'rescue' craft. Before I met her, Marion was struck by one, and suffered a cracked rib. Some fifty meters offshore, there was a resting-place, constructed of three large pipes embedded in the sand and joined on top. I watched with envy as boys swam out to this point, climbed and dived off it. I'll never forget the thrill of achievement I felt when I managed to dog-paddle out there and back. The same feeling returned when, left to guard a friend's bicycle while he was getting a haircut, I managed to mount and ride it. As far as I can remember, the Seligmans were not enthusiastic beachgoers. In any case, Max was probably too busy for such idle pastimes.

Primness was not a prominent feature of my parents' quasi-bohemian circle, and I observed a lot of good-natured "messing around", in which Max obviously shared with relish. I remember one occasion, a garden party *à la anglaise* at the Bernstein villa in Rishon le Zion outside Tel-Aviv: fragrant ladies in pretty summer dresses and wide-brimmed hats, daintily traipsing in high heels across the lawn. A long table by the pool, generously laden with bite-sized square and triangular cucumber, tomato and salmon salad sandwiches on thin white bread, lemonade, iced tea, and angel-food cake, all delicacies never seen in our nutrition-conscious home. The Goddards were among those present: British police inspector Harry Goddard, who lived with his family in Tel-Aviv, and whose son and daughter attended Hebrew schools. The Goddards' friends were mostly Jewish, and the British establishment looked askance at this fraternizing with "natives." Our mothers arranged for us to meet—the Goddard boy and I—though he was a couple of years older. (I remember him telling me he wanted to become a pilot. He later enlisted in the RAF and was killed in action over Germany.) Max was an avid bridge player, much sought after as a partner. He had been playing inside, and now emerged for a change of pace and refreshments: suave, debonair, his silver-tipped malacca cane in one hand, a *Players* in the other, he was joking with friends, kissing one lady, casually caressing another's bottom. My young heart beat faster: this was my hero.

The celebrated concert violinist Bronislaw Huberman founded the Palestine Orchestra at that time (1936), and for its inaugural concert, Arturo Toscanini was invited to conduct. The gala affair took place at the grounds of the Levant Fair, which was held the previous year. Everybody who was anybody attended, of course, the Seligmans and my parents included, with me in tow. The concert consisted of Beethoven's Ninth Symphony, with it's majestic and rousing choral finale. After the concert, the cream of Tel Aviv society gathered backstage, and Maestro patted me on the head.

There was a symphony concert over the radio every Friday night, and as we did not have a radio, we'd go over to our friend Helen Tannenbaum's house nearby. That was how I discovered and fell in love with Schubert's *Unfinished* Symphony. There were also Concerts for Youth at the Ohel Shem theatre, where Malcolm Sargent gently led his youthful audience into the world of the masters, in a series that lasted several weeks. I was well on my way to becoming a certified music addict, and when family friend Rae Berger gave me her portable wind-up phonograph for my Bar-Mitzva, I was really launched. Another friend, Jack Brinn, manager of the Tiberias Hot Springs, was a chamber music lover, and would bring over some of his records when he'd come for tea of a Saturday afternoon. I'm sure I was not able to appreciate the bittersweet subtleties of Mozart and Schubert quartets, but it was a good start.

On holidays we would sometimes travel to Netanya, where my uncle Zion and his family lived, or to Jerusalem, where another uncle, Peretz (both on Father's side) lived in the suburb of Rehaviah. My cousin Danny was a couple of years older, one of the five children of my uncle Peretz and aunt Rachel. Danny was my favorite. He was tall, broad-shouldered and could easily walk around on his hands! Like the rest of the family on my father's side, he was right-wing and a member of *Beitar*, the Revisionist youth movement (Beitar was the last Judean stronghold to fall to the Romans during the Bar Kochba revolt in 130 A.D., following which the emperor Hadrian changed the name Judea to Palestine.) Danny taught me many things, most importantly to stand tall and proud when dealing with Arabs. During WWII he rose to the rank of Captain in the Jewish Brigade (his older brother Mattie was a Major!), while I left the R.A.F. a lowly Aircraftsman/mechanic[4]. Both brothers went on to become senior officers in the Israel Defense Force, and certainly had the experience and personalities to go to the very top, were it not for their rightist political orientation.

One year we were in Jerusalem for Passover. The day after the *Seder*, I went along with my parents to tea at friends of theirs, the Maurice Bassans. Virtually all houses in Israel's capital are built of the ivory-hued, locally quarried Jerusalem stone, giving the city its unique golden glow in the soft sunlight of dawn and at the end of day. The Bassans' house was very nice and had a lovely garden, but I was quite unprepared for the sight that greeted my eyes upon entering the living room: a record collection lined an entire wall, floor to ceiling! I had no idea such things even *existed*! A highly polished ladder leaned against the record shelves, and nearby stood a record-player, a quality instrument with adjustable louvers for controlling the volume and direction of the sound. Our hosts noticed my interest and very kindly asked if there was something I'd like to hear. Would I, indeed! I knew there and then that someday, I too would have a fine record collection, with all the music I loved within easy reach.

Buying records was of course practically out of the question, but eventually I managed to purchase a two-record set of Mozart's *Eine Kleine Nachtmusik*, Walter Susskind and the Vienna Philharmonic on two ten-inch 78's. I also enjoyed popular music, and discovered a source for cheap records: a store on Nachlat Benyamin Street that had the latest imports, cracked but still playable, and for pennies. I turned as deaf an ear as I could to the click, click, click and proudly played for Max a record of *Amapola*, a popular dance tune of the day. I knew he liked to dance, and was not profoundly interested in the classics (he later developed a liking for opera and symphonic music, when his lifestyle became more tranquil). He then handed me a crisp Pound note (a fortune!) and suggested I buy some new records. The man was generous to a fault!

KNIGHT ERRANT

In 1939 Max was sentenced to prison for complicity in aiding immigrants enter the country illegally. We were all naturally dismayed, but Max put on a brave front and was making all sorts of jokes about going to jail. His release four months later was accompanied by a lot of publicity and a great round of parties. It was only much later that I found out what he had undergone, what traumas he suffered, and how well he bore up under the ordeal.

Yitzchak Gurion was the courier who carried messages between the political prisoners and their families on the outside. He was of course a member of the Irgun, but as far as the British authorities were concerned, he was simply a clerk in Max Seligman's law offices. Eventually, they caught up with him and he was interned. After sentencing, he was transferred to the central prison in Jerusalem. He relates the following anecdote:

There was one prison officer of the Jewish faith there, in the Jerusalem prison, who did not know I was coming this time as an ordinary inmate. He knew me quite well from a previous tour of duty in the Acco (Acre) fortress prison, and then from his more recent duty here. And he knew that whenever I came to visit, I'd cross his palm with silver (paper money, actually), to let me do my work smoothly. So he came over, as usual, ready to serve me with a cordiality that bordered on obsequiousness. There was nothing he was not ready to do for me. And since, as it happened, Max Seligman the attorney was also "inside" for a six-month term, for helping in an operation to bring in Jews illegally—this officer was convinced I had simply come to see Mr. Seligman, my employer. So he blandly turned to the prison guard and told him to inform Mr. Seligman that there was a visitor to see him. Then he brought me a chair, and said apologetically: "Reb Aryeh (the prison rabbi) is now in the prison synagogue with the Jewish inmates, and none of them would be willing to come out for a visitor as long as he is there." In his effusive friendliness he then suggested that I go to a nearby cafe for a cup of coffee, and come back in about half an hour.

Had it been four or five years later, I would not have hesitated to take full advantage of this Jewish officer's generous mistake and walk off nonchalantly and disappear. It would have caused me no pain if on account of his cordial friendliness he lost the star he wore on his epaulet. But in 1939 I was far from prepared for an anonymous life hidden in the underground movement.

In a few moments I saw Reb Aryeh coming from the cells in his slow, steady walk, accompanied by Seligman. They perceived my situation, and did not make the same mistake as the Jewish prison officer. When he (poor fellow) now realized his error, Reb Aryeh smiled at him benignly, but Seligman could not suppress his laughter.

My memory leaps now to Yom Kippur (the Day of Atonement) in 1939. Cell 29 was converted into the temporary synagogue of the central prison. We were all there, close together. Yet at the same time, how far apart one inmate was from another. Here was a man who had murdered his wife . . . sentenced to fifteen years. On the other side there was a group of hashish-smokers. And over there was the "business group": merchants and shopkeepers who went bankrupt. Side by side with murderers and criminals of various kinds stood some of the finest sons of the Jewish people, who risked every danger (as fighters in the underground movement) to free their homeland from crippling foreign rule . . . three students who invented a special kind of explosive for the *Irgun*; and nearby, two who faced the gallows until their sentences were commuted to life imprisonment: Yehezkel Altman (Ben-Hur) and Yaakov Kotek. Only one thing united this strange, motley crowd into a congregation of worshipers: the deep respect, even reverence they bore for the kindly rabbi, short in stature, who blended his voice with the sweet chant of the *hazzan*, Max Seligman, when the solemn prayer of *Kol Nidrei* was heard.

Immediately after he began serving his sentence, Max received the following letter from Vladimir (Ze'ev) Jabotinsky, exiled leader of the Revisionist movement:

Vals-les-Bains (Ardèche)
July 12th, 1939

Dear Mr. Seligman,

For weeks and weeks I wanted to write you but I was not sure if my letter would be welcome. I hope my son* has told you what I wrote on the subject to him at least. Now I hear from a mutual friend that you did expect to hear from me during this ordeal. I am glad to learn it; it is in keeping with all that attitude of frankness and courage of which you have become a living lesson in a society that badly needs such lessons.

I want you to know that, despite the base pusillanimity of some, there are hundreds of thousands—there will soon be millions, without any exaggeration, and we shall take care that they do not forget,—who bless you from afar. You are the first victim in a fight that seems to be destined to become (one of) the loveliest chapters in the history of Zionism.

No decent person the world throughout pays any attention to the silly charge framed up against you. Let me only add that, having been brought up in the judicial atmosphere of pre-war Russia, I had never heard of stool-pigeons produced as evidence in a Court of Law. It is a practice which reminds me of some of the less clean features of the Stawski trial, things beyond the pale of civilisation. The bigger the courage and the merit of those who struggle under such conditions to make right a substance.

I feel that we in Europe have too long neglected what ought to have been our main care from the first: to help in that struggle. It was almost a crime to have let down such an important initiative as "Zechutenu"—an association bent on following up, stubbornly and relentlessly, any big or small violation of equity in Palestine, bringing it before the English Courts, before Parliament, keeping that Pekidut under constant fire. But it may not be too late. I fervently hope being able soon to approach you with concrete schemes and suggestions aiming to revive that institution on sound and durable foundations.

In the meantime, let me shake your hand on behalf of all those whose gratitude you have earned.

Kindest regards from my wife who joins me in all I have said; and I hardly need assure you that I also express the attitude of all my colleagues on the Nessiut who have always admired you for the staunch and generous knight errant you have been in our crowd in Palestine, giving unstintedly not only of your time but your money to ensure their defence.

Please remember me to Mrs. Seligman, who must be one of the proudest women in Israel.

Yours very sincerely
V. Jabotinsky

*Eri Jabotinsky

THE ARLOSOROFF MURDER

The Arlosoroff affair had always been a mystery to me—something awful that happened soon after we arrived in Palestine. The whole truth emerged years later, after Max was released from prison.

Late one night in the summer of 1933, a man was murdered on the beach in Tel-Aviv. The victim was Chaim Arlosoroff, brilliant head of the State Department of the Jewish Agency (whose secretary then was Moshe Sharett, later Prime Minister of Israel).

At that time the Revisionist party was gaining in popularity. A bitter rivalry existed between it and Mapai, the Labor party, which often led to open conflict and violence. Soon after the murder of Arlosoroff, rumors were spread that it was the work of the Revisionists. Three Revisionist leaders, Aba Achimeir, Zvi Rosenblatt and Avraham Stavsky were arrested as the murder suspects.

Arlosoroff's wife later identified Stavsky as one of the attackers. She was unable to identify either Achimeir or Rosenblatt, but Mapai did its best to implicate them in a "plot to assassinate Mapai leaders." The case for the prosecution, nominally handled by the police, was actually prepared by Mapai's lawyer, Dr. Bernard Joseph, aided by Jewish police officer Bechor Shitrit (both of whom later became ministers in the State of Israel).

On the day following the murder, a couple of escaped Arab convicts were caught in Jaffa. Both had long criminal records, including murder. During preliminary investigation, they admitted being at the scene of the crime, adding that all they were looking for was "someone to rob", that they intended to harm no one, and that in fact they had no idea who it was they shot.

The Yishuv was rocked by the murder and its aftermath. Demonstrations took place demanding the release of Stavsky and his colleagues, and in London Jabotinsky assembled a defense team headed by Horace Samuel, and also asked Max to join the defense. Samuel and an assistant went to the jail and took a statement from the Arab prisoners. Apparently he told them that since they were under life sentences for murder anyway, they would probably not be sentenced to hang if tried for this crime. He then proceeded to show the signed confessions to the Chief Justice, an unprecedented move to make during the preliminary stages of a criminal case. It appears they were later visited by a Jewish police officer, who advised them that unless they withdrew their confession, they were sure to hang. They came to believe that the three Jews accused of the crime would be released for lack of evidence against them.

As a result, the court ignored the confessions when the case came to trial. The charges against Achimeir and Rosenblatt were dropped, but Stavksy was convicted and sentenced to death. The verdict was later reversed by the court of appeals, and Stavsky was completely exonerated.

After he was released from prison, Max wrote about his experience:

> I began serving my sentence at the Central Prison of Jerusalem on 7 July 1939.
>
> A few days later, I was told by several Jewish fellow-prisoners that among the Arab inmates there were two men under life sentence for murder, and who had admitted being the killers of Arlosoroff.
>
> A couple of the fellows who spoke fluent Arabic introduced me to them, telling them I would like to hear their story about the incident. They readily agreed, and told me the following: On the night in question, they were walking along the beach in Tel Aviv, looking for someone to rob. It was very late at night when they noticed a couple slowly walking towards them. They approached, and one of them who spoke Hebrew asked the man for the time. The man (Arlosoroff) first hesitated, then shone a flashlight he carried at them. One of the Arabs had a gun, which he said was only intended for menacing his victims, but when blinded by the light, he panicked and fired, not having any idea who was shot. They then ran from the scene, and spent the night on a bench on Rothschild Boulevard, before continuing to Jaffa, where they were captured.
>
> When I asked them why they recanted after admitting to the crime, they confirmed that a Jewish police officer advised them to do so. They also expressed their surprise that Mrs. Arlosoroff identified Stavsky as one of the attackers, since he bore no resemblance to either one of them, beyond the fact that one of the attackers was stockily built, like Stavsky. They also stated they were sure the Jewish suspects would be released for lack of evidence.

Max's trial and subsequent incarceration had wide repercussions at home and abroad. A few samples of the reactions it aroused follow.

THE JEWISH CHRONICLE
August 18, 1939
SCANDAL OF SELIGMAN TRIAL
Conflicting Evidence for Prosecution
"IMPLICATE SELIGMAN IF AT ALL POSSIBLE"

The High Commissioner has made it known to Mr. Max Seligman, the Swansea-born lawyer of Tel Aviv who was recently sentenced to four months' imprisonment on the allegation of having assisted an "illegal" immigration association, that he must decline to grant a pardon. It would perhaps be appropriate to review the circumstances of this unfortunate case in their legal aspects in view of the very grave political implications involved.

At the outset, it would be instructive to examine the background of the trial. By an order under the Emergency Regulations, which supersede ordinary legislative practice in Palestine and from which there is no appeal, the Attorney-General directed that the hearing of the case against ex-Police Inspector H.G.G. Goddard and Mr. Seligman should be held in Jerusalem, although both are residents of Tel Aviv. The idea behind the Attorney-General's action in transferring the case was possibly that a Jewish judge would not convict. And the full implication of this maneuver was apparent when Mr. Seligman in fact appeared before a British judge and an Arab acting judge. It will be seen that the choice of an Arab judge was particularly unfortunate as the trial followed shortly after the publication of the White Paper, and questions were asked by the prosecution based upon the restrictions upon immigration contained in that Statement of Policy. "If I were an Arab" said Mr. MacDonald in Parliament, "I should be passionately opposed to Jewish immigration." The inference might not be lost upon a judge who happens to be a member of that race selected to hear charges against a Jew alleged to have been assisting "illegal" immigration into Palestine.

THE APPEAL

Then came the question of the appeal. The Chief Registrar of the Supreme Court, Mr. L.W.A. Orr, had been present throughout the District Court proceedings in Jerusalem. It is customary for appellants to file their appeal within ten days after a sentence has been pronounced by the Lower Court. Yet apparently the Chief Justice was apprised beforehand of certain circumstances prevailing in this case, since His Honour himself fixed the date for hearing the appeal and ordered that the grounds should be lodged without delay. In other words, the instruction to file the appeal came from the head of the Palestine Judiciary even before counsel for the defence had formulated the substance of their submissions to the higher court. At such direction, the formulation of the appeal had to be rushed through in three or four days, although the law specifically allows ten days as the period of grace. It was apparently the Chief Justice's wish to preside at the hearing of the appeal in view of his projected departure on leave. In his petition to the High Commissioner for a pardon, Mr. Seligman submitted that the Court of Appeal and the District Court referred to his visit to the Chief Secretary and the Attorney-General, and appeared to believe he had called upon both officials to ascertain whether any proceedings were pending or contemplated against him in connection with "illegal" immigration. That was not so (as the High Commissioner subsequently agreed in his reply). Mr. Seligman had applied for the interview with the Chief Secretary several days earlier because he (Mr. Seligman) was about to proceed to England. It was at the Chief Secretary's own suggestion that he went to see the Attorney-General, and the purpose of his call was to communicate in confidence complaints made to him by clients that they had been approached by the police for bribes in order to secure their freedom from arrest.

IN THE PUBLIC INTEREST

The Attorney-General thanked Mr. Seligman for the information, which he said was in the public interest. No information was conveyed by Mr. Seligman concerning direct activity of police officers in "illegal" immigration, and the reference to such information having been given was, consequently, a misleading and unwarranted maneuver by the prosecution and wrongly embodied in the judgments of the District and Appeal Courts. Mr. Seligman in his petition analysed the evidence given against him by Mr. Walter Gilpin, Assistant Superintendent of Police, and pointed out that testimony by a police officer stated to have heard only one conversation failed to corroborate Mr. Gilpin's version in a number of most important particulars. No statement was recorded to show that Mr. Seligman was personally connected with any "racket" or conspiracy. Moreover, it was inconceivable that he should have freely confessed guilty participation in an illegal conspiracy to a police officer who stated on oath that he had never previously had any intimate conversation with Mr. Seligman and never discussed the matter with him before. (Minutes of District Court Case.) Such a suggestion concerning the confession could not be believed of any person of intelligence, more particularly an advocate of some standing in the profession.

There were other statements made on which the prosecution failed to secure or attempt to secure corroboration, and Mr. Seligman submitted, in his petition to the High Commissioner, that they were patently untrue. No attempt was made to trace a number of five Pound and ten Pound currency notes, yet the prosecution, stating that it was impossible for notes to be traced, made the allegation, which the court apparently accepted without due corroboration, that these notes had actually been passed to Mr. Gilpin by the accused. Nevertheless, it is well known in criminal investigations throughout the world that notes of high denominations can be traced. Mr. Seligman at this point referred to a sum of 200 Pounds missing from the safe of the C.I.D. at Jaffa. No public report had yet been made as to how this amount in currency notes disappeared from a police safe, although the fact of the disappearance was public knowledge.

In conclusion, Mr. Seligman dwelt upon his difficulty in believing a Court of Law could have set against his known professional standing the uncorroborated and conflicting statements of a very young and ambitious officer (Mr. Gilpin is twenty-six years old) who had, as he admitted in court and as was specifically declared on a police memorandum, instructions "to implicate Seligman if at all possible."

ENGLISH ZIONISTS AND MAX SELIGMAN
A Petition Urged
To the Editor of the Jewish Chronicle

Sir.—Max Seligman is an English Jew who, like his father before him, has rendered yeoman service to the cause of Zionism in England. It is therefore a matter for surprise and regret that no single voice has been raised on his behalf. As for his "crime" in helping "illegal" immigrants into Palestine, the reports of the trial suggest that it was intended that he should be trapped. Max Seligman is being punished not for the offence preferred against him but for the zeal which he has always displayed in helping those who were unable to help themselves, especially those who were unable to speak the King's English. It is well known that he is the only Englishman, certainly the only English lawyer in Palestine, who has stood up fearlessly against the police and other authorities whenever their action tended to be arbitrary or in disregard of the rights of the individual. What wonder then that he has incurred their odium in championing the cause and defending successfully the many Jews who have sought his aid.

He is now undergoing his four months' sentence in Jerusalem and thereafter there may be many even who may desire to see his future career arrested. Apparently it should be a matter for our Jewish Agency to protect him, but to anyone having a knowledge of Jewish politics in Eretz Yisrael and of the fact that Seligman has always been a freelance, their intervention on his behalf would appear to be doubtful. I would therefore strongly appeal to the Zionists of England either through the Zionist Federation or by the collective action of Zionist bodies of whatever shade of opinion to petition the Palestine Government through the Colonial Office to remit the remainder of his sentence.

I am, &c.,
AN ENGLISH JEW

THE PALESTINE POST
7 November, 1939
MR. SELIGMAN RELEASED

Tel Aviv, Monday. When the advocate, Mr. Max Seligman, returned here this morning after serving four months' imprisonment in the Jerusalem Prison for conspiracy in connection with offences under the Immigration Ordinance, he was greeted at the entrance to the town in Rehov Herzl by friends and sympathisers.

HAMASHKIF
12 November, 1939

Tel Aviv, Sunday. The attorney Max Seligman wishes to express his heartfelt thanks to the many individuals, friends and institutions who sent flowers, gifts and congratulations upon his return to Tel Aviv, and wishes them to accept his appreciation via the press, as it would be impossible for him to do so in person.

Aura recalls: "I remember very vividly a torchlight procession in Rothschild Boulevrad when Abba came out of prison. We stood on the balcony and watched them pass by honoring Abba's release."

THE JEWISH CHRONICLE
April 5, 1940
MR. MAX SELIGMAN
Wins Appeal Against Law Council

Readers will remember the case of Mr. Max Seligman, the Tel Aviv lawyer, who was convicted by the Palestine Courts last July for conspiracy to assist refugees to defeat the immigration laws. Mr. Seligman served a term of four months and was released last November. The case was taken a further, and probably a final, stage recently when he appealed to the Supreme Court against a decision of the Law Council to suspend his licence for six months. Mr. Seligman conducted his appeal in person, and the Law Council was represented by the Senior Crown Consel, Mr. E. Bell. The Supreme Court allowed the appeal, holding that as Mr. Seligman's offence did not involve either moral turpitude or unprofessional or disgraceful or fraudulent conduct, the decision of the Law Council could not be maintained. The Attorney-General, as Chairman of the Law Council, was ordered to pay the costs of the appeal.

Soon after the outbreak of WWII, the brave Italians sent over 'planes and dropped bombs on a wide area of Tel-Aviv, a one hundred percent undefended civilian target. Mussolini wanted to impress his new German ally that Italy was doing something concrete in the war, and took the cowardly path of hitting where he was assured of suffering no losses, and his pilots returned victorious.

In 1940, Rommel's *Afrika Korps* was advancing unimpeded across Egypt and it seemed like only a matter of time before the Germans overran Palestine, where they had a ready-made Arab Fifth Column in place. Things looked grim indeed, and the Seligmans decided it would be best for Aunt Millie and the girls to go to Canada, leaving Max to hold the fort. The girls thus spent their formative years without benefit of their father's company (years later, Sheila, the younger of the two girls, was to tell me that she had to become re-acquainted with her daddy, as she was too young to remember him very well when they were separated).

Their apartment was rented out for the duration, and Max took a room at the Brandstaetter Pension a block away from our house. The establishment was run by Mrs. Brandstaetter, a handsome German-Jewish lady, aided by her daughter, who was a real beauty and who apparently had a huge crush on Max. Between the two ladies, and our home just down the street, Max was quite comfortable. I took over the care of the Seligmans dog Coushy (Blackie), a dachshund-and-something-else mix, given to them by the Goddards. Coushy was jet-black, hence his name, and was quite a rover. He couldn't quite decide which he liked better, our place near the beach, or Rothschild Boulevard. I ran into him at different places all over town—it's hard to train a grown dog. Whenever Max would come over—which was quite often—he always delighted in romping with Coushy.

I don't believe Max ever made a great deal of money, although in a country where poverty was widespread, especially during hard times, he lived well and was considered wealthy. The general appearance of the man in the street, particularly that of middle-aged and older people, tended to be on the shabby side in the 'thirties, 'forties and even later, but Max was always impeccably dressed in English-style three-piece suits. He never owned a car—in fact, I doubt that he could drive one—but he did have a keen interest in them, as did I, and we held long and lively chats on the subject. Max dined well, drank only the finest brandy and whiskey[5], and smoked *Players* cigarettes exclusively. He also enjoyed a fine cigar, and as these were extremely hard to come by during the war (and after), he was always asking friends travelling abroad to bring him a box. Nevertheless, he could always smoke or switch off on command (as when he had a cold, for example)—such was his self-control. (Anti-smoking campaigns are making some headway, mostly in the western U.S.A., but for those who did not live through WWII, it would be difficult to grasp the importance of smokes.

They exerted a powerful social and economic influence and were a very important daily item. English cigarettes, taken for granted by the military and other like-privileged classes, were very expensive on the civilian market—actually the black market—since they were simply unavailable otherwise. The only affordable brand in wartime Palestine which did not smell like camel-dung were *Victories*[6]).

It was decided for safety reasons that I should leave the city, and so I went to Yavne'el, near Tiberias, where my uncle Nachum Sandler and aunt Ella (on Father's side) had a farm. I remained there a year. At that time, the Vichy French, who were allied with the Axis, were in control of Syria. They began shelling the border towns of northern Palestine. Uncle Nachum's brother and his family lived in Metulla, and when things got too hot, they came en masse to Yavne'el to sit it out. They arrived on horseback and in several mule-drawn carts, a whole tribe of giants: the sons, like their father, all stood well over a raw-boned six feet, and sported fierce-looking mustaches. Nor was there anything subtle about their womenfolk. They spoke in a Hebrew dialect that was at least ten per-cent Arabic, uttered in a unique drawl, and accompanied by broad Oriental gestures. During the fortnight these Upper-Galilee superfolk stayed at Yavne'el, I can remember feeling particularly insignificant. (It was about this time, incidentally, that Moshe Dayan lost his eye. As a scout for the British army, he was leading an Australian patrol in Vichy-held territory. They came under fire, and he was hit by a sniper's bullet when he held up his binoculars, the impact driving metal and glass fragments into his eye. In his memoirs he said he was never free of pain for the rest of his life.)

On the farm I shoveled a lot of cow-dung and did all the other things a boy does on a farm. Yavne'el was one of a cluster of three communities in the Yavne'el Valley, Beit Gan and Mishmar Hashlosha being the other two. The Sandler farm was actually in Beit Gan, and that is where our family buries its dead. Whenever there was a wedding, everyone was invited. I remember one such occasion, a rollicking affair which in later years was to remind me of that famous *Peasant Wedding* by Pieter Brueghel. There was a barrel of sweet red wine, which was tapped by everyone to fill their glasses. Some didn't bother and drank right out of the spigot. I too had a few draughts, and was roaring drunk as I rode my mule home in the moonlight, a quite unforgettable experience (as was the monumental hangover the next morning!)

Relations with neighboring Arab villages were good on the whole, and Arab outlaw activity went into low gear when war broke out. Still, one could never be too sure, and our village perimeter was regularly patrolled at night. I believe most settlers owned firearms, legally registered, for self-defense. My cousin Yitzhar (so named in honor of the Balfour Declaration, when he was born) was in charge of the family *Mauser*. This 9mm German-made machine pistol (along with the *Parabellum*) were the two most popular guns in use since WWI. When mounted on its wooden holster, the Mauser became a submachine-gun, a formidable piece of equipment. One windy, rainy winter night when it was Yitzhar's turn to patrol, he dared me to come along, feeling sure I'd decline. I surprised him by not only accepting, but telling him he need not bother, I'd go alone. Up since dawn every day, seven days a week, the poor fellow was in a constant state of weariness. He readily accepted, and I put on the heavy gun (which he had previously showed me how to use), high rubber boots and coat, and ventured forth into the night. To say I enjoyed the experience would be an overstatement; but it was part of growing up.

All in all, my year on the farm was a truly valuable, if not always pleasant experience, and it taught me to put my values in perspective. Since I had no pocket-money, I would bicycle to Tel Aviv when I got homesick—a distance of some two hundred kilometers, which took about fifteen hours to cover. Home is probably not the proper word to use, since my parents agreed to disagree: our apartment was rented out, Father went on an extended business trip to Turkey (whence he sent me interesting postage stamps), and Mother rented a room with board (they made up after his return). I remember the shock I gave her when I appeared unannounced, all grimy from my day-long bike ride. I made several such trips, always on my own: the few friends who agreed to come along always chickened out at the last moment. It hurt me that Max did not believe I made these trips unassisted.

Like every other boy I knew, I was in the Hagana. Belonging was such a natural process that I don't even recall how it came about. But I soon became disillusioned with the repetitive, boy-scout type tasks given me, such as making diagrams of areas bordering on Jaffa, noting escape routes, or passing endless chain messages. All this was useful, admittedly, but unexciting. We had unarmed combat training, long, sometimes overnight hikes, and eventually graduated to the use of rifles and grenades. But all this seemed too tame while (to quote the Irgun posters pasted on walls and billboards) *The Nazo-British beasts ran rampant.* During training sessions, the subject of what to do in case we were caught came up in conversation. Boys enjoy name-dropping no less than do their elders, and I never missed an opportunity to brag about my uncle Max.

1942 was my last year in high school, and I transferred to the *Montefiore School*, which offered technical courses that interested me, especially the course in auto-mechanics. I was very keen on cars and hoped to own one at the earliest opportunity. In the basement of the school there were two cadavers, a Morris Eight and an ancient Reo truck, upon which so many post-mortems had been performed over the years that all bolt-heads were rounded and the threads were stripped. Our instructor Mr. Rudich was later to become a bigwig in the Motor Vehicles Department of the State of Israel. This training enabled me, when I got out of the R.A.F. in 1946, to earn my living as a mechanic.

There were only three girls at the school, all in my class. I concentrated on Marion Waxman, the prettiest of the trio. Not only was she cute, but she also had a scholarship (very impressive!), and was to my joy, a *Yekit* (a girl from Germany). I liked German Jews—they were very civilized, unlike most others. Marion was a brunette, petite but very well-formed and athletic, and an enthusiastic swimmer, as I soon found out when I set to work on getting to know her. We enjoyed the same hobbies and had, unbeknownst to each other, frequented the same tidepools, pinched cactus cuttings from the same places, and haunted similar nature sites. I was *very* excited, as only a schoolboy who had found his first love can be.

Early in the war, The *Parita*, a ship carrying refugees, beached at Tel Aviv, and soon after that another, the *Tiger Hill*. I used to swim out to the *Parita* and dive off it. So did Marion, and after we met, we haunted the old wreck together. The ships were eventually blown up by British sappers, probably to remove these reminders of British foreign policy and prevent them from becoming shrines of some sort. They had a good excuse for the dismantling: the scrap metal was needed for the war effort. (In 1948, the Irgun ship *Altalena* beached at almost the exact spot where once the *Parita* had lain.)

We had been dating for several months before I discovered (and not from Marion) that she was in the Irgun. So was her older sister Ruth (also a scholarship alumnus of the *Montefiore* school) and her boyfriend Niko, who was later deported to Eritrea. It was a long while before Marion conceded that she indeed was a member. I told her of my frustration with the restraint (Havlaga) policy shown by the Hagana, of which I was a member. The news about the Holocaust was appalling beyond belief, and Max, who was consumed by it to the point of obsession, would speak of nothing else. The British were acting their brutal colonial worst, and Max was kept busy saving boys from the gallows. As if she had to be told any of this! She gave me the name of a contact, who swore me to secrecy and told me where and when to report, for induction into the Irgun, I thought. I arrived at the appointed place, a school near Jaffa. It was the pitch-dark of wartime blackout, and I was proceeding slowly when I felt something cold pressed into my neck, and a strong hand clamped over my mouth. After giving the password, I was taken upstairs, where two men and a woman sat behind a powerful lamp, rendering them all but invisible. A large *Parabellum* pistol lay on the table, a bible alongside it. I was asked countless questions, many of which seemed to me irrelevant, although my relation to Max was obviously not. Then I was told I'd be notified, and was asked to swear, one hand on the *Parabellum*, another on the bible, that I not disclose anything which took place, under threat of severe penalty.

I felt the melodrama was overdone, I told Marion. As it turned out, I got her into a lot of hot water, since during my questioning I divulged the name of my contact—something I had sworn not to do. My indiscretion all but caused Marion to be court-martialled. At that time I began cramming for my matriculation exams, after which I joined the R.A.F. Thus I missed joining "The Firm", as the Irgun was fondly referred to by its members.

SELIGMAN'S HUMOR

Max was born to be a Public Person. He had all the qualities needed for a successful diplomatic career, and undoubtedly would have shone in such a role, were it not for his political orientation, which precluded his holding high office in any left-wing government. One of his greatest gifts was a keen sense of humor that made him such delightful company, and the despair of his adversaries. His was a British brand of whimsical humor, of the kind his English-speaking interlocutors, in social as well as court situations, could and did appreciate. His ready wit undoubtedly helped Max win acquittal for many of his clients (as in the case of the man accused of possessing illegal leaflets, which Max claimed the defendant only kept for sanitary use). On a few occasions when I was home on leave, my uniform enabled me to get into Military Court where I could observe Max in action. But those were solemn occasions, matters of life and death. I would have given anything to be present, however, or view films, had they existed, of some of the civil cases he defended, and which involved quaint, colorful Arab and other oriental characters, about which he would tell us later.

Max's younger brother Arnold tells of the time he came to Israel for a visit, and made a luncheon appointment with Max at the Diplomat Hotel in Tel Aviv. They had not seen each other in many years. At the appointed hour, Arnold was walking towards the hotel when he spotted Max ahead of him. Pulling up alongside, Arnold said something along the line of *Dr. Livingstone, I presume*? Without a sideways glance, Max muttered: "Bloody decent of you to be on time for a change!" Then they embraced in a great bear-hug.

A *raconteur* of the first order, Max loved to tell stories and jokes with flair, assuming, it seemed to me even then, a lot of sophistication on the part of younger members of his audience. He had the knack of making even the most serious matters appear comical, so much so that it was sometimes disconcerting, not knowing whether he was in earnest or merely jesting. Nor was he averse to practical jokes: Aura told me he'd disguise his voice on the telephone, announcing: "This is the Saudi Embassy calling." His humor was so infectious that one couldn't help being swept along by it. He would without warning engage in mini-comedies. Fixing me with a stern gaze, he would thunder in his best courtroom basso: "Who are *you*? No, no, don't tell me. You're Yakobovitch, right?" and one was expected (and did) make the appropriate response. His Yiddishisms were outrageously funny because they were so completely unexpected: he would nudge the person next to him, and looking at whoever happened to be speaking at the moment, would ask in a loud voice, "Vus zugt er?" (What's he saying?), or, sighing deeply, he would wail, "Oy, siz schwer zi zein a Yid!" (Oy, it's hard to be a Jew!) Or little gems like: "What were Gandhi's last words?" "Mahatma geharget!" (They've killed me!) Whenever we'd meet, Max would always have new additions to his repertoire.

In his book *In My Time*, Lord Elwyn-Jones[7] writes about a visit to Israel where he addressed a gathering of lawyers.

> Brought up on the Bible as I was In the Tabernacle Chapel, Llanelli (Wales), I was greatly moved looking out of my bedroom window in the Saint David Hotel in Jerusalem to see the site of some of the Holy Places I had learned about as a child.
>
> When I sat down, the chairman of the meeting said genially that they knew King David was a great king, but until I spoke they had not realised that he had been canonised by the Church of England.

The chairman was Max Seligman.

Max's stories were invariably top-drawer, but that did'nt really matter. The magic was in the telling. Max was one of the funniest men I have ever known.

NOTES TO UNCLE MAX

1. Aura recalls: 'There was no lift in 87 Rothschild Blvd.—to our perspiring lot. How my parents made that climb day after day for years I'll never know. But it kept them fit, so much so that in his eighty-fourth year, Abba was still able to climb up to the seventh floor of their London flat when the lift there broke down—which happened often!'

2. Falafel is Israel's national snack—a sort of spicy vegetable hamburger eaten in a *pita* with *tahini* (sesame sauce) and hot pepper sauce. To quell the fire in one's mouth, a glass of *gazoz* or freshly-squeezed orange juice are good antidotes.

3. Sheila recalls: 'In London, many years ago, Max had meetings with Arab individuals willing to talk peace with Israeli representatives. He went to a great deal of trouble to set up the meeting (I think with Israeli Embassy officials). Imagine how he felt when the Israelis did not show up! I cannot provide any proof, names or dates, only how incredulous he was when he mentioned it.'

4. Although I had begun training as a WOP/AG (Wireless Operator/Air Gunner), it was late in the war and the training program, to my great disappointment, was terminated.

5. I've often seen Max drink socially, but never remember him drunk or even slightly tipsy.

6. In the 'thirties and 'forties, everyone smoked as though cigarettes were about to be banned (were this only so!). Hollywood did its bit to cultivate the macho, nonchalant image of the smoker. Cigarette butts were everywhere, and on the beach and in the streets, Arab urchins would collect them in tin cans. These were later recycled in a factory in Jaffa and marketed under the "Victory" brand name. They were cheap and I recall they tasted quite good, as they contained a high ratio of English tobacco. Max smoked non-filter *Players*, and the fingers of his right hand bore the tell-tale brown stains of the chain-smoker.

7. Lord Elwyn-Jones who was Attorney-General in the Labour Government from 1964–70, evinced a warm regard for the Jewish people and championed among other human rights causes that of Soviet Jewry. He had been a member of the British War Crimes Executive at the Nuremberg trials of Nazi war criminals (1945) and he was insistent, in speeches both inside and outside Parliament, that the evils of Nazism should never be forgotten. He frequently voiced anxiety at the recrudescence of Nazism in Germany and elsewhere. He was a staunch friend of Israel and visited the Jewish State as an honored guest on several occasions.

Illegal Immigration

THE FOLLOWING CHAPTER was written by Max Seligman. The typewritten MS bears his name and a handwritten "Notes for Book." The twenty-three legal-size sheets appear to have been typed in haste by Max himself, possibly begun when he was in prison and completed much later. It may be that he intended to revise the text once the other chapters were written. The writing is essentially in memorandum style, laced with legal terminology. I left the English usage intact, and the only changes made were the correction of typographical errors.

"ILLEGAL" IMMIGRATION

In the early days of 1939, I was very friendly with a number of British Police officers, among whom was an Inspector named Harry Goddard. Goddard had had an excellent career in the British Army in India and had served for about twenty years in the Palestine Police Force. He was a very sociable fellow and was very well liked in the community. He had assisted in the training of the Jewish Supernumerary Police and had also taken an interest in the Maccabee Sports Organisation. He was married to a vivacious blonde Irish woman, who also lived on excellent terms with her Jewish neighbours, and they had two children, a son and daughter both of whom were educated in Jewish schools and spoke fluent Hebrew. The son was killed during the war when he was shot down over Germany while on an R.A.F. strafing mission.

One afternoon Goddard dropped in for tea and in the course of a conversation told me that he had just seen a decoded message which had been received that day by Major Gilpin, the officer in charge of the Post and Marine Police warning them that a boat of "illegal" immigrants was on its way to Palestine and was expected to land near Herzlia that very night. I did not know who was likely to be concerned, although it was common knowledge that, despite objection by the Jewish Agency, the Revisionists and the Agudat Yisrael were running ships of refugees from Europe to Palestine. I decided I would first try to contact the Revisionists in order to warn them of the fact that the authorities would be waiting for the boat, and one of the first persons I met was Dr. Buxspan, a Revisionist leader, who said that they were expecting such a boat and that he would take steps immediately to divert its course. I learned later that this had been successfully accomplished and that the refugees had been landed safely elsewhere in Palestine.

A few days later I met Goddard again and thanked him for his kind "tip". He told me that he thought that Gilpin, who was a good friend of his, might be willing to help the organisation which was landing "illegals" if he was paid for it. I communicated this information to Dr. Buxspan who was delighted to hear it and who requested me to make all necessary arrangements in that respect. I was most reluctant to become involved directly and suggested that someone of their organisation should be introduced to Gilpin and should make arrangements directly. He said this was not desirable as the authorities might thereby learn the identity of the organisation involved, of which they were not aware.

I told Goddard that he was free to agree to any reasonable terms with Gilpin and I would advise the organisation concerned. Later, Goddard told me that Gilpin had agreed to help, that financial arrangements could be agreed at a later date, and that, if I would telephone to him whenever a boat was expected, merely saying "Thumbs up", he would direct the coastal patrol. This was actually done on two or three occasions, the message being phoned by me as arranged, and, so far as I was aware, the immigrants landed without any trouble. No money passed, and I might here state very categorically that, despite all the malicious rumours which were spread to the contrary, I never demanded or received a single penny in connection with these matters, whether by way of fees or for my expenses or otherwise. Even the cost of the defence in the criminal proceedings which later ensued were all paid out of my own pocket and I was never reimbursed. Moreover, it would have been useless to ask for money because the Revisionist organisation had no money and were unable even to pay me for professional services which I had rendered at their request in the military courts and elsewhere on behalf of many alleged "terrorists".

Towards the end of April or early in May I received a telephone call from Major Gilpin requesting me to call upon him at his office in Jaffa for an urgent private discussion. At the time I was extremely busy and could not comply with his request. He said that the matter was one which could not be delayed, and I finally agreed to call upon him in the afternoon at his home. He then resided in a flat in Rothschild Boulevard, Tel Aviv, only two blocks from my own flat.

When I called at the flat, he offered me a drink and told me that he had been asked by his superiors to make recommendations as to measures to be taken in order to prevent illegal immigration into Palestine. He said that it had been suggested, among other innovations, that a number of forts should be erected all along the coast which should be manned by guns which would open fire on all persons attempting to land. He said I was one of the very few representative Jews which he knew personally and he should like to have my view on the probable repercussion on the part of the Jewish Community.

I told him that, in my opinion, the restrictions on immigration were already sufficiently severe and that, having regard to the desperate plight of so many hundreds of thousands of Jews in Europe, these restrictions were inhuman and ought to be eased. I said that, if steps were taken as now suggested and Jewish refugees should actually be fired upon, the patience of the entire Jewish community might be overtaxed and they might rise in armed revolt against the Government. I added that if he was really friendly disposed, as he indicated, then he ought to advise the Government to abandon their plans and that, if they could not officially permit immigration of these refugees, then they might have an unofficial policy of turning a blind eye to their landings. Gilpin replied that he fully appreciated my contentions and that he would advise his superiors along the lines suggested by me. During our conversation I told him that some British Army officers were rumoured to be very friendly disposed to help this "illegal" immigration, and that a story was then going the rounds that there was an arrangement with an Army Officer in Nathanya whereby he permitted refugees to be landed illegally against payment of one Pound per head, that on one occasion there were some three hundred such immigrants and the man in charge could only raise 299, and the officer then said "Well, never mind, let him land; there will be one illegal immigrant".

A week or more later, on the 25th of May, I called in Jerusalem upon the Chief Secretary of the Palestine Government in connection with an appeal which I had lodged against an order for the deportation of a Jewish client from Palestine. In the course of the discussion the Chief Secretary, who appeared to be very embarrassed, told me that I had better not continue to talk on that subject as he knew that I was involved in certain investigations which were then proceeding. He suggested that I ought to see that Attorney General. He then telephoned to the Attorney General telling him that I was with him and asking him to receive me. I then called on the Attorney General who told me that it had been alleged that I was involved in "illegal" immigration and that he believed that proceedings were already pending against me. I expressed my surprise, and he advised me to await possible further developments.

On my return that afternoon to Tel Aviv, I happened to meet Gilpin and I asked him whether he knew of any investigation or proceedings in which I was involved. He professed to be completely ignorant thereof and promised to make enquiries and to let me know. I did not hear any further from him.

A few days later a British Policeman called upon me at my office and delivered to me a Charge Sheet containing twenty-two counts alleging conspiracy with Inspector Goddard to defeat the Immigration Laws and with bribing Goddard. Goddard was charged similarly.

At the same time, the Attorney General, in exercise for the first time of powers vested in him under the Emergency Regulations (which Regulations were enacted for the express purpose of subduing the Arab revolt which was then in progress), made an order removing the venue of the trial from Tel Aviv to Jerusalem. The reason for this was the apprehension which was felt that the Court in Tel Aviv would never convict me on the charges laid.

This step on the part of the Attorney General caused me no little inconveniences and interference with my defence because at the time there was a curfew at night on the road between Tel Aviv and Jerusalem and in any event witnesses were naturally reluctant to travel because of the shootings and stoning by Arabs of Jewish vehicles.

When the case came on for hearing before the Chief Magistrate in Jerusalem, both Goddard and I elected to be tried before the District Court, and an order was made accordingly. On the advice of numerous mutual friends, it was decided that I should not conduct my own defence but to brief Mr. M. Eliash to appear for me and Mr. E.D. Goiten, now a Judge of the Israel Supreme Court, to appear for Goddard.

Before the case came on for trial before the District Court, we requested the Prosecution to furnish us with the names of the witnesses who would be called for the Prosecution and for access to the file containing the statements made by these witnesses. This they refused to do. We thereupon applied to the High Court for an order directing the Attorney General to deliver to us the names of the witnesses and to permit us access to their statements.

In consequence of these proceedings, we were furnished with a list of the names of the witnesses and copies of several statements. The only item of any real interest which became apparent from these statements was an order from the head of the C.I.D. to Gilpin in which he was directed to "get Seligman if at all possible". The reason for this extraordinary and malicious order was, of course, that I had become a nuisance to the C.I.D. in my unrelenting struggle with them on behalf of the hundreds of men and women who were suspected of being terrorists or of being connected with terrorist organisations.

The case came on for trial on the 15th June 1939 before Judge Shaw, and as Goddard and I elected to be tried separately, the case proceeded only against Goddard who had been named as the first accused. In the course of that trial, it transpired that the only real witness for the Prosecution was Gilpin who, despite his friendship with the Goddard family, testified against him and told a long series of falsehoods as became patently obvious as the result of a very able and effective cross-examination by Mr. Goiten. I also testified on behalf of Goddard and remained completely calm under a severe cross-examination by Crown Counsel, largely relating to matters which were entirely irrelevant, such as my political affiliations and beliefs. Nevertheless, Goddard was convicted on all twenty-two counts and was ordered to be bound over to be of good conduct for a period of two years.

The hearing of the case against me was fixed to commence on the 27th of June. It might be of some interest to record that, although summonses were served upon me as well as upon Goddard on several occasions, we were never arrested nor were we even required to attend at any police station in order to make statements or furnish a bond to ensure our attendance in Court. I mention this because in Israel, it is the invariable practice of the police to require accused persons to attend at a police station and to make statements and to arrest them or require bonds to be given to secure their attendance when called to trial. In fact, their fingerprints are also taken today, even though they might never in fact come up for trial before the Courts.

Another matter which I think is deserving of mention is that, before the trial took place, a number of advocates expressed their desire and suggested that representations should be made by the Jewish Bar Association to the Jewish Agency to intervene with the Government with a view to staying the proceedings against me. One morning, in my presence, several advocates raised the matter in the Court at Tel Aviv with Dr. Bernard Joseph, who was then the Legal Adviser to the Jewish Agency. His reply was that, although he felt sympathy, such representations would be useless because the Jewish Agency could not become involved in any matter involving "illegal immigration". It was not until several years later that Dr. Joseph joined the chorus of Jewish leaders who at a very belated date contended that such immigration was not illegal. In the summer of 1939 they were still reluctant to approve of this immigration and in fact were still officially condemning it.

The hearing of the charges against me commenced in Jerusalem on the 27th of June, but on this occasion the Court was otherwise composed, there being a different British Judge, Mr. Curry, and an Arab judge, Mr. Khoury, who was a Magistrate and had been specially appointed to hear the case. This composition was significant and immediately gave rise to the feeling that the case had been "fixed" by someone in authority. The case was one dealing with the question of Jewish immigration into Palestine, and the British judge was not particularly friendly towards the Jews, while no Arab, however friendly he might be, could be expected to indicate any sympathy with Jewish immigration, whether legal or otherwise. In fact, only a few weeks earlier, Mr. MacDonald, the Prime Minister of England, speaking in Parliament, had said; "If I were an Arab, I should be passionately opposed to Jewish immigration". *Verb sap.* Nevertheless, when the case was closed, Mr. Khoury confided to a friend that he was not satisfied with the evidence and wished to acquit me but that he was told that, unless he agreed with the judgment of Judge Curry, he would lose his post and that he had no option but to agree. At this point I might also mention the point that, when I was released from prison, a Police Officer offered for a price of one hundred pounds to extract from the files of the C.I.D. a note which he had seen therein written by the head of the C.I.D. in which he stated that, prior to the commencement of the hearing of the case, he had spoken to Judge Curry and impressed upon him the necessity of delivering a judgment against me which would serve as a warning to the community. Unfortunately, by the time arrangements had been made to extract this interesting document, the offices of the C.I.D. had been blown up by the Irgun Zevai Leumi and the file had been destroyed. When the hearing of the case was commenced, the Court was crowded to capacity and at every subsequent hearing there was not a vacant seat. Two or three seats were reserved at every hearing for some Consuls of East European States.

The first witness for the Prosecution was Gilpin. The Prosecution was conducted by two Senior Crown Counsel, Mr. Bell and Mr. Hogan. Gilpin stated that he was in charge of the Post and Marine Patrol. He said that he had made certain overtures to Goddard in the hope that the latter would be able, having regard to his friendship with Jews in Tel Aviv, to lead him to the people who were in charge of the illegal immigration. Later, he stated, Goddard came to him and said that he, Gilpin, could earn a lot of money if he would agree to divert the patrols. On being pressed for names, Goddard told him that the only person he knew was Seligman. He made arrangements with Goddard whereby he would receive a fee of 100 pounds for every boat load which he allowed to land and that he would divert the patrol on receiving a telephone message of "THUMBS UP" whenever a boat was expected. He said that he had received from Goddard altogether only 25 pounds. On instructions from Headquarters in Jerusalem he had asked me to call upon him and I had called at his flat where he had placed another officer, Inspector Christie, under a rug in order to overhear and take notes of the conversation. He said that I had stated that a number of Army officers were assisting illegal immigration and that it was the wish of the Colonial Office to turn a blind eye to it.

Christie testified that he had heard my voice and that I had spoken about Army Officers. He admitted that it was difficult to hear the conversation; that he had missed a great deal of it, and that there had been no mention of the name of Goddard.

This was the only material evidence for the Prosecution. It was never even alleged that I had been seen to meet together with Goddard or with Gilpin. There was, therefore, no evidence of conspiracy other than Gilpin's own statements and conclusions.

In giving evidence, I denied all of Gilpin's allegations and his version of what took place at the meeting which took place in his flat. Gilpin had said he was informed that I was a Revisionist and was being paid an annual retainer of 1,000 pounds for my legal services to the Revisionist Organisation and that was the reason for my readiness to pay money to Goddard and Gilpin. This, as I testified, was totally untrue. I was not a member of the Revisionist Party (for some years past, in fact, I had been a member of the General Zionist Party and was for a time a member of the National Executive Committee), I had no such retainer, they had never paid me such fee and that, although I was their lawyer they were not able to pay my fees but were actually in debt to me for moneys which I had disbursed for Court fees, etc.

I was severely cross-examined by Mr. Hogan, particularly regarding my sympathy for persons who had been arrested on charges of entering the country illegally and regarding my friendly relations with British Police Officers. I told him that, in my view, every Jew had a right to come to Palestine; otherwise the term "Jewish National Home" had no meaning. I agreed that I was in favour of a Jewish majority in Palestine. I said that I was not a member of any organisation dealing in illegal immigration but that I saw nothing for a Jew to be ashamed of in assisting Jews to enter the country. His cross-examination did not direct a single admission which could be construed against me. Evidence on my behalf was given by Major

Harrington, Chief of the District Police who testified that, in the course of a very close friendship over a period of twenty years, I had never made any improper suggestion to him.

Mr. Julius Meltzer, a prominent journalist, and Mr. Ittamar Ben-Avi then testified confirming various statements which I had made in the course of my evidence.

A representative of the Revisionist Organisation testified that I had rendered professional services to that organisation but that I had never received any fixed retainer and that they were still indebted to me even for out-of-pocket expenses.

Mr. Lubianiker of the Histadruth (Labour Federation) testified in support of statements made by me and agreed with me that, in view of the cruel and illegal provisions of the White Paper of 1939 prohibiting Jewish immigration, there was nothing wrong in "illegal immigration".

Several other prominent Jewish personalities who had expressed a desire to testify on my behalf, such as the late Mr. Pinchas of the Mizrachi Organisation, were unable to do so because of the difficulties then involved in travelling from Tel Aviv to Jerusalem owing to the curfew.

Judgment was delivered the following day. Although the impression made on everybody else by Gilpin was that he was patently lying, as, in fact, he was, the Court stated that they believed him and that Christie's evidence, though incomplete, corroborated him. There was no evidence, however, of bribery or of suborning Police Officers, and the Court accordingly acquitted me of nineteen charges. They held me guilty, however, on three charges of conspiracy to defeat the immigration laws by assisting Jews to enter the country illegally.

Judge Curry stated that the offences were serious and merited an exemplary sentence. It would not be sufficient to impose a fine and the Court accordingly imposed a sentence of imprisonment for a period of six months. My wife, who was seated in the well of the Court, screamed out: "Shameful! It is a disgrace to the Court".

According to all newspaper reports, the judgment and sentence made a bitter impression upon the crowded Court. As the spectators left the Court, they demonstratively filed past me, and each one shook my hand, told me I should be proud of myself and wished me luck in the appeal which was bound to follow.

I immediately applied for my release on bail pending an appeal. This was granted, but at the time, to the astonishment of all of us, I was notified that the appeal could be heard the following Friday, a week hence. It was the invariable practice for appeals to be fixed for hearing only months after they had actually been filed. Here, it was fixed for hearing at record speed even before a formal appeal had been lodged. No explanation for this extraordinary haste was forthcoming.

Upon being released on bail, I was notified by the Police authorities that I could not return home to Tel Aviv, but must remain in Jerusalem. The explanation offered for this was that it was feared that my appearance in Tel Aviv might lead to serious disturbances, and in fact the Army and Police had been given orders to stand to.

I remained in a hotel in Jerusalem until Sunday when, after further approaches to the Police, I was permitted to return to Tel Aviv. There appeared to be no real justification for the fear of trouble, although whenever I appeared in public during that week, i.e. in a cinema or a cafe, I was greeted by spontaneous and vociferous demonstrations of sympathy and solidarity.

The appeal was heard on the 7th of July. With one solitary exception, so far as I am aware, it was the confident belief that the Court of Appeal would reverse the judgment of the lower Court and would acquit me. The one exception was the late Mr. Menachem Ussishkin, the President of the Jewish National Fund, whom I met on the eve of the hearing of the appeal and who said to me: "Do not trust the British here. They want you to go to prison and you should be ready to go. You should be strong and proud of yourself".

As I have stated elsewhere, the Court of Appeal held that they could not interfere with the findings of the lower Court which had heard Gilpin and stated that they believed him. Despite a hostile, separate judgment by the Jewish Judge, Mr. Frumkin, the British Judges agreed to reduce the sentence from one of six months to one of four months imprisonment and directed that I should be given "special treatment" while in prison. This "Special Treatment" was a provision of the law which could be exercised in the discretion of the Court in favour of privileged prisoners. It meant that they need not work, could wear their own clothes, could have their own food sent in to the prison and could sleep on a bed.

I was immediately taken to the Central Prison in Jerusalem. There I was greeted by the Jewish prisoners, including a number of former clients, who were expecting me as a result of a "grape-vine" communication from a British Police Officer to the effect that my appeal would be rejected.

My four months in prison were a most unpleasant and gruelling experience. In the course of my professional career, I had probably paid more visits to the various prisons in Jerusalem, Jaffa and Acre than any other person in the country, but until I was actually confined as a prisoner I had no real notion of what conditions inside were like. The prison was an old Russian building which had been used prior to the first World War to house Russian pilgrims to the Holy Land. There were over six hundred prisoners in it, about fifty of whom were Jews, the remainder, except for three Englishmen, being Arabs. The prisoners were kept in large bleak rooms containing from twenty to forty prisoners in a room, the Jewish prisoners occupying two separate rooms. The three Englishmen, former British policemen, were enjoying the privilege of special treatment and shared one room with me. Two of them had been sentenced for manslaughter and one for forgery and embezzlement. They admitted to me they had been convicted by Courts or Army Courts Martial before they had joined the Palestine Police Force. Two of them had been sentenced for the killing of an Arab prisoner whom they were escorting and who, they maintained in Court, had attempted to escape from the Police van in which he was being taken to prison. Their story was a very far-fetched one, but the Court, apparently reluctant to convict them for murder, found a solution by holding that it was "attempted manslaughter", the first time such an offence had ever been discovered in Palestine legal history. Although the three of them got along fairly well with me, they made little bones about being viciously anti-Jewish.

In our cell, we slept on beds of a sort, but in the other cells all the prisoners had to sleep on the bare cold stone floor with some poor rags or pieces of blanket as their only protection. Their food consisted mainly of olives and "pitta" (the Arabic flat bread) and water. They never received any tea or coffee or any other warm beverage. They were allowed out to exercise twice daily, once in the early morning and once in the early afternoon for a total of about two hours. They were employed mainly in the printing press, where the Police Gazette was printed, a furniture manufacturing shop, an iron foundry and a laundry. There was no form whatsoever of cultural activity or of any entertainment or training. The only relaxation was the possibility of borrowing some uninteresting books from a sparsely filled Prison library. The warders were all Arabs. The Superintendent and his assistant were British and there was a Jewish Inspector and for a time also a Jewish Sergeant.

Among the Arab prisoners, there were at least twenty who had been sentenced to long terms for murder. Homosexualism was common among the Arab prisoners. There was one open old Turkish form of lavatory and one room containing showers to which the prisoners were taken in squads on days when water was available. None of the cells contained any running water or any lavatories. The occupants of my cell, if caught short, could go to the public lavatory if we succeeded in catching the eye of the warder or if the warder happened to be friendly disposed. In the large cells, all the prisoners had to relieve themselves in the communal bucket which was cleared every morning.

The warders were mostly illiterate and brutal unless they were bribed. Most of the warders added to their poor monthly wages by taking bribes from prisoners in order to smuggle letters or messages in and out of the prison or to bring razor blades, cigarettes or cards, all of which were confiscated if discovered during the searches which were made periodically.

A large number of the Jewish prisoners were men who had been sentenced by the Military Courts or who were being detained pending trial or pending dispatch to a concentration camp. I made a practice of slipping whenever possible into the cell containing the majority of the Jewish prisoners and would share with them sweets and other delicacies which I was receiving and also the newspapers which were smuggled in to me. I was in prison during the High Holidays of 1939, Rosh Hashana, Yom Kippur and Succoth, and I acted as Cantor during the religious services. A Rabbi also attended from outside the prison, Rabbi Arie Levin, a very kindly man who was a source of great comfort to many of the prisoners with his ready advice and encouragement and by conveying messages to and from their families.

Most of the prisoners, other than those who had been convicted for political offences by the Military Courts, maintained that they were innocent, and I was consulted by many of them, Jews and Arabs, in the hope that I might be able to assist them after my release. One prisoner who did give me the impression that he was innocent was Reuben Sheinzwit, who was serving a fifteen years sentence for murder and who was released after serving for about ten years. He was obviously a man of superior character and upbringing to most of the prisoners, but his repeated petitions to be granted special treatment were all refused.

The fact that I was being consulted daily by most of the prisoners and that I was helping some of them in drafting petitions came to the knowledge of the Superintendent of the prison and he was extremely indignant. He resented the fact that I had become, as he termed it, a "mukhtar" of the prison, and he sought means of curtailing my privileges and freedom. He finally succeeded in trapping a warder who was smuggling a letter out for me, and he punished me by revoking all my privileges for one week, including the right to have my own food sent in. It was doubtful whether he had the right to do this, but an appeal to superior authorities would have been useless as he would have delayed its transmission for several days if he would have forwarded it at all.

During my stay in prison I received many messages of cheer and encouragement. They include a long letter written by Vladimir Jabotinsky from New York, which letter has strangely disappeared, and a cable from Isaac Allen, a well known American lawyer and Mizrachi leader, who said he would deem it an honour to share my imprisonment. Oral messages were conveyed to me from Judge Aressal, the British President of the Jaffa District Court urging me to "keep my chin up" and from Mr. Stubles, the British Director of one of the Government Departments, saying that he "hoped the Jewish people appreciated what I had done and would later elect me Mayor of Tel Aviv".

Touching on "appreciation", I am glad to record that my conviction had no prejudicial effect upon my legal practice. Only one client, a Mr. J. M. Tocatly, who represented a foreign insurance company rushed to withdraw his business from me. Mr. A. E. Mulford, representative of the Prudential and other English insurance companies, was actually approached by another local lawyer, a member of the English Bar, to transfer his work to him, but he declined to do so stating that I was convicted for political offences with which his companies were not concerned. Before I entered prison, Mr. Victor Ellern, the Director of a local bank, said to me: "Remember, Max, that I was your client even *before* you had this case".

A number of active leaders both of the Irgun Zevai Leumi and the Stern Group were arrested during my stay in prison and were kept in the same prison for some time. Among them was Stern himself, and I must say it was a real pleasure to get to know him. He was a very quiet and learned person, and in the early evenings the Jewish prisoners would gather around him and listen to his reasoned and logical discourses on political and religious and other subjects. Some years later I had the occasion to meet Stern again in connection with preparations for the defence of some members of the Stern Group, but that is another story.

A month or so after my arrival in prison, information reached me of the disappearance of a large amount of money in cash from the office safe of Mr. Gilpin, who had been promoted in the meantime to the rank of Major, presumably as a reward for his services in securing my conviction. An official enquiry into the disappearance of the money led to no conclusions. I made a point of this incident in an appeal which I addressed to the High Commissioner for a free pardon.

Although I indicated a number of facts which now showed beyond any doubt that Gilpin had lied when testifying against me, the petition was rejected.

The second World War broke out while I was in prison. I immediately sent a letter to the authorities volunteering for service in the British Army, but I heard nothing further on the matter and I doubt whether my letter was even forwarded by the Superintendent of the prison. The only noticeable effect of the war upon life in prison was the behaviour of the Arab prisoners. There were frequent demonstrations by them particularly when Arab prisoners were being hanged, in the course of which they would yell in unison "Heil Hitler; Down with the Jews; Down with the British; Long live the Mufti". On days when Arabs were being hanged, the cells of the Jewish prisoners were locked and the Jews were not allowed out at all. This was a reasonable precaution as the Arab prisoners were a very violent lot and many of them were armed with razor blades and even with knives.

The hangings took place in the main yard of the prison, and prisoners were not allowed to be present. But from early morning, until the hangings were over, the Arab prisoners would bang on the cell gates and kick up a terrific din shouting curses on the British and encouragement to those going to the scaffold. It was a most unpleasant atmosphere, and there was even present a real danger that some of the Arab prisoners might succeed to break out of their cells, in which case nothing could have prevented them from murdering Jewish prisoners.

When a prisoner seriously misbehaved, i.e. when he would strike a warder, the usual punishment would be a whipping. Such punishment would be ordered by the Superintendent of the Prison, but was subject to approval by the District Commissioner. The whipping would take place in the main yard of the prison in the presence of the Superintendent, a representative of the District Commissioner and the visiting medical officer. All the other prisoners were also ordered to be present to view the whipping. They would refer to these spectacles as "cinema balash", i.e. free performance. The prisoner concerned would be stripped in front of all the other prisoners and then tied to a piece of high scaffolding so as to be in full view of all the other prisoners, with his hands and legs outstretched and pinned down to prevent him from moving them.

My last few weeks in prison were the most painful. The hours seemed to drag by so slowly, and I would be almost counting the minutes. However, they at last came to an end, and on the morning of 7th November I was called to the office of the Superintendent of the

Prison, and from there, following the formalities, I was led outside the prison. I was greeted by a large crowd and there were a number of cars lined up. Some people had come all the way from Tel Aviv just to shake hands with me immediately upon my release. Several girls presented me with bouquets. I was then taken to the Vienna Cafe in Jerusalem where included were many personal friends and some representatives of the Revisionist movement including Dr. Arie Altman. Being anxious to get back to Tel Aviv in order to see my daughters, we left Jerusalem very soon. The drive through the main street of Jerusalem (the Jaffa Road) was a slow one because of the crowds stopping the car and throwing flowers inside. At the entrance to Tel Aviv, there was a crowd awaiting my arrival and we were greeted with cheers. I spent the afternoon at home where bouquets of flowers were arriving every few minutes from friends and various organisations. In the evening I went with my family and Mr. and Mrs. Julian Meltzer to a cinema, as I had not seen a performance for over four months. On returning home I found a surprise party which had been organised by my office staff and Mr. Juda Nedivi, the Town Clerk of Tel Aviv, and the festivities lasted until the early hours of the following day.

The next morning I attended at my office and found that a case was to be heard that very morning by the same judge who had convicted me, Mr. Curry. I decided to appear before him, and although he was obviously taken aback, he was most courteous and I even succeeded in obtaining judgment for my clients.

Moves to Revoke my Licence

On the morning of the 8th November, just over 24 hours after my return home, I received a telephone call from the Secretary of the Legal Board. He informed me that the Attorney General had moved for disciplinary action to be taken against me on the ground that I had been convicted of criminal offences, that a meeting of the Board would take place that afternoon to deal with the matter, and that I was requested to attend and give reasons why the application should not be granted. I replied that I had just returned to Tel Aviv after spending four months in Jerusalem as the guest of the Government, and I was in no mood to return to Jerusalem in such a hurry. I added that I would deal with any application if a copy of it was sent to me and if sufficient time were given to me to study the position. He said he would convey my remarks to the Board.

A couple of weeks later I received a formal communication from the

Board informing me of the move of the Attorney General and requesting me to submit in writing the representations which I might care to make. In reply I submitted a long memorandum in which I denied guilt of any of the offences for which a lawyer could be disbarred or suspended from practice, and I indicated my readiness to be tried again by any impartial Court before which I was confident I would be able to establish my innocence. In reply I received a letter a few days later stating that the Board had considered my representations and had appointed a special sub-committee to make recommendations, that this committee would meet in Jerusalem on a date fixed and that I could appear before it and argue my case. The Committee was comprised by Judge Plunkett, then President of the District Court of Jerusalem, Mr. M. Smoira, now President of the Israel Supreme Court, and Mr. Moghanam, a Christian Arab lawyer who was also the Secretary of the Palestine Arab Executive.

Abcarious Bey, a leading Arab lawyer, met me at this time and had expressed a desire to help me in the matter. It was agreed that he should appear before the Committee in Jerusalem and argue on my behalf. On attending at Court on the morning fixed for the hearing by the Committee, however, Mr. Abcarious informed me that, to his great regret, he could not appear as he was engaged in a case before the Supreme Court from which he could not be excused. I had no alternative, therefore, but to conduct my case in person and to do so extemporaneously. I replied to various questions put to me by members of the Committee and then made a plea to their conscience. I argued that the right of the Jews to Palestine did not stem from the Immigration Ordinance nor even from the Balfour Declaration. It was a historic and religious right. I asked them whether, if they were placed in the position of seeing fellow co-religionists die by drowning at sea if they did not assist them to land, they would act differently than I was allowed to have done, and I depicted the sufferings of the Jews in Germany and Poland, their dreadful ordeals in escaping from the Nazis and their terrible tribulations on the primitive vessels which carried them to the shores of Palestine. The Chairman was a very kindly Irishman, and I asked him what he would do if Irish refugees wanted to land in Ireland before the British left Ireland and if the British prohibited their landing.

After some further questions, the Chairman said that it was the duty of the Committee merely to make recommendations and that they would forward their conclusions to the Legal Board. Later I met Judge Plunkett who wished me good luck, and I was later told by Mr. Smoira that I had made a very deep and favourable impression on the Committee.

The next development was a report which appeared about a week later in the newspapers to the effect that the Board had decided to suspend me from practice for a period of six months. I was told confidentially that the Arab members of the Board had demanded that my name should be struck off the Rolls, that the British members had been content to dispose of the matter by severely reprimanding me, and that the Jewish members had suggested the compromise of a temporary suspension.

When the report appeared in the newspapers, I was bombarded by telephone calls congratulating me and suggesting it was not a bad thing and that I should take a holiday for six months. The law, however, provided that an appeal could be made to a Special Tribunal of the Supreme Court, and I decided to make such an appeal, which was the first of its kind in the legal history of Palestine. The question then arose who should conduct the appeal for me. Several offers were forthcoming from leading members of the Bar, but Mr. Smoira expressed the view that, having regard to the excellent showing which I had made before the Special Committee, I was the best person to conduct the case, notwithstanding the old adage that "A lawyer who defends himself has a fool for a client". In the preparations for my appeal I received a number of friendly suggestions from various lawyers, and in particular I was indebted for some very valuable tips given to me by a South African lawyer, Colin Gluckman, who is now an Assistant Attorney General.

The appeal came on for hearing at the beginning of April, 1940, and was heard by the Chief Justice, another British Judge, Mr. Justice Rose, and an Arab judge. Mr. E. Bell, Senior Crown Counsel, appeared on behalf of the Attorney General and the Law Council. After a lengthy hearing which was conducted *in camera*, the Court unanimously upheld all my submissions and ruled that, even if I was guilty as convicted, which they must assume, my offences did not involve either moral turpitude or unprofessional or disgraceful or fraudulent conduct, one or more of which were necessary to maintain the decision of the Law Council. The Court, therefore, allowed the appeal, ordered that the decision of the Law Council be set aside and further directed that the Attorney General should pay all Court costs in connection with the appeal.

The large crowd of lawyers and other curious well-wishers who were waiting outside the Court bombarded me with congratulations.

The newspapers had been extremely friendly to me in their treatment both of my prosecution and my case against the Law Council. In particular, I was deeply satisfied to note a most sympathetic editorial which appeared in the "Davar" (The newspaper of the Jewish Labour Federation) on the 11th July, 1939, in which they warned that what had happened to me might very easily happen to other members of the Jewish Community as a consequence of the repressive anti-Jewish legislation of the Mandatory Government. This article was particularly gratifying because in official Jewish quarters and especially in Histadruth circles I was extremely unpopular because of my services to the men and women of the Irgun and Stern Group.

After my return to Tel Aviv, a number of organisations hosted a dinner in my honour to celebrate the decision of the Court. I was also presented by my Masonic Lodge with an inscribed plaque, and received a certificate from the Jewish National Fund. It was highly gratifying to note that the inscription on the Masonic plaque was subscribed to by all the brethren, including a number of Englishmen and Arabs. Still a little later, the Lodge unanimously elected me to serve a for second period as Master of the Lodge, and at the subsequent banquet there were present most of the English Government officials, including high Police, Judicial and Administrative officials, who then publicly demonstrated their friendship and esteem despite my "Criminal" record.

Gilpin—Retribution?

As time went by and I was kept tremendously busy with legal work, particularly in connection with the disturbances and the defence of "terrorists", I practically forgot all about Mr. Gilpin, the man on whose false evidence I had been convicted.

At the end of April, 1943, nearly four years after my trial, an elderly Jew named Leib Berger called on me to enlist my aid in what appeared to be a hopeless matter. It appeared that late one evening some five months earlier, in November, 1942, he was riding a bicycle along a street in Tel Aviv when he was suddenly knocked down by a motorcar which proceeded on its way without even stopping to enquire whether he had been hurt or to offer any help. He had suffered injury in the form of a broken thumb as well as some damage to his bicycle. Passers-by had taken the number of the car, had tried to stop it and had noticed that it was being driven by a British Police Officer. The facts had been reported to the Police, but despite constant enquiries, nothing had resulted, and he had been informed by the Police that they were unable to take any action owing to the fact that they could not trace the identity of the driver of the car.

I felt that something ought to be done on behalf of the old man and that the conduct of the investigating authorities could not be justified. I therefore addressed petitions to the Inspector General of Police and to the Chief Secretary in which I contended that it was not credible that the Police Officer in question could not be traced at a time when the movements of all cars and Police Officers were being carefully checked because of wartime restrictions. As a consequence, a high-ranking Police Officer, Major Broadhead, was specially ordered to conduct an investigation. A few days later, a friendly British Police Inspector confidentially tipped me off to the effect that the driver of the car was Major Gilpin but that he had completely denied all connection with the incident.

From meetings which I had later with Major Broadhead and Crown Counsel, I learned that the car was the property of a junior Police Officer who was stationed in Beersheba; that on the date in question, the said officer and his wife were dining at Cafe Piltz in Tel Aviv and with them were Gilpin and a lady friend (it transpired that the lady friend was an Italian war detainee who had no right to be out at all); that during the dinner Gilpin had asked and received permission to borrow the car in order to go for a drive with his lady friend and had returned much later that evening without having said anything about being involved in an accident. On being questioned, Gilpin denied all knowledge of the facts, even to the extent that he had driven the car.

As a result of the fresh investigation, Gilpin was compelled to admit the facts, and he was then prosecuted before the District Court in Tel Aviv. The charges laid against him were 1) failure to report an accident, 2) failing to stop after the accident, and 3) using a Government vehicle for personal purposes contrary to the terms of the licence. For no apparent reason, he was not charged with making a false statement to the Police in the course of the earlier investigations.

The case naturally attracted very wide attention and the Court was packed with spectators, including a large number of Court employees. The scene of Gilpin standing in the dock in his Major's uniform being prosecuted by the man he had caused to be sent to prison four years earlier was, of course, a most unusual one. It was also interesting to note that the Judge trying the case was Judge Plunkett, who had been the Chairman of the Special Committee of the Law Council which dealt with the question of my licence. The Judge made no secret of his feelings when he convicted Gilpin and fined him 50 pounds or to serve in prison for six months and to pay 50 pounds in damages to the cyclist. The comment made by one newspaper was that it was "poetic justice". Ten days later, Gilpin was dismissed from the Police Force and left Palestine. According to reports which reached Palestine about two years later, he was caught in a criminal conspiracy in Eritrea and sent to England to serve a long term of imprisonment.

Caring For The Prisoners

PRESS REPORTS

(From Haboker, 15 September 1938)

Some 70 Jewish prisoners are being held in Acre at this time. They asked visitors to announce via the press that (a) they wish to thank Max Seligman publicly for the help and support he continues to give them in the collective matter of moving them to a prison located in Jewish surroundings, and for the individual attention given by him to each and every case, all this without charging a fee; and (b) that as of a few days ago, the Haifa Community Council stopped supplying food for the prisoners from Tel-Aviv and Jerusalem, who actually constitute the majority of inmates. Only 19 prisoners received rations: those from Haifa, and a few others who were able to pay for the food. Since these 19 cannot eat while their comrades go without, they share their rations. Consequently, all 72 prisoners are going hungry. The reason the Tel-Aviv and Jerusalem Community Councils were unable to continue supplying rations was that collections have fallen off, and even after the intervention of Mayor Israel Rokach of Tel-Aviv, only 43 rations were supplied, and that too on a temporary basis, and will be reduced to 19 again. If that happens, the prisoners are threatening a hunger strike; (c) The prisoners request their families, especially those outside the Haifa area, to refrain from visiting them, due to the dangers of travel on the highways; (d) They wish to inform their families that rumours about a typhoid fever epidemic in Acre prison are untrue. All prisoners are well.

The Zionist Revisionist Organisation wishes to inform the families that they may receive news of the prisoners through the Z.R.O. (44 Nachlat Benyamin, Tel-Aviv).

The Acre Prisoners Welfare Committee announces that couples will canvass every grocery store in Tel-Aviv, and request that they be given supplies for the inmates. We are also informed that Advocate Max Seligman and the Chief Rabbi applied to the Police Commissioner for permission to send a Torah, prayer books, etc. as well as to allow a cantor and shofar blower to visit the prisoners during the forthcoming High Holidays.

(From Ha'Aretz, 18 October 1938)

Advocate Max Seligman wrote two memoranda to the authorities, pointing out the dangerous conditions in which Jewish prisoners live, in the midst of hundreds of hostile Arab prisoners. The prisoners wish to be removed to a jail located in a Jewish area, and failing that, to be released on probation. The Memoranda were sent to the Prison Director and the Chief Secretary and detail the danger to the safety and even lives of the Jewish prisoners in their daily encounters with the Arabs in the yard, shower, infirmary and other locations.

The prisoners put the authorities on notice that unless their demands are met, they will have to resort to the only method of protest available to them: a hunger strike.

(From Ha'Aretz, 3 November 1938)

Chief Rabbi Herzog informed Advocate Max Seligman, who is handling the affairs of Jewish prisoners in Acre, that he has had no word from the Police Commissioner, although he was promised a reply in the matter. He has therefore decided to withdraw from handling the matter. Our readers will recall that the prisoners postponed their hunger strike for a week, at the suggestion of Rabbi Herzog. The deadline runs out tonight, and unless the prisoners are transferred to a concentration camp located in a Jewish area, they will begin the strike.

THE PRISON SYSTEM

It might be useful at this point to examine the various prisons and detention camps in Palestine, and those in the African exile, through which over the years many thousands of underground members passed.

ACRE: In 1937, the British built a detention camp within the walls of the ancient fortress, to hold Irgun detainees. This became necessary when large numbers of Irgunists were detained following its campaign of reprisals against Arab terrorists. The camp was surrounded by hostile Arabs, and Max Seligman labored mightily first to improve conditions within the camp, and later to move the camp to a location less dangerous to the prisoners. The camp was closed in 1939, and the 120 remaining prisoners transferred to Sarafand.

BETHLEHEM: This was a women's prison, adjacent to which there was a detention camp where underground women were held without trial. When first admitted, the girls were in the main prison with women sentenced for various crimes, until their transfer to the detention compound. Over one hundred members of the Irgun, Lechi and Hagana passed through this prison, which was closed in the last months of the Mandate, when the inmates were transferred to Atlit. Seligman organized a Committee for Women Prisoners in Bethlehem[1], headed by Lady Wedgwood in England. The committee, along with the constant intervention of Seligman and Kritzman, were instrumental in improving conditions for the detainees.

SARAFAND: This camp was opened in 1939 when prisoners from Acre and other overcrowded detention centers were moved there. When the Irgun suspended its anti-British activities at the outbreak of war, most inmates were released, and the remainder transferred to Mizra. (Sarafand was the largest military base in Palestine).

MIZRA: The first inmates here were those members of the Irgun command who opposed the suspension of anti-government operations, ordered at the outbreak of WWII. Other extremist elements, along with Communists, Trotskyites and others were also included. In June, 1940, the police released all members of the Irgun command, except those they suspected of being close to Ya'ir Stern's Lechi (Fighters for the Freedom of Israel). More Lechi adherents were added, until the camp was closed in 1942, when the one hundred and fifty or so inmates were moved to the new camp of Latrun.

LATRUN: This is where, when war began, the authorities held enemy nationals, Nazi agents, and Arabs known for their sympathy to Germany and Italy and their hostility towards Britain. The camp was divided into four parts, the last having been added in December of 1942 to house the transferees from Mizra. When Irgun renewed its war on the British, Latrun became so crowded that Arab prisoners were moved elsewhere and it became "all Jewish", and in fact all-Irgun and Lechi. Later still, during the period of civil disobedience when all three arms of the underground cooperated, leaders of the Yishuv, including the heads of the Jewish Agency and National Council, as well as hundreds of Hagana and Palmach personnel, were also sent to Latrun.

LATRUN II & III: Among the several hundred persons detained following the blowing up of the King David Hotel in Jerusalem, there were several dozen women. The police constructed a new camp for them, Latrun II, just off the Tel-Aviv to Jerusalem highway. Most of the women were released a few weeks later, and only a few were transferred to Bethlehem. In August 1947, about a week after the two British sergeants were hanged[2], the camp became a V.I.P. center: among the fifty new arrivals were the chiefs of the National Movement (Revisionist) and the mayors of Tel-Aviv, Ramat-Gan and Netanya. A third compound, Latrun III, was wired off to accommodate Netanya residents suspected of being connected with the hanging of the two sergeants. In the autumn of 1947, most detainees of Latrun II & III were moved to the main camp, and later to Atlit.

ATLIT: The main purpose of this camp was for the detention of illegal refugees caught at sea; later, the British would bring them directly to Cyprus. During the last days of the Mandate, Atlit became part of the British enclave ("Bevingrad"), which surrounded the Haifa bay area, and where the British continued to incarcerate Jews, even after statehood was proclaimed. Lawyers Seligman and Kritzman devoted a lot of time and energy to obtain the release of citizens of a sovereign state, held in a temporary enclave, even after the British announced their date of departure. Seligman met with the army commander and heads of the government administration, already in the process of dismantling, but they refused to acknowledge the existence of the State of Israel, and continued to detain Jewish prisoners in Atlit. Seligman then pointed out that members of the underground were liable to come to the assistance of their imprisoned comrades. But the British were afraid that the release of "these terrorists" might endanger their withdrawal. When the lawyer suggested the prisoners be released into the custody of the state, the British adamantly refused to recognize its existence. They finally agreed to release them into the custody of Mayor Joseph Sapir of Petach Tikva, if he could guarantee they would not endanger the British withdrawal. After obtaining Irgun and Lechi command assurances that the released prisoners would not be forcibly released from his custody, Sapir agreed. The entire maneuver was a charade, since there was no place in Petach-Tikva large enough to hold that many prisoners. Even so, the British held back a dozen prisoners, who were transferred to Bat-Galim.

BAT-GALIM: This small camp near the port of Haifa is where on 27 May, 1948, the British moved six Irgunists which they suspected of being implicated in the hanging of the two sergeants, and six Lechi men caught during a raid on the railway workshops in Haifa. They had been sentenced to death, and their sentences commuted after the sergeants were hanged. They were held until the end of June, 1948, when the last Englishman left Israel. On the last day, the jailer opened the gates, gave the prisoners the keys, and parted from them with an emotional farewell.

THE AFRICAN EXILE: For a period of some three years—October 1944 to the end of British rule in Palestine—439 members of the underground (including Palmach) were sent to detention camps in Africa. The first shipment consisted of some 250 prisoners, mostly from Latrun. As soon as the location of the camp became known, efforts were begun to countermand the order to exile Jews from their homeland illegally. Not only did the lawyers approached in this matter not respond, but a campaign *justifying* (my italics) the exiling got underway. The Histadrut daily *Davar* editorialized that "The Yishuv does not support their deeds and there is no readiness to help them (the terrorists)".

When the deportations took place, Seligman was in England and his partner Kritzman was himself detained in Latrun. Seligman returned when he received a telegram from Tel-Aviv, and immediately set to work to prevent further exiling of prisoners. Meanwhile, Kritzman was released and together, they addressed countless memoranda and held numerous meetings with the military and civilian authorities, but at the end of six months, they realized that, given the negative attitude of the Yishuv's institutes and press, they were fighting a losing battle. Three more groups were shipped to Africa during a three-month period beginning in December, 1944. The camp meanwhile was moved from Eritrea to the Sudan.

A TEST CASE

Seligman and Kritzman then decided on a test-case, which, if successful, would put a stop to the deportations, and the precedent could be used to force the return of all prisoners from Africa. In July of 1945, they submitted an *order nisi* on behalf of Eli'ezer Zabrowsky, the father of detainee Aryeh ben Eli'ezer (Zabrowsky), against the Commander in Chief, Middle East Forces and the Commander of H.M. Forces in Palestine and Trans-Jordan, as well as the Chief Inspector, Palestine Police Force concerning the illegal deportation of his son. The British administration, civil and military, did its best to avoid answering the charge, claiming the deportation was legal, based on the Emergency Regulations. Seligman's response was that the regulations do indeed permit the authorities to detain any suspect without trial, and even deport him, but under no circumstances are the authorities permitted to detain the deportees in a foreign country.

Seligman had won the first round: the High Court granted the order and obliged the authorities to show cause why Zabrowsky was being detained in Africa. But the government decided to drag its feet, and it took over a year from the time proceedings began until a response was given. It was a masterpiece of deceit. An order signed by the governor of Eritrea stated that Zabrowsky was held under the Emergency Regulations of Eritrea! For what it was worth, Seligman pointed out that (a) the detention order was signed by the governor of Eritrea in July of 1945, nine months after Zabrowsky arrived there; and (b) at which time, Zabrowsky was no longer in Eritrea, but in the Sudan. Finally, the document was signed after the High Court's granting of the *order nisi*, obliging the Palestine authorities to show cause for Zabrowsky's deportation and detention in a foreign country.

As expected, the prosecutor's reply was arrogantly high-handed: The governor of Eritrea is not on trial in Palestine and is not required to explain why he signed the document. Hence, this court has no jurisdiction over the case. Adhering to the strict letter of the law (such as it was), the presiding judge had no choice but to concur with the prosecutor. He must have felt uncomfortable about this, however, since he added: "I know of no law that gives the government of this country the right to hold a Palestinian citizen in custody in another country." A second judge commented: "I am sure that if the Government of Palestine wished, it could order the Governor of Eritrea to release him, and have him brought back to Palestine." When in December, 1945 Seligman asked for leave to appeal the verdict to the Privy Council, he received a written reply: "This case is outside the jurisdiction of this court, but were this not so, it would have given counsel leave to appeal, as the case touches on many important matters."

The deportations continued, and the new concentration camp in the Sudan became too small. The inmates were shipped back to Asmara in Eritrea, which now held many of the senior commanders of the Irgun and Lechi. The main camp and a second, smaller one adjacent to it were guarded by Sudanese soldiers, who were constantly incited against the "Jewish terrorists who are killing Moslems in Palestine and are wrecking mosques." The Sudanese in turn did their best to provoke the Jews, and on 17 January, 1946, opened fire, killing two and wounding twelve of the prisoners. Seligman asked for permission to visit the prisoners, but his request was denied by the C.I.D. Four prisoners managed to escape, but two were caught in Addis Ababa, and the Ethiopian authorities were about to hand them over to the British in Asmara. Seligman bombarded the Ethiopians with cables to the Department of the Interior, the Justice Department, and to Emperor Haile Selassie, citing international law which requires giving asylum to political refugees. The Emperor granted Seligman an entry visa, but the C.I.D. again forbade him to leave the country.

Through his colleague Dr. Sullivan Kaufman in London, Seligman now made a direct appeal to the Privy Council. Seventeen months after he and Kritzman made their initial appeal, the Privy Council agreed to hear the Zabrowsky case. Now Seligman could no longer be prevented from visiting Asmara, which he did, arriving in October 1946. He met with most of the inmates over the course of a four day stay. Before leaving, he addressed the prisoners, telling them that in spite of everything, he still felt confident British justice and fair play would prevail. In London, meanwhile, a board was convened, consisting of five senior judges, but including none of those who agreed to hear the case originally. After three days of deliberation, their verdict upheld the deportations, giving no reason or explanation. Seligman instructed Dr. Kaufman not to accept this verdict until it was accompanied by the arguments and reasons behind it. This the Privy Council did: a month later, the explanation given was that the High Court in Jerusalem had to approve the application, which was not given. It disregarded the subsequent leave to appeal granted to Dr. Kaufman on Seligman's behalf.

The deportees, who never put much faith in British justice, attempted many escapes, and several senior commanders managed to get away, including Aryeh Ben-Eli'ezer (Zabrowsky), who escaped in January, 1947. In March of the same year, the camp was moved from Asmara to Gilgil, in Kenya (to discourage further escapes). Here the prisoners, along with fifty new deportees from Jerusalem, sat it out until set free in May, 1948.

(From The Day, New York, May 23, 1947)
MAX SELIGMAN, UNDERGROUND DEFENDER
His Mission to America
By Dr. S. Margoshes

Max Seligman, fortyish, large, raw-boned and looking more like the prize-fighter he isn't than the lawyer he is, belongs to the small company of Palestinians with a message who have recently arrived in this country. His message, to put it in a nutshell, is simply this: If you believe in the resistance movement in Palestine you've got to help those of its members who have fallen by the wayside!

As defender of Dov Gruner, among many others, before the Palestinian courts, Seligman knows full well how costly are the various legal steps that must be taken in the long drawn-out fight for justice. Without funds to wage this fight even such important delaying tactics as appeals for carrying the suit to higher courts or for a stay of execution of sentence, would be impossible. And surely the least we owe those who risk their heads for us is to try to save them with our money, if not with our manpower, as long as possible. Another obligation we owe our underground fighters is to help their dependents after the tide of battle has made it impossible for the fathers of families to take care of their wives and children. Someone, to be sure, ought to look out for those who had lost their providers in the struggle for national Jewish independence in Palestine. The official Jewish agencies and institutions cannot and will not do it for reasons that seem valid to them and sometimes opportune to us. A special fund is therefore required, if the work of caring for the casualties in the war for Jewish independence in Palestine is to go on.

The Prisoners of Zion Fund or Asirei Zion Fund is such a fund. And Mr. Seligman, who more than anyone else in Palestine had to do with the legal ramifications of the Jewish underground fight, is here to help in arousing American Jewry to the realization of the great need of swelling that fund as speedily as possible.

As Palestine's outstanding lawyer who dared to take up cudgels repeatedly for the hunted outlaw, as well as a Jew who suffered imprisonment for his convictions, Seligman has an authentic story to tell of prison conditions and British justice in Palestine generally. Only part of this story reached the American public when some months ago after meeting Mr. Seligman in London, I published in the Day and in P.M. a letter to the District Commissioner in Jerusalem from the Seligman firm describing in detail the almost incredibly barbaric treatment of Dov Gruner and his comrades by the Palestine prison authorities on the day of their capture. Mr. Seligman, having in his possession a vast amount of authentic information, can, I am sure, paint a correct picture of the Hitlerian practices which today pass for British justice in Palestine. British-born and educated, Mr. Seligman can hardly be dubbed anti-British. He may rather be styled as anti-Bevin and pro-Balfour. Yielding to no one in his devotion to the high principles of law which are the glory of the British genius, he is bitterly opposed to the police state imposed by the current masters of Britain on Palestine and regarded by him as a direct contravention of the most solemn British pledges to the Jewish people. Max Seligman does not believe that to be loyal to the British tradition of fair play one must be loyal to Mr. Bevin's policy of going back on Britain's pledged word on Palestine.

Mr. Seligman's mission to this country has been undertaken, I am informed, under the auspices of the Zionist Revisionist Organization. I trust no Zionist will withhold his support from the Asirei Zion Fund on that account. The Zionist Revisionist Organization is now numbered among the parties represented in the World Zionist Congress, which means it is a legally recognized Zionist group on a level with the Mizrachi and the Labor Zionists. And then again, Mr. Seligman rates a hearing and a helping hand regardless of the auspices he happens to travel or speak under. The most significant thing, as far as I can see, is the fact that the Jewish underground in Palestine is in need of legal and medical help and that its foremost legal champion is here asking help. It should be given in the fullest measure and without hesitation.

DR. WOLFGANG VON WEISL

The series of letters which follow tell the story of one man's arrest on "Black Sabbath" [3], and Seligman's relentless efforts to obtain his release. His very German name notwithstanding, Wolfgang von Weisl was a distinguished Jewish physician and journalist, a cultured man who counted Max Seligman among his many friends. The mere fact of being under arrest so rattled Dr. von Weisl that he undertook a hunger strike, which very nearly killed him. Even after his (apparently unconditional) release from police custody, he had to be dissuaded from "rocking the boat" in his vigorous attempts to clear his name of any wrong-doing. It is interesting to note Seligman's frequent allusions to information he suspects was fed to the government, leading to Dr. von Weisl's arrest, and which may well have been political account-settling on the part of anti-Revisionist elements.

28 July, 1946

The General Officer Commanding,
Troops in Palestine and Trans-Jordan,
Force Headquarters,
Jerusalem.

Sir,

We beg to submit the following humble petition that you may see fit to direct the release from detention of our client, Dr. Wolfgang von Weisl, of Gedera.

Our client was arrested at his home in Gedera in the course of the military operations which took place on or about the 29th June, 1946, and was taken to the Detention Camp at Latrun where he has been detained ever since.

Our client is a physician of repute and conducts a sanatorium in

Gedera to which he has devoted all his time during the past few years.

It is to be presumed that our client was arrested on the grounds of suspicion or information that he is a member of or in some manner associated with an illegal organisation or that he was a political leader whose expressed views were considered dangerous by the authorities.

We are specifically authorised to state that our client has never been a member of any illegal organisation. He has never been associated with the Hagana, the Irgun Zevai Leumi or the Stern Group.

So far as his political activities are concerned, he was at one time an active Revisionist, but owing to differences of opinion with leaders of that movement, he severed all connections with it over two years ago, and since then he has not been a member of any political organisation.

We are assured of the truth of the above statements of fact, and in view thereof it is respectfully submitted that any information which may have been received against our client is ill-founded and that there is no reasonable ground for his detention. We would, therefore, most urgently beg you to enquire into the matter with a view to directing the immediate release of our client whose business is suffering seriously by reason of his continued absence and whose family is naturally greatly distressed.

Yours respectfully,
Max Seligman

*****

Mrs. Wolfgang von Weisl, 22 August, 1946
Gedera.

Dear Mrs. von Weisl,

I enclose copy of a reply which I have just received from Army H.Q.

I am afraid nothing further can be done just now. We must just wait, and I hope it will not take much longer.

Yours sincerely
Max Seligman

*****

HQ Palestine
tele 4651 Ext 169
GSI 0-46-4

M. Seligman & Co.,
1, Bialik Street,
TEL-AVIV.

Dr. WOLFGANG VON WEISL.

Referring to your letter of 28th July 1946, regarding the above named detainee.

It is regretted that no action can be taken at this stage to release Dr. Von WEISL.

E. Quinn, Major
for Brigadier,
General Staff.

TOS 1940MS

*****

4th September, 1946

Mrs. W. Von Weisl,
Gedera.

Dear Mrs. Von Weisl,

I enclose for your information copy of a further letter which I have today addressed to the G.O.C with copy to the C.I.D.

Yours sincerely,
Max Seligman

*****

4th September, 1946

The General Officer Commanding,
H.Q. Palestine.

Sir,

re: Dr. Wolfgang Von Weisl.

We beg to refer to our letter to you of 28th July, 1946, and to your reply thereto, Ref. No. GSI-0-46-4, dated the 8th August, 1946.

Our client is still detained in Latrun, and we understand that he has declared a hunger strike as a protest against his continued detention.

Dr. Von Weisl is a person of very high principles, and any statement made by him may be relied upon as being truthful and strictly in accordance with the facts. He has asserted that he is not guilty of having had any part whatsoever, neither directly nor indirectly, in any illegal activities. We have no doubt that that statement is absolutely true. Moreover, we are assured that for over two years he has not even engaged in any political activity, having severed all connections with any political party.

We submit that, if he is detained on the strength of information to the contrary, then such information must be untrue and unfounded and should be disregarded.

In these circumstances, there is no just reason for the continued detention of our client. Moreover, he is a sick man, and the hunger strike upon which he has entered and his detention generally can only be calculated to affect his health most injuriously.

We would, therefore, most respectfully beg you to reconsider the case with a view to directing the immediate release of our client. We hope you will see your way to giving this matter your urgent and sympathetic consideration, and we thank you in anticipation of your courtesy herein.

Yours faithfully,
Max Seligman

Copy to:—
The D.I.C., C.I.D.
Police Headquarters,
Jerusalem.

*****

16th September, 1946

The General Officer Commanding,
Troops in Palestine and Trans-Jordan,
Force Headquarters,
Jerusalem.

Sir,

re: Dr. Wolfgang Von Weisl.

We beg leave to submit what we feel is a last-minute appeal for it is the general belief that your decision herein will decide whether our above named client shall live or be doomed to die. We, therefore, approach you with the most urgent request to give this appeal your most immediate and favourable consideration.

As you are aware, our client was arrested on the 29th June, 1946, and was thereafter detained in Latrun without ever being charged or brought to trial or convicted for any offence against the law and without even being informed of any reason for his completely unjustified arrest and for his continued detention for a period which appeared to be indefinite.

Our client, being a man of high moral principles, and whose belief in human justice and equity were profoundly shaken by this treatment of him, could not bear the humiliation inflicted upon him and decided at the risk of his own life to assert his complete innocence by declaring a hunger strike.

We would respectfully reiterate the assertions made in our letter to you of the 4th September, 1946, that our client never had any connection whatsoever, either directly or indirectly, with any illegal organisation.

It is an undeniable fact that our client has devoted the best part of his life to the Zionist cause and by his untiring efforts he has been recognised as a leading personality in the Zionist movement, a movement which enjoyed and still enjoys the ardent support of most civilised and enlightened nations. It surely cannot be suggested that he can be punished for his Zionist activity by being deprived of his personal freedom.

It is obvious that our client has indicated his preparedness, if necessary, to sacrifice his life only because he is innocent and absolutely convinced of the justice of his cause. Whatever affiliations might be alleged or suspected against the other persons who were arrested at the same time as our client, we are confident that no such allegations or suspicion can have any serious or honest foundation as regards our client.

We are profoundly convinced of his innocence, and we feel that an unbiased and careful investigation will satisfy you also of our client's innocence.

It will be seen from the attached certificate from the Tel Aviv Hadassah Municipal Hospital, the facts stated in which are supported and endorsed by all the leading local medical and health institutions of all political creeds, that the life of our client is now in the gravest danger. Any delay in effecting his release may prove fatal. Whatever provocation there may be for taking extreme measures against many people in this country, including deprivation of personal liberty, we cannot believe that you will wish to be a party to the death of a person who is wholly innocent. Dr. Von Weisl is a highly respected member of the local community and a doctor and journalist of international repute. Not only his immediate family, but the entire Jewish community pray that you will see your way to avert a tragedy for which there is no justifiable cause.

Yours faithfully,
Max Seligman

TRANSLATION FROM HEBREW

Municipal Corporation of Tel Aviv
Municipal Hospital Hadassah. No. 2025.........
Tel Aviv - 17th September, 1946.

CERTIFICATE

We hereby confirm that Dr. Von Weisl was ill in our Internal Department in May 1946, due to

HAEMORRHAGE OF THE
GASTRO-INTESTINAL TRACT
DUE TO DUODENAL ULCER

It is our opinion that a prolonged hunger strike is liable to involve dangerous complications causing death.

We apply to you to appreciate his dangerous condition and to release him immediately.

(Sgd.) - Dr. A. Abramovitch

The following join in the demand to release Dr. Von Weisl:

1. MUNICIPAL HOSPITAL HADASSAH
   TEL AVIV.
2. FEDERATION OF PALESTINE MAGEN DAVID ADOM
   FIRST AID SOCIETY, EXECUTIVE COMMITTEE.
3. NATIONAL LABOUR ORGANISATION
   NATIONAL SICK FUND CENTRAL.
4. PUBLIC SICK FUND
   TEL AVIV.
5. PALESTINE JEWISH MEDICAL ASSOCIATION
   CENTRAL COMMITTEE.
6. SICK FUND OF THE GENERAL LABOUR
   ORGANISATION.

*****

When matters appeared hopeless and Dr. von Weisl's condition worsened, Seligman sent him the following telegram:

18 September, 1946

WOLFGANG VON WEISL GOVERNMENT HOSPITAL, JERUSALEM. ON EVE MY DEPARTURE FOR ERITREA AND LONDON FEEL MUST IMPLORE YOU TO CEASE YOUR STRIKE STOP BELIEVE YOUR CASE RECEIVING CONSIDERATION AND ONLY PAIN AND SUFFERING CAN RESULT FROM PERSISTENCE YOUR STRIKE KINDEST REGARDS SELIGMAN.

*****

Subject: Detainee

Brig. J.R. Cochrane
Brigadier General Staff
HQ Palestine
Tel 4651
GSI 0-46/4
24 September, 1946

Sirs,

The General Officer Commanding British Troops in Palestine and Transjordan has instructed me to acknowledge your letter of 16th September in regard to the case of your client, Dr. Wolfgang von Weisl, and to reply to it.

As you will be aware, Dr. von Weisl has been released since your letter was written, but matters dealing with his detention are purely a matter for the Government of Palestine, and do not fall within the province of the G.O.C. All communications should therefore be addressed to them.

Yours truly

(Sgd.)

Messrs. M. Seligman & Co.,
1 Bialik Street
TEL AVIV
Palestine

*****

Government of Palestine

Chief Secretary's Office
Jerusalem
28 September, 1946

C.S. 778

Gentlemen,

I am directed to refer to your letter of the 16th September regarding Dr. Von Veisl which was addressed by you to the General Officer Commanding and forwarded to this office.

Dr. Von Veisl has since been released from detention on health grounds.

(Sgd.)
(J.R. Smith).
CHIEF SECRETARY

Messrs. Seligman & Coy.,
P.O.B. 627,
Tel Aviv.

*****

30th September, 1946

Dr. Wolfgang Von Weisl,
Gedera.

Dear Wolfgang,

I enclose for your information copy of a letter which I have just received from Army Headquarters in reply to my application for your release.

Do you wish me to address a further petition to the Chief Secretary or the High Commissioner? A copy of my last petition to the G.O.C. was also sent to the C.I.D. so that Government is fully aware of the representation which I have made.

All best wishes.
Yours sincerely,
Max Seligman

*****

1st October, 1946

Dr. Wolfgang Von Weisl,
Gedera.
Dear Wolfgang,

I enclose herewith copy of a letter which I have just received from the Acting Chief Secretary. From this letter, it would appear that your release is an unconditional one as there is no mention of the possibility of your being rearrested.

In these circumstances, I think it would be wiser not to address any further petition in the matter to Government.

Yours sincerely,
Max Seligman

NOTES TO CARING FOR THE PRISONERS

1. Bethlehem prison was used to hold most long-term women prisoners.
2. See *The Military Courts*.
3. *BLACK SABBATH* (29 *JUNE*, 1946): following a coordinated action by units of the Irgun and Palmach in which eight strategic border bridges were blown up, the British retaliated with massive collective punishment against the Yishuv and its institutions. A curfew was imposed on most of the country, and systematic house-by-house searches took place in Tel Aviv, the Jewish quarters of Haifa and Jerusalem, and in many other locations. The offices of the Jewish Agency in Tel Aviv and Jerusalem were seized, and 2,700 persons, mostly Hagana members and activists, were arrested. Among them was David Remez, chairman of the Va'ad Le'umi (his son Aharon, a veteran of the RAF, became the first commander of the Israel Air Force). A warrant was also issued for the arrest of Ben Gurion, who was out of the country at the time. Black Sabbath ended the brief period of cooperation between Hagana and Irgun. The latter now had strong support from an embittered Yishuv. The blowing up of the King David Hotel in Jerusalem which housed C.I.D. headquarters followed in July.

PART II
In The Military Courts

THE FIRST DEATH SENTENCE

In the autumn of 1937, gangs of Arab marauders had made most roads in Palestine too hazardous to travel. The Irgun decided to launch a country-wide counter-terror campaign, with the center of operations in Jerusalem. There were two reasons for choosing Jerusalem. The first was that the Arabs always sought to isolate it from the rest of the country, attempting to cut the only road link between it and other cities. Within Jerusalem, they tried to cut off the Old City, where inhabitants were for the most part defenseless students and old people—easy targets for the Arabs. The second reason was that in Jerusalem, Irgun fighters could function in a sympathetic atmosphere, where their many supporters and friends did not forget Jabotinsky's part in defending the city in 1920.

On the Castel Heights overlooking Dir Yassin and two other Arab villages, there was an abandoned quarry, which the Beitar now took over. It was a source of income—always sorely needed—but the quarry was also strategically located on the road to Kiryat Anavim, and was an excellent place for training. The explosions required for quarrying the stone effectively masked the detonation of grenades and the sound of firing. The rifles used were those belonging to the Jewish auxiliary policemen, posted by the authorities to protect the quarry. In November, five Jews were killed by the Arabs in nearby Ma'aleh Hachamisha; Kiryat Anavim was not spared either. The men at the quarry fumed at not being able to respond to the attacks. Finally, one of the auxiliary policemen, twenty-three year old Yechezk'el Altman, decided to take matters into his own hands. He took his rifle, went down the mountain, and took up a position overlooking the highway. He fired a total of seventeen shots at a number of Arab vehicles; the exact toll inflicted by him is in dispute. He then returned to base and reported to his commanding officer, and was arrested the following morning. Max Seligman warned Altman that if he took a political line in his defense, he would be compromising the other men at the quarry. He agreed to this, and when the trial opened before a military court on 2 February 1938, he accepted full responsibility for his actions. The prosecution claimed shots were fired from at least two guns and from both sides of the road. Conflicting evidence was given by several witnesses, and Seligman's skillful cross-examination resulted in much of this evidence being dismissed. Yet enough evidence remained against his client, and in spite of Seligman's emotional appeal, Altman was sentenced to hang.

The accused man remained remarkably calm, but Seligman was devastated: this was the first death sentence to be pronounced on a man he defended, and he now regretted telling Altman not to adopt a political line of defense. As soon as the court adjourned, Seligman went to the judge's chambers to plead for clemency. While in the judge's chambers, he spotted an open file, and in it a description of Altman, with a note that he was a member of Beitar and the Irgun. Picking up the file, Seligman confronted the judge, asking: "Is this sufficient excuse for hanging a man?" The judge was embarrassed. "Submit a plea for lenience" he said, "and I'll endorse it". Seligman was delighted, but deciding not to take any chances, he mobilized all his contacts and resources, including high civilian and military officials, the Chief Rabbinate, and even the leadership of the Yishuv, in spite of their disapproval of the Irgun.

(From the Manchester Guardian)
JEW NOT TO DIE
Sentence of Death Commuted

Jerusalem, February 7

By decision of the General Officer Commanding it was announced to-night that the sentence of death on Ezekiel Altman, a 22-year-old Jewish auxiliary constable, has been commuted to life imprisonment.

Altman, the first Jew to be sentenced to death by the special military courts, was found guilty of firing at an Arab omnibus, near Jerusalem, on December 27. The trial lasted three days. Altman was defended by Mr. Max Seligman, a former Cardiff man. A plea for clemency was made on Saturday by Dr. Isaac Herzog, the Chief Rabbi, formerly of Dublin.

(The following year, Seligman was sentenced to a prison term and sent to the central prison in Jerusalem, where he met Altman, who served seven years and was released in 1944. Four years later, he was one of the commanders on the Tel Aviv-Jaffa border, where I was serving as a member of Israel's army-in-the-making. —G.C.)

A second death sentence was pronounced, this time on Shlomo ben Yosef, who was tried with two other young men from Rosh Pina. He and the two others, Avraham Schein-Amikam and Shalom Zurabin, ambushed an Arab bus near Rosh Pina, in retaliation for Arab attacks on Jews in the area, in which several people lost their lives. The attack failed, and all three were apprehended and brought to trial before a military court. When asked to defend the trio, Seligman was ill in bed with a high fever. He telephoned his colleague Phillip Joseph, asking him to visit the prisoners. Joseph went further, and had them sign a power of attorney, authorizing him to appear in their defense. Zurabin was given a long prison term; Ben Yosef and Schein-Amikam were sentenced to death, but the latter's sentence was commuted to life imprisonment because of his youth. All efforts to save Ben Yosef's life were in vain. He went to the gallows at Acre prison on 29 June, 1938, singing Beitar songs, the first Jew to be hanged by the British in Palestine.

AN ARMS DEAL

In response to Ben Yosef's execution, the Irgun stepped up its activities in early July, 1938. The C.I.D. was instructed to do likewise. One of its officers, a Jew named Valentine Beck, knew a dealer who was known to have sold arms to the Irgun. This dealer let Beck know that a shipment was due to be made that day, at the offices of the Revisionist Labor Organization in Tel Aviv. Beck decided to catch the dealer red-handed, and arranged an ambush. The dealer became suspicious and stayed away, and the police caught the courier, Jacob Kotek with the arms.

The dealer, a gentile, disappeared. Seligman invited detective Beck for tea at his home, where he admitted he set the trap in order to apprehend the dealer, but was now afraid of reprisal by the Irgun. Seligman could not admit to any direct connection with the Irgun, but suggested to Beck that if he gave testimony favorable to the accused, he should have nothing to worry about.

(From the Palestine Post, 4 October 1938)
KOTEK SENTENCED TO DEATH
"Informer" Gives Evidence

Jacob Ben Moshe Kotek, aged 25, a mason of Tel Aviv, was yesterday sentenced to death by the Jerusalem Military Court on the charge of carrying three automatic pistols, 405 rounds of revolver ammunition, eight detonators, seven sticks of gelignite and two lengths of safety fuse.

At the continuation of the trial yesterday, the "informer" who was called by the Defence, stated that he was in Tel Aviv on August 20 to meet a certain person (he gave the name in writing to the Court) from whom he had bought arms two months ago and was going to buy arms again. He met him in a cafe in Tel Aviv and the two of them went to the offices of the Revisionist Labour Organisation, where the witness was to collect the arms. The witness stated that he did not know the accused, and had not heard his name before his arrest. He was not cross-examined by the Prosecution.

Alleged Scheme

In his summing-up, Mr. M. Seligman said the case was an arrangement on the part of the police to arrest a person who dealt in arms. Their scheme miscarried, as that person became apprehensive, and instead, one of the persons who attempted to take away the arms was arrested. The accused picked up the case a moment before his arrest, and it was quite clear the man who should have been arrested was someone other than the accused. He was a person who dealt in arms, and was known to the informer, who had bought arms from him before the incident.

"Innocent Victim"

Mr. Seligman said it would have been safer for the accused and his friends if they had revealed to the police what they had known about the case, but it was also the duty of the police to find the real culprit, and they should have used the accused and the others for this purpose. It was scandalous on the part of the vendor to use the offices of the Revisionist Labour Organisation for this purpose, and it could not be suggested that the accused had dealt in arms. He was an innocent victim, and had been sufficiently punished by his arrest and the agony he had undergone.

Defence a "Farce"

In his reply, the Prosecutor said that if he might employ an analogy from a chess game, he would say that two plays had been enacted before the Court—a "straight" play, that of the Prosecution witnesses who told the Court just what they had seen and done, and a "farce", that of the Defence, when the witnesses contradicted themselves and were apparently not telling the truth. The story of the Prosecution, he said, was not involved. Three policemen saw the accused coming from a dark place underneath the stairs on the ground floor of the offices of the Revisionist Labour Organisation in Tel Aviv. The accused was seen carrying the attache case containing the exhibits, and was arrested as he attempted to take it away. These facts were not disputed.

Deal in Arms

The Prosecutor then dealt at length with the evidence of the witnesses for the Defence, and said that Tudnovsky and the informer had apparently arranged a deal in arms at the cafe, but as the latter left, the suspicions of the former were aroused and he hid the attache case below the stairs. Tudnovsky tells Wilner, one of the witnesses for the Defence, to remove the arms, but the latter gets cold feet and asks the accused to take the attache case away. Whether the accused learned from Wilner of the real contents of the case, or was merely the catspaw, was a matter which the Prosecutor said he would leave in the hands of the Court. After a short deliberation, the Court announced that they had found the accused Guilty of the charge. The Prosecution produced a record of two previous convictions of destruction to property and fines of five and three Pounds, and after hearing a plea of mitigation by Mr. Seligman, the Court passed the sentence of death, which is subject to confirmation by the General Officer Commanding.

No one was allowed to leave the Court before the accused was taken away.

Seligman went into the judge's Chambers, where he was told that, as in the Altman case, a plea for clemency would be favorably received. After this was done, Kotek's sentence was commuted to life imprisonment. A week after the death sentence was passed, Valentine Beck was shot by persons unknown.

THE SEARCH FOR JEWISH IDENTITY IN HIS MAJESTY'S FORCES

When tens of thousands of Jews volunteered for service in H.M. Forces in WWII, the British resisted the establishment of autonomous Jewish units, to fight the Nazis alongside the Allies. If such units were established, they reasoned, that would strengthen Jewish demands for statehood when peace came.

When Rommel's forces came uncomfortably close to Egypt, the Colonial office and Winston Churchill finally yielded to Weizmann's entreaties and agreed to the formation of a "Palestine Regiment", comprised of an equal number of separate Arab and Jewish units. As expected, only a handful of Arabs joined up. The mostly Jewish regiment included in its ranks members of Beitar and the Irgun. It served with distinction in France, and a commando unit drawn from its ranks played a key role in the liberation of East Africa. In addition to the obvious fight against Germany, there was the practical objective of training with and getting close to sources of British equipment, which could be appropriated for use by the underground.

Politics, unfortunately, could not be kept out of the lives of Jewish soldiers serving in H.M. Forces. The perils of war and soldier's camaraderie had served to break down the mistrust between Revisionist soldiers and those of other political views, but the Jewish Agency saw fit to keep the division and discrimination alive. A number of soldiers in the Third Battalion were transferred by their (Jewish) commander to other units, the excuse given being that all were subject to the authority of the Jewish Agency, and there was "no place for others" in the unit.

A Mutiny?

The creation of Jewish units had its own obvious merits, and this was now followed by an effort to obtain for them a unique badge. As early as 1942, some Revisionist soldiers of The Buffs began wearing Eretz-Israel shoulder-patches and painting the Star of David on their helmets. In some units, the white and blue flag was raised on holidays. When news of the holocaust reached the soldiers, many units requested permission to raise a black-draped flag to half-mast, and fast for a day. Only the permission to fast was granted. By late 1943, the British finally came up with a special shoulder-patch, which was immediately deemed unacceptable. It had the word "Palestine" in the three languages, forming a circle around the olive branch taken from a 100 mil (2 Shilling) coin, with the usual E.I. (Eretz-Israel) added in parentheses. The new badges were handed out during pay parades with the order for all ranks to wear them. The Jewish Agency ordered all service personnel to comply, but sixty-nine soldiers, (all Revisionists except for two Hagana members, who later joined the Irgun) refused. The entire group was arrested and brought to trial at Sarafand, the largest military base in Palestine[1].

(The poster distributed to all Jewish units: Hundreds of Jewish soldiers in the Hebrew battalions are facing courts-martial for their refusal to wear the yellow patch—this Palestinian badge. Scores of them will be tried on Thursday, 2 December 1943 for this "offense". The community of soldiers and the entire Yishuv will never agree to calling Hebrew youths in uniform "anonymous Palestinians!")

Disobeying a direct order, especially by such a large number of soldiers, is a serious matter: it constituted a mutinous act, technically punishable by firing squad.

Seligman was abroad at the time, but hurried back to Palestine when Kritzman cabled him. A team of sixteen lawyers was assembled, and as witnesses the defense called the country's highest religious and spiritual leaders. A joint letter addressed to the court stated: "These men, who of their own free will offered to sacrifice their lives and took an oath of allegiance to the British Crown, would feel revulsion if forced to wear a badge in which the sacred name of their land is hidden by parentheses, and in the form of initials.

Seligman met with the military prosecutor and asked him point-blank whether it was conceivable that sixty-nine men could be shot for refusing to wear a badge which violated their beliefs. The military now knew they could not impose a severe sentence in this case, as it would arouse the indignation of servicemen (and not only Jewish ones) throughout the Empire, if carried out.

It must have been with great relief that the military accepted Seligman's suggestion that one soldier be tried, his sentence to set the precedent for the others, who would be tried in small groups. The authorities were thus able to back down without losing face. Some unit commanders ignored the matter entirely. The sentence handed down was sixty days at hard labor—the only one to get ninety days was the unfortunate soldier in the test-case.

There were more flag-raising incidents, and all this agitation hastened the eventual arming of the units and sending them into action. Finally, the Jewish Brigade Group was formed, and fought under its own colors until disbanded in 1946.

DEFENDANTS TURN ACCUSERS

When in 1920 Ze'ev Jabotinsky was tried for "illegally" defending Jerusalem,[2] he turned the tables on the court. Dispensing with legal counsel, he became the accuser on behalf of himself and his nineteen co-defendants. Similarly, in March 1944, five members of LECHI were arrested and brought to trial very quickly. As Seligman and Kritzman discovered, the reason for the hasty trial was that an amendment to the Emergency Regulations, which now carried the possibility of a death sentence for the possession of arms, was made *subsequent* to the arrest of the accused. The four men and young woman of 18 were all tried separately. In each case, they announced they waived their right to counsel, and that they wished to make statements. Seligman and Kritzman were unable to dissuade them from taking a political approach to their defense, but secretly hoped that the new amendment to the Security Regulations would not be applied. In the event, only one of the men was sentenced to death, and that was commuted to life imprisonment. The statement read by Zvi Tavori is typical of the others:

I admit possessing the gun and bullets. I refute your claim that I had them without permission or logical justification. I got my permission from the only authority I recognize in Eretz Israel, and that is the Hebrew freedom fighters' movement, that wishes to return to the people of Israel its just place among nations, in the form of a Hebrew state in this land. The laws by which you are judging me were made by an authority which I do not acknowledge. This authority, given to you in order to establish a Hebrew state here, has turned in your hands into an occupational, imperialistic regime. Your laws are illegal by virtue of your international commitments, as well as incompatible with moral and juridical standards. I therefore challenge your authority to try me under these unacceptable laws. I also challenge your contention that there was no logical justification to my bearing arms. Because when British policemen and officers murder Jews in their homes and in the streets, even with their hands up or tied; when British policemen drive away from the shores of my homeland my brothers and sisters, survivors of the Nazi hell; when British provocators continuously incite the Arabs to attack the Jews, under these conditions, not only is there a logical justification to bearing arms, but it is the obligation of every Hebrew youth to bear these arms. Because your government and laws are meant to stifle the Hebrew nation's last hope, your trial and verdict are of no concern to me, and I will answer no questions. You are obliged at the very least to try me not as a criminal, but as a political prisoner who fell into your hands. I therefore demand the status and rights given to all prisoners of war.

Replying to the statement made by another of the defendants, David Meiri-Begin, the presiding judge made the following comments:

The Court has listened patiently to all you had to say, but before passing sentence, the Court would like to make a few remarks.

For several years now members of your nation have been suffering in Europe, and many thousands have been destroyed. The civilized world has viewed this awful scene with horror, but has been unable to begin the rescue effort earlier and endanger its armed forces before the time was right. Many of those wretched people in Europe would have been glad to accept the shelter given by the British Mandate in this country, and which you have found right to insult.

The crime of which you are accused is of stabbing in the back the people who would shed their blood to protect you. You have emulated Nazi methods and helped them by providing propaganda material, which they are sure to distort in a diabolical manner. These ideas could pave the way for your own destruction.

You have demonstrated knowledge of arms and explosives; you could have employed this knowledge successfully and honorably, as do the true fighters of the nation of Israel, fighting side by side with the Allied armies against the Nazis, and whom we are proud to call comrades-in-arms. Whatever punishment you are given by this court, you will serve a harder sentence, that of your conscience; because your conscience will tell you, if not now then later, that what you have done is wrong, not only in the eyes of this court, but in the eyes of your own compatriots.

And to eighteen year-old Hassiah Shapira, sentenced to four years in prison:

It is very sad to see a young girl like you, with your kind of education, standing accused of such crimes before this Court. Judging your case has put this Court in an awkward and unpleasant position. Your entire behavior as described here proves you were a foolish girl, influenced by others to do the wrong things. These people mean to disrupt the peace in this country. What you have done was to commit a crime for which the punishment is severe, up to life imprisonment. As young and foolish as you may be, you cannot go about with guns and bombs, all the more so when what bothers you most was that you were not able to use these arms against the police. Taking into consideration your tender age, and the fact you were influenced by others, the Court sentences you to four years in prison and recommends special privileges for you in prison, although you do not deserve it.

It would be hard to accuse either side of lack of sincerity; each held the courage of its convictions, deeply rooted and firmly felt: complete polarization was the inevitable outcome.

BRUTALITY

During a raid on a government parking lot, one of the attackers, Iyov Avtalion, was caught by the police. Irgun command received a report that Iyov was being tortured, but it took several days before the police would admit the boy was in custody, and "did not know where." He was found in the Ramleh prison, but only after Seligman threatened to appeal to the Supreme Court.

When Kritzman returned from visiting the prisoner, he told a tale of horror: the boy's entire body and face were a mass of wounds. Seligman immediately addressed a strongly-worded letter to the Justice Department, complaining of torturing the prisoner and not allowing a lawyer to visit him. He demanded that a doctor be allowed to see him. In order for Kritzman to qualify as a witness (since he was the only one who saw the boy wounded) the case was transferred to Asher Levitzky, Seligman & Co.'s colleague in Jerusalem.

On 19 April 1944, the trial began. There were four charges: blowing up of vehicles at the parking lot, possession of a gun, ammunition and explosives. Following testimony by prosecution witnesses, Avtalion, a twenty-four year old diamond worker and a graduate of the Hebrew Gymnasium in Jerusalem, mounted the dock and told his story. On Friday evening he had been to dinner at his mother's home. Later he went for a walk with his girlfriend, and after he escorted her to her house, was returning home when he noticed a couple of suspicious fellows looking in a shop window. Then he heard an armored car approach, and was struck on the head. He fell to the pavement, causing him further injury. He was taken to the first-aid station, where his wounds were dressed, and from there was taken to the police station. He was asked for his name and address, and gave that information. From there, he was taken to Jaffa prison, where he was interrogated and beaten. During two days of interrogation, he was given nothing to eat. The worst interrogation took place in (officer) Stewart's office, where a number of men in civilian clothes were also present. The officer himself grabbed him by the hair, knocked him down, and two men stood him on his head. He was beaten on the soles of his feet until they swelled, and when raised, was unable to stand. He was shoved on the floor, from one man to the next, then put on a chair and another officer entered the room. He was interrogated but not beaten. When this officer left, Stewart pointed a gun at him and threatened to shoot him if he did not talk. Beaten, hungry and confused, he finally broke down. He was led to a room where two officers made him sign a confession that was dictated to him. Only then was he offered food, which he was unable to eat due to his injuries. He was then taken to a doctor, and warned enroute not to complain, or he'd be beaten again.

Max Kritzman was called to the stand. He testified how it took two days to verify that the prisoner was at Ramleh. Later yet, he was able to visit Avtalion, and he described in what terrible condition he found him. Permission for a doctor to visit him was denied. A fellow prisoner at Ramleh confirmed that Avtalion was beaten, tortured and humiliated. His feet were so swollen he could not stand.

Levitzky demanded that charges be dropped, as the confession was obtained from the prisoner by violent means. As expected, the court disregarded the torture charges, and sentenced Avtalion to twelve years imprisonment. Seligman's appeal resulted only in special privileges being given the prisoner.

POLICE OFFICER ON TRIAL

The case of Assistant Superintendent of Police A. G. Bedwell was unusual in more ways than one. It resembled the Goddard case in one respect: both officers were charged with aiding illegal Jewish immigration. But while Goddard was charged with accepting a bribe, this was not the case with Bedwell. This made matters worse for him: the British could understand how a man could be bribed, there was nothing unusual about that. What they could not comprehend (and what really angered them) was how a fellow British officer could feel pity for survivors of the holocaust attempting to enter the country. Nor could they forgive him for marrying a Jewish girl, and insisting on living in Tel Aviv. The case was being tried, ostensibly, before a police court, but it had all the appearances of a military tribunal, held at Military Police H.Q. in Jerusalem, which was heavily guarded. Only police officers and senior government officials were admitted.

(From the Palestine Post, 5 September 1944)

COURT MARTIAL OF POLICE OFFICER

Admitting People Without Visas

A General Court Martial, presided over by Colonel Bighton, with Major W. Russell Lawrence as Judge Advocate, sat at the Police Depot on Mount Scopus yesterday to hear the case of Mr. A.G. Bedwell, A.S.P. who is charged with ten offences under section 40 of the Army Act. Nine of the charges deal with admitting people into Palestine without a visa despite the fact that he had no authority to do so. The tenth charge is of giving false reports to the Inspector-General of Police in respect of the number of entry permits issued by him by omitting the names of 57 persons.

The case should have been heard a fortnight ago in Ismailia as most of the prosecution witnesses come from Egypt, but as the Defence called police officers from Palestine, it was decided that the Court should convene in Jerusalem.

The Defence raised several preliminary points, objecting mainly to the jurisdiction of the Court. The defending counsel argued that the High Commissioner had no authority to convene the Court and that the proclamation of the Palestine Police as a military force by the High Commissioner applied to the limits of the command of the Inspector-General of Police in Palestine, whereas the offence in the case was committed in Kantara in Egypt.

Not a Member of Force

He further argued that the accused had not been a member of the Police Force at the time the offences were committed. Mr. Bedwell was discharged from the Police in 1938 on being transferred to the Immigration Department as an Immigration Officer. He wore the uniform of an A.S.P. and received the pay of that rank but did not enter into a contract with the Police and was not sworn in. He was sworn in May 1944, but the offences were committed during the period between April and September 1943.

The hearing was then adjourned to this morning in order to hear evidence for the prosecution and the defence as to whether Mr. Bedwell was a Police officer or not.

At the close of the hearing the defending counsel told the Court that should the Court Martial hold against his client on the tenth point, he would apply to the High Court for a Writ of Prohibition to order the Court Martial to stay proceedings as it had no jurisdiction. The Crown Counsel, Mr. I.C.C. Rigby and Mr. M. Beham prosecuted. The accused was defended by Mr. M. Seligman and Mr. M. Kritzman.

(From the Palestine Post, 6 September 1944)

The General Court Martial sitting at the Police Depot on Mount Scopus yesterday to hear the continuation of the Bedwell case, decided to overrule the submission of the defending counsel, Messrs. M. Seligman and M. Kritzman, that it had no jurisdiction to deal with the case as the accused was not a police officer.

Giving evidence yesterday morning, the accused stated that he had been discharged from the Force in September, 1938, with the rank of Sergeant, upon transfer to the Immigration Department. He had never officially been appointed A.S.P. and had never been sworn as such. During the Syrian campaign in 1941 he was ordered by the Assistant-General of Police, Mr. Giles, to wear the uniform of an A.S.P. He first learned of his appointment as A.S.P. from the Palestine Post in December, 1943, when it was reported that he had been appointed A.S.P. with effect as from 1941.

Cross-examined by Crown Counsel Mr. I.C.C. Rigby, Bedwell admitted that on his transfer to the Immigration Department he was notified that the High Commissioner reserved the right to transfer him to other posts. He also admitted that he was notified in March, 1939 that the Frontier Control Force had been transferred from the jurisdiction of the Director of Migration to that of the Police. He further

The Exodus *on its arrival in Haifa, July* 18, 1947, *its passengers being "processed" by British troops.*

Prime Minister David Ben Gurion welcoming President Chaim Weizmann (under picture of Herzl), *September* 30, 1948.

Convoy of home-made armored-cars on the road to the besieged Jerusalem (1948). The remains of some of these vehicles are still in place along the road, where they were ambushed.

Defending the suburbs, June 1948.

The author (right) *at a defensive post on the Jaffa border, December* 1947.

Dr. Chaim Weizmann being sworn in as Israel's first President, February 17, 1949 (standing on right: Moshe Dayan).

Honor guard receiving the remains of Theodor Herzl on their arrival for reinterment in Jerusalem, August 1949.

Max Seligman (profile, left), *Chaim Herzog, Ralph and Edgar Seligman, Jerusalem, April* 1981.

Druze members of the Israel Border Police.

At an Israel, Britain, and the Commonwealth Association function honoring Abba Eban.

At a Masonic function, Tel Aviv, October 1979. (left to right: Ralph D. Seligman, Max and Millie, Mr. And Mrs. Yehuda (Jack) Jacoby.

Lord Robert Boothby (left) *with Max Seligman.*

Birds of a Feather

Robert Boothby was born in 1900. He attended Public School and Oxford, and became M.P. for East Aberdeenshire. He served as Parliamentary Private Secretary to Winston Churchill when the latter was Chancellor of the Exchequer. He also served as British representative to the Consultative Council for Europe, and was made an Officer of the Legion of Honor. After he was knighted, he served in the House of Lords until his death in 1983. Boothby was a flamboyant and charismatic character, a snappy dresser with a theatrical manner and a delightful sense of humor. As President of the Anglo-Israel Association, he and Max Seligman became fast friends.

Max Seligman at Eighty.

admitted that he used to sign documents as an A.S.P., send regular reports to the Inspector-General, and received the salary of an A.S.P. His transfer from one frontier to another, including his last transfer to Kantara, had always been announced in Police Force Orders. Mr. G. Farley, Assistant Secretary, brought Bedwell's personal file to Court. He read a telegram from the High Commissioner to the Colonial Secretary requesting the approval of the transfer of the Frontier Control Force to the Police, and said that no reply to that telegram had yet been received.

At this point the Defence asked whether the High Commissioner had the authority to transfer the Frontier Control Force to the Police. Other witnesses were Lt. Colonel S. Prosser, who at the time the offences were committed was Assistant Director of Migration, in charge of Frontier Control, and the Chief Clerk of the C.I.D.

"Chaos and Disorder"

Summing up for the defence, Mr. Seligman stated that the prosecution had not proved that the accused was a police officer and that the Court therefore had no jurisdiction to try the case. He also argued that the Inspector-General could not appoint a man to the post of A.S.P. and that such appointment could only be made by the High Commissioner. The evidence had revealed chaos in the two departments concerned, said Mr. Seligman, who went on to criticise the disorder prevailing in the Police Force where a man could act for more than two years as an A.S.P. without an official appointment.

The Crown Counsel, Mr. Rigby, analyzing the evidence heard, requested that the submission of the Defence be overruled as it had been proved that the accused was a police officer at the time he is alleged to have committed the offence.

Another session took place at the court on Friday afternoon, in Mr. Seligman's absence. Mr. Kritzman pointed out that as the Sabbath was approaching, the Court should be adjourned. His request was ignored, and two more witnesses were called. Meanwhile, Mr. Seligman arrived in Court. He had been to see the Chief Secretary and warned him that an unprecedented scandal was about to erupt unless the Court respected the law of the land and recessed before the Sabbath. The presiding judge thought better of it, and announced that although he was entitled to continue the case during the Sabbath, he would require special dispensation for this from the High Commissioner, and since it was too late for that at this time, the case would be continued to the following Monday.

(The surprise verdict read: "The Court trying the case of A.S.P. Bedwell has found the defendant guilty of three of the ten charges brought against him. He has been found guilty of illegally admitting people into the country, and of two counts of submitting false reports to his superiors. Conviction of the defendant on these charges, and the penalty he is to receive, are in the jurisdiction of the High Commissioner."

It was later learned that Bedwell and his family were secretly ordered by the High Commissioner to be deported from Palestine.)

Word of Seligman's moral victory resulted in hundreds of congratulatory letters, wires and telephone calls. On 29 April 1944, the popular journalist Uri Keisari wrote the following editorial in *Yedi'ot Achronot*:

REMEMBER THE SABBATH DAY, TO KEEP IT HOLY

It was not Rabbi Herzog, not Rabbi Uzi'el, nor Rabbis Amiel or Toledano who evoked the old commandment, the admonition, the warning. Without a skullcap, not wearing sidecurls nor a great beard, not in a synagogue nor even a house of learning were these words sounded. An everyday Jew, a secular, bareheaded man with forward-looking views is the one who invoked this commandment. Max Seligman, the advocate Max Seligman, is the one who uttered these words in military court, in the presence of high-ranking officers, and in an atmosphere of impending verdict, he quoted this part of the Ten Commandments, reminding the gentiles and Israel of the sanctity of the Sabbath. The trial had lasted several days. Seligman was the only Jew at the proceedings. The defendant, prosecutor, and judges, were all non-Jews. At the end of Friday's proceedings, the Bench decided to continue the next day, but the Jewish lawyer stated that the following day was Sabbath, and that neither he nor his partner, Mr. M. Kritzman, were prepared to desecrate it.

Military law requires every person, every Jew, to obey its dictates without question. Sabbath or weekday, no Jewish lawyer is exempt from fulfilling his duty. By taking this stand, Max Seligman placed his professional position in jeopardy. The presiding judge told him so, Mr. Seligman understood it, yet he refused to desecrate the Sabbath. The Court recessed for consultation, and returned to announce that it saw no reason for not continuing on Saturday. But the Jewish lawyer followed the dictates of his conscience, and refused to reconsider. The presiding judge had to turn to the highest authority, the only one able to make a decision in this matter. He addressed the Deputy High Commissioner, and Mr. Shaw deserves the highest praise and thanks. He understood the spirit of the situation, and opted for that over the form. He was able to fathom the ascendancy of the Ten Commandments over the law of the land. He understood this, and was able, along with the entire administration of this land, to defer to ancient tradition. Mr. Seligman received thanks from the Sabbath Keepers' League, but what is missing is a widespread public and press reaction. It may be that certain narrow-minded persons view this deed as a merely ritual matter. They are wrong. Max Seligman did not protect the Sabbath. Holy Sabbath needs the protection of none of us. What he did was to protect all of us, and our rights in this country, now and forever.

Thus, with a gesture by one of its members, the entire legal profession has been instantly elevated.

TWENTY IRGUN MEMBERS ON TRIAL

In the summer of 1945, a group of twenty Irgun officer cadets were arrested at their training camp at Shuni, an old Roman fort south of Zichron Ya'akov. They were taken to the Atlit police station, where they were searched, fingerprinted and booked. The official communique relating the incident stated:

> At dawn on Thursday, the settlement of Shuni (Tel Tsur) near Benyamina was surrounded by police and military forces. 18 men and 2 women were found sleeping there. North of Shuni, a search uncovered 9 cases containing 2 rifles, a submachine gun, a quantity of gunpowder and fuses, 15 revolvers, 4 hand-grenades, and 36 sticks of gelignite. In addition, the searchers found weapons instruction pamphlets, 100 live rounds, a bottle of acid, and training manuals. All 20 persons were detained and charged with possession of firearms. Shortly before the assault, an explosion was heard. It transpires this explosion was a warning signal for the people there to disperse, but it came too late, as the place was already surrounded.

Such a mass trial was bound to attract a lot of attention, and as I was home on leave at the time, I managed to get into the Court[3]. A British Broadcasting Corporation crew was also present to report on the trial, and I heard its spokesman remark that if this (terrorist activity) has attracted the educated youth of the country, then it was clear British rule here was facing difficulties which it may not be able to surmount.

Prominent educators and rabbis testified during the long trial. The defendants elected a political line of defense, and all had their say. The moving testimony of Ya'akov Genzweig , a recent immigrant, is brought here in full:

Your Honour, respected Gentlemen;

I wish to deliver a personal message. I want to give you some details from my recent past, not that these are of much significance in themselves, but because they reflect especially upon Jewish fate and the relations between Britain and our nation. I leave it to your own consciences to draw the conclusions from what I have to say.

I have the honor to inform you, gentlemen, that I am arrived from the killing fields of Poland. I came to Eretz Israel a mere year and a half ago. You will find on me no marks to distinguish me as a fighter. My brethren and I arose in the ghettos and escaped to the forests, where we attacked German convoys. A handful of anonymous, hungry and lonely men, we took on the mightiest and cruelest military power ever to arise in Europe. No one took cognizance of our deeds, no one appreciated our sacrifices. Were it not for this trial, were it not for the need I feel to appear before a British court, not as an individual, but as an emissary, a representative of Hebrew blood that is shed as water, and of Jewish isolation the like of which has not been known in history—were it not for this, I too would remain anonymous among the thousands who fought in the hardest battle of all—the battle of destroyed Jewry against the destroying Vandal.

Now that I have introduced myself in my invisible uniform of honor, I would like, I have the right to demand of you, that you focus your attention on the following question: *how is it that a Jewish fighter from Poland stands accused, not before a German court, but before a British one*? Assume the Germans still had military power; if caught, there is no doubt I would get my ration of lead. But the question is, why am I standing before a *British* court? Why am I detained in a *British* jail?

A year and a half ago, my brothers and I were still your allies. Unacknowledged allies, albeit, unknown allies, but allies in fact. We manned the same side of the barricade. You killed Germans, and we killed Germans; you destroyed their highways, and we too sabotaged their railways. Of course there is a vast quantitative difference between what you did and what we were able to accomplish, just as there was a huge difference between the means at your disposal and ours. But morally, according to the soldier's code, we were in effect brothers-in-arms. We had a common enemy, and we fought him in common according to the means we each had. And now—what a difference?! You are the accusers, and I the accused.

I, gentlemen, am "there"; I descended into the nether regions of hell. Dante masterfully described the reality of Satan's messengers on earth. Real Hell was there in Poland, in the heart of Europe. There, people were burned alive, synagogues were turned into cemeteries, babies were smashed against rocks; there, people were turned into beasts of prey, into strange creatures, kept alive by mysterious powers. And who were these people who were trampled, strangled, burned, butchered? They were my father and my mother, my sister and my brother, relatives, childhood friends—all those I loved, all those who loved me.

Can you imagine our feelings? Can I with my poor powers of expression make you realize that before you stands a man who stood up to his neck in blood; who has trudged through a never-ending graveyard, who has seen what man's eye has not seen since the beginning of time? I want to tell you the truth, English gentlemen: we Jewish fighters hated the Germans passionately, unto death. For us the word "revenge" took on the aspect of a plan, a duty, a sacred vow. Although we knew it was naive of us to think we could avenge everything they had done to us—still, the awareness that we have done something against them was a consolation. We killed them, these mad dogs that would wipe out an ancient nation, and would enslave the entire world.

But the Germans were not the only ones cursed in the ghettos. You too were cursed. I tell you this to your faces, as I know I speak for millions of people who perished with a double curse on their lips: damned be our murderers, they whispered, and damned be that "enlightened" world that left us in their hands, that did nothing to save us, or at least save our children.

Thus spoke the martyrs. And we the fighters added another count to your terrible indictment. Day and night we looked skyward, waiting for help. Waited for arms, waited for food. We had no doubt that you could have sent us the bare necessities for continuing the struggle, in the burning ghettos and in the deep forests. But you did not do that. The heroes of the ghettos had to make do with homemade weapons, and face Nazi Germany's mighty war machine with a few pistols and tiny bombs. You abandoned people who were ready to give their all, unconditionally, but whose hands were empty. For if our hands were not empty, not only could we have hit harder at our common enemy, but also—or mainly—we could have saved hundreds and thousands from slaughter. Can there be an indictment more severe than that you face from the remnants of a destroyed nation, who bore on high the standard of anti-Nazi resistance?

God willed that I live and not die; that after endless wanderings, I should come to my homeland. And what did I find here? Oh, respected judges, if you only had an idea how we yearned for Eretz Israel from the depths of the bunkers, if you only knew how we dreamed of her in our days of terror! Early in the war, there were rumors about in Poland, that the Hebrew State was a fact, that there was a Hebrew Army! You would call that wishful thinking, but the condemned Jews wanted a state that would be their salvation, and imagined it to be already in existence. On the other hand, there were logical reasons that lent substance to the wonderful rumor. War broke out. The entire Hebrew nation would face mankind's enemy. Our nation would therefore be recognized as an ally, and England would change her policies. There would be a Hebrew Army and a Hebrew Government would be set up. Dreams, wouldn't you say? But that is what we all believed, walled up in the stinking ghettos, whence we addressed our prayers, our faith and our hopes eastward, to Zion! Only after coming here, did the full horror of reality dawn upon me. Not only did we not have a state, not only did we not have our own army—even the White Paper was still in force, and the gates were closed, and remained closed. I must confess: at first I could not believe my eyes. I thought reality was a dream, just as there we thought dreams to be reality. Is this how we are to be paid for our blood? Is this how we are to be compensated for our victims? Is England, too, among our destroyers? But reality was undeniable. Eretz Israel was barred and locked. People may leave; none may enter. It was then, respected judges, that I swore an oath on the blood of my parents, brothers and sisters: that I shall not rest until these gates to our only land will open—or will be forced open. I am one of the few that managed to come here, while tens of thousands remain there, in the great prison, in hell. I asked myself: why have I been spared? How am I better than my brothers, that I have not perished like them? And I found in my soul one answer: if great God has brought me thus far, it must be a sign that He wants me to bear witness for all those still on the other side of the wall, that I fight for them to save them, for their salvation and their future. Otherwise, there is no point to my life.

If this mission, sacred not only in my view but in the eyes of every honest man, Jew or gentile—if you view this mission as a crime, it is proof that the Jewish tragedy is endless, just as there is no forgiving your crime of helping in the destruction of my people.

(According to Max Kritzman, who regularly smuggled mail into prison for his clients, the speeches delivered by Irgunists who chose to take a political line of defense were written by Menachem Begin, the commander-in-chief. Indeed, it would seem unlikely, given the gut-wrenching emotional content of these addresses, that they originated with the young men and women who delivered them.)

A long silence ensued. I doubt there was a dry eye in the Court. Even the British judges were visibly moved. Now it was Max's turn to sum up for the Defense, and he uncharacteristically had to clear his throat a number of times before he began:

This has been a long and tiring trial; unnecessarily so, I might add. When the Prosecution rested, I told the Court there were no grounds for continuing this case. Now today, there are two trials being heard. One is the case against the criminals of Bergen-Belsen, the other here. In the former, the defendants are all despicable murderers. Yet in spite of the hideous crimes they have committed against civilization, they are entitled to the best defence attorneys England can provide, while in the case before you, the defendants are twenty Hebrew youths, educated and of good families. They must rely only on the help I and my partner Mr. Kritzman can give them, poor indeed when compared to the help given the Bergen-Belsen defendants.

During my twenty four years of work here and in England, I have never until now come across a case where the prosecution has failed from beginning to end. It has been unable to prove any connection between the indictment and the defendants. The charge is of possessing the exhibits without reasonable justification, but possession has not been proved. The prosecution has based its case on the fact that the twenty youths were caught together, and were searched, but no one has stated that the exhibits in question were in their possession, and there is no proof that they belonged to them. They were removed from the place, and only then was a search made—and then too, no one bothered to connect the exhibits with their owners. In my considerable experience as a lawyer, I can state that in a civil court, this case would have been dismissed when the prosecution rested. Here we are concerned with a military court, but such a court too cannot go so far as to place blame without proof. The prosecutor begged the court to believe him when he said the defendants came to that place for arms training, but the court is not concerned with beliefs. It needs proof, and no witness has stated that the defendants were arrested as they were about to commit a crime. Can a person be punished for a crime he did not commit? From the testimony given by witnesses for the prosecution, it is evident that none of them attempted to identify the defendants as the owners of the arms in question. The search itself was not conducted as required by law. None of the defendants were present during the search, not even the local mukhtar. I am not accusing the police of planting the exhibits, but the place is a popular hiking area, and what proof is there that the defendants were those training with the arms exhibited?

This is an unusual trial. The defendants have chosen a different kind of defence, one supplementary to their plea of Not Guilty. They contend that the accusation itself is unjustified, since had they indeed been in possession of the exhibits, then too they should not have been accused. This is a political point which justifies the bearing of arms. We recommend the Court proceed with caution and examine what has happened to the Jewish nation. This is a terrible tragedy, and the defendants, being of this nation, are linked to it.

For thousands of years the Jewish nation has been persecuted all over the world. For thousands of years the Jew has prayed: "Next year in Jerusalem," meaning to return to the land given to him by the law of the Bible, which came before British law. During the past fifty years, a lot has been done to make the Zionist dream come true, and England deserves much credit in this endeavor, not the England of Bevin and Passfield, but that of Disraeli, of Joseph Chamberlain and Balfour. The Balfour Declaration was given in 1917. This declaration breathed new life into the land. Towns and villages were built, and tens of thousands of Jews came and settled in Eretz-Israel, your humble servant among them.

World War Two began. Millions of Jews perished and were burned in the Nazi gas chambers. There isn't a Jewish family in the world that is not mourning. Only a few Jews remained in Europe, but wherever a Jewish heart beats, its thoughts were of Eretz-Israel, promised to Abraham by the covenant with God, and in our day by Britain's finest sons. For the remnants of the European holocaust there is only one place left on earth—Eretz-Israel. The elders want to live out their lives in peace. The younger ones, survivors of the German hell, want to build their future in their land, but the gate to their hopes is locked.

It's only natural that every Jew should wish to help his brother. Jewish youth is entitled to believe that even if there are certain laws—there is something which is above the law—and that is their conscience. This conscience will not allow them to forget the Jews in exile.

The defendants claim alternatively that even if the prosecution had been able to prove that they possessed and trained with arms, they had a right to do so.

If you release the defendants, you will be doing justice. If you do justice, you will inculcate in our hearts here and all over the world the belief that British justice is above all else. Based on both the evidence presented and the alternative plea by the defendants, I beg you to set them free.

The judges remained silent for a long while. The prosecutor then requested a recess while the Court considered its verdict. When it reconvened, a guilty verdict was announced. Following testimony by character witnesses and the appeals by Seligman and Kritzman, two boys and two girls were released, and the remaining defendants were sentenced to relatively short prison terms with special privileges.

ALL IN THE FAMILY

On several occasions, Max asked whether I'd like to study Law. Neither one of his daughters Aura and Sheila gave any indication of interest in following their father's profession. In any case, woman lawyers were a rarity in Palestine at the time. The implication in his request was quite clear: he would have liked me to become a lawyer, and presumably work for him, and later—who knows? My parents thought this was a good idea. I too appreciated the sentiment and respected Max's wishes, but really felt no inclination in that direction. Along the same lines, Max's nephew Ralph Seligman (born in Dublin in 1919) wrote me:

I had always wanted to be a doctor, but in 1936 a younger brother of my father, Hymie, paid a visit to Max in Tel Aviv and came back to Dublin and told me Max had a successful law practice in Palestine, being one of the few English-speaking lawyers there—that he had no sons, and that if I became a lawyer I could become a partner of Max in due course. Thinking this might be a good idea, I became a law student at the University of Dublin, Trinity College. In March 1938 I went to Palestine to visit and stay with Max and see if I would like living there.

I stayed at Rothschild Boulevard until some time in May, paying visits to Jerusalem to see my godfather (Sandek) Chief Rabbi Herzog (who had left Ireland in 1937) and my friend his son Chaim who had become a member of the Hagana[4]. I also went to Petach Tikva for a few days and attended a Seder on April 15th presided over by the venerable Shimon Zahavi and a legion of children and grandchildren totaling about fifty and including a spinster sister who had kept the surname Seligman. Amongst Shimon Zahavi's grandchildren was a member of Betar aged about eighteen whom Max had defended. However, Max's social life was radically different from that of his Zahavi relatives, with whom he had little contact.

My initial impressions of Palestine as a place to live were not favourable—there was a lot of Arab violence in 1938 and in the end I was glad to leave.

Ralph was returning to Britain from South Africa in 1948 when the 'plane on which he was traveling had to make a detour and landed in Palestine (which was about to become Israel). He told me of an adventure he had after landing:

We flew to Lydda Airport (which towards the end of April was still occupied by British forces). We were told we had to stay the night inside the airport before continuing on to Athens the next day. I managed to get a message to Max through an American I met at the airport, and received a pass to travel in a convoy of two armoured cars which, unknown to me, were carrying a cargo of gold bullion (which had been flown to Lydda by KLM) to Barclays Bank in Tel Aviv.

When the trucks rolled out of Lydda I was startled to see a Sten gun being assembled. I was told to keep my head down especially when passing through Ramleh which we did without incident. We finally came to friendly territory (I believe I remember seeing a signpost to Petach Tikva) where we disembarked for a cigarette. However, when we reached Ben Yehuda Street in Tel Aviv, a car blocked the road, and when we stopped, a number of armed youths wearing hoods appeared and at gunpoint I and the guards dismounted and the youths (whom I later learned were from the Lechi) then proceeded to unload the bullion. The boy guarding me could not resist turning away and joining in the loading—I found myself unattended and just outside the door of TWA Airlines offices—I darted in and telephoned Max. The Lechi car sped off with the stolen gold as I was on the 'phone. The windows of Max's flat on Rothschild Boulevard had bullet holes from the fighting in Jaffa the previous night. The following morning I returned to Lydda in an armoured convoy along with a number of people including Rabbi Kopul Rosen.

Max had three younger half-brothers, born after his widowed father had remarried. David kept the name Seligman, while his brothers Leonard and Arnold changed theirs to Selwyn. David was a member of the Chalutz Youth Movement and came to Palestine in 1946, where he joined Kibbutz Ma'ayan Zvi near Zichron Ya'akov, He writes:

> Max always wanted me to study Law and go into his practice in Tel Aviv. Max and Millie could not understand how I could reject the fleshpots of Tel Aviv and Jerusalem for the simple life on a kibbutz. With hindsight perhaps he was right.

David and his wife Philippa returned to England in 1951, where Max helped him through law school. He now works in Cardiff. Again from Ralph Seligman:

> In 1949 my younger brother Donald was called to the Irish Bar and Max came to Dublin for the occasion. I arranged a meeting for him with President Eamonn de Valera who lamentably compared the apathy of the Irish to the attempted revival of Gaelic, and the enthusiasm in Israel for the revival of Hebrew. My brother left for Israel immediately after his call and joined Max's brother David in Kibbutz Ma'ayan Zvi near Zichron Ya'akov. He spent a year there before returning to Dublin.

YOU'RE A TERRORIST IF YOU ASK FOR MAX SELIGMAN

At the completion of a platoon leaders course in August 1946, a group of trainees went to an orange grove near Netanya to practice dismantling and reassembling of a machine gun. In charge was Chaim Wasserman; a newcomer from Romania, Yosef Rosenzweig, was on guard duty. While working with the gun, they were surprised by soldiers of the 6th Airborne. Wasserman ordered everyone to disperse, while the armorer, Yitzchak Wilenchuk, took the dismantled Bren-gun parts and buried them in the ground, hoping to somehow retrieve the valuable treasure later. In his haste, he dropped three magazines, a loaded pistol and his Irgun-made false identity card, in which he appeared as Yitzchak Gil'adi. Wasserman (the commander) and the two men were now surrounded, and the British soldiers fired warning shots; they had no choice but to surrender. The British searched the grove and found the ammunition clips, revolver, identity card and a training manual.

They were taken to the police station of Beit-Lid, where they were booked, then to Nablus where a judge ordered them held for fifteen days at the Tul-Karm prison. The health of Wasserman, a veteran of the Jewish Brigade, was a matter of concern to the Irgun command, as he appeared to be suffering from the after-effects of combat. When Seligman and Kritzman got word that the prisoners wished to defend themselves politically, they objected: It was out of the question for Rosenzweig, who spoke none of the languages used in Palestine, to deliver a political speech. Then there was the concern for Wasserman's health: in a conventional and not anti-British line of defense, the outcome would most likely mean detention in Latrun, far better than a prison sentence. And since Rosenzweig was a salaried guard at the orange grove, his presence there could be proven to be entirely innocent.

The trial opened in Jerusalem. The defendants pleaded not guilty. A police sergeant from the Beit-Lid station testified that they were brought to the station with the exhibits, which were in serviceable condition. Kritzman then stated that nothing has been proven against his clients and asked for their release. This was denied, and a date was set for continuation of the trial three weeks later. Pointing out that the fact the defendants appeared in court with a defence attorney and did not use it as a political platform is evidence that they were innocent, and should be released on bail, so as not to be in jail during the High Holidays. The prosecution countered by claiming that *the very fact that they called on the services of Seligman and Kritzman is evidence that they belong to an illegal organization* (my italics.) Kritzman reacted sharply, and the prosecutor apologized and said that what he meant was that when an accused person felt he needed the services of one of the top lawyers in the country, he must believe himself to be in serious trouble.

When the trial reopened, Wilenchuk, a plumber by trade, testified that he was asked by the owner of the grove to repair a broken irrigation line, and went there with an assistant, Wasserman. While at work, a group of armed men entered the grove and told them to leave. They heard shots, and ran away. Their story stood up well under the prosecutor's cross-examination, who now decided to concentrate his efforts on Rosenzweig, who was new and inexperienced in such matters. The following exchange took place:

Prosecutor: Why did you request at the police station that Mr. Seligman should be called on your behalf?
Defendant: I read in the paper that he was a successful lawyer.
Prosecutor: You mean you knew he defended terrorists?
Presiding judge: Defendant has stated he knew Seligman defended arms cases. That would imply he defended terrorists.
Kritzman: Your honor, this is not the same thing. Must I reiterate what the duty of every lawyer is in such cases in a democratic state? The way the question was phrased is not fair.
Defendant: I heard he defended people accused of carrying arms.
Prosecutor: And I maintain that you belong to an illegal organization, where you were told that if you get into trouble, you ask for Seligman to defend you.
Defendant: What organization?
Presiding judge: You were asked whether it was true that some organization instructed you that in case of trouble you should ask for Mr. Seligman, and since you answered neither yea or nay, I am noting that you refuse to answer the question.
Kritzman: It is a typical Jewish custom to answer a question with another.
Presiding judge (angrily): This is a British Court, not a Jewish one. Please confine your remarks to the subject at hand.
Kritzman: I beg your honor's pardon, but Jews are on trial here, not Englishmen, and I would ask the Court to provide a Romanian interpreter, as this is the defendant's language.

Prosecutor: If it is a Jewish custom to reply to one question with another, what use would an interpreter be?
Defendant: I belong to no illegal Organization and no one told me to ask for Mr. Seligman. I read papers and know he defends such cases.

The defense presented witnesses that corroborated the defendants' statements, and the orange-grove owner testified that he is a member of the General Labour Organization, a body vehemently opposed to terror and one which has collaborated with the police in efforts to eliminate terror. The court found all three men guilty, and sentenced them to ten years, with special privileges. Two months after the trial, the following letter from the prosecutor was received by Seligman & Co.:

It was never my intention to infer that any defendant asking for lawyer Seligman & Co. is by implication a terrorist suspect. What I wanted to say was that a man who was arrested and who asks for the services of one of the top criminal lawyers in the land, like Mr. Seligman, reveals the burden of heavy guilt he must feel.

FLOGGING

Like every other war, the one against the British required financing. Public support, if any, was minimal, and the Irgun had to resort to other sources, preferably British. Two branches of the British-managed Ottoman Bank were targeted on 13 September, 1946. The first operation, at the Tel-Aviv branch on Rothschild Blvd., went without a hitch. The second holdup, the Clock Square branch in Jaffa failed. This failure snowballed into a series of arrests, trials, and the execution of Jews and Englishmen.

After the Irgun men entered the bank, they rounded up all the employees, and the manager was told to open the safe. When he said he did'nt have the keys, he was shot in the leg. The keys in fact were held by the Arab assistant manager, who showed courage and presence of mind by darting into the safe and locking it from within. The attackers lost precious minutes trying to force the door, but had to give up and leave empty-handed.

In order to sow confusion and throw off pursuers, burning tar blocked the street outside the bank. Because they were delayed inside the bank, the fire went out, and when the attackers emerged, they found themselves facing an angry Arab mob. The cover unit had to withdraw because of the mob and the proximity of the police station, and the attacking unit scattered, the men attempting to make their way back to Tel-Aviv. One man was killed by the Arabs, two others captured and handed over to the police, and five more were also apprehended, two of them wounded. The toll, in addition to Irgun casualties, were two Arabs killed, and a number of Arabs and British wounded.

All seven were transferred to Jerusalem and booked on suspicion of attempting to rob the bank. Fearful of Irgun reprisal, all witnesses called to identify the attackers declined, with one exception. This one identified two of the men, who were under eighteen, and therefore not in danger of the death penalty. The others wanted to use the court as a political platform, but were not permitted to do so, because of Dov Gruner, who had been condemned to hang. The Irgun did not want to risk any more death sentences, and preferred to have each man defended separately; the evidence against them was not conclusive, and separate trials would emphasize the lack of connection between them. One of the teen-agers was tried first, and sentenced to eighteen years imprisonment and eight strokes. The defendant, Benyamin Kimchi, smiled as he told the judge: "I may be flogged, but do you really think you'll be here another eighteen years?" It was the flogging that brought on an escalation of hostilities. Flogging was viewed in some quarters as worse than hangings. In his book *Defenders of the Underground Fighters*, Yitzchak Gurion gives a description of this barbaric custom. Gurion was the liaison man between Seligman and Co. and the Irgun; both he and Seligman were prisoners in Jerusalem in 1938. He writes:

> In jail with us was one Abdul Majid, an underworld type from Jaffa, who confessed to murdering Chaim Arlosoroff, and later changed his mind about it. He was under life sentence, a "big shot" in the prison, who would strut about as though he owned the place. Once, when a British policeman insulted him, he drew a razor and attacked him. He was sentenced to receive eighteen strokes.

During the "ceremony", all Arab prisoners were herded out into the courtyard and made to squat in a semicircle around the victim, "so they may see and learn a lesson." The Jewish prisoners were exempted from this pleasure. We viewed the happening from our window. Majid, naked from the waist up, was tied hand and foot to two steel pipes erected in a corner of the courtyard. The lower part of his body was covered with leather. Nearby stood a bucket of salt water, and in it a leather whip whose thongs were reinforced with steel. The Prison Director counted the strokes, and a sergeant administered the blows. Each blow left a blue and red welt on Majid's back. After the third blow, his back started bleeding profusely. When all eighteen blows were given, Majid was barely conscious, but when he was about to be untied, he looked with contempt at the Director, and shouted: "Minshan mudir, kaman wachad!" (For the Director, one more!) The

רק כך

אזהרה!

חייל עברי, שנפל בשבי האויב, נידון ע"י "בית-דין" של צבא הכבוש הבריטי למלקות.

אנו מזהירים את ממשלת הדכוי מפני הוצאה לפועל של עונש משפיל זה.

אם הוא יוצא אל הפועל, יוטל אותו עונש על קציני הצבא הבריטי. כל אחד מהם יהיה עלול ללקות 18 מלקות.

הארגון הצבאי הלאומי
בארץ-ישראל

כסלו תש"ז

WARNING!

A Hebrew soldier, taken prisoner by the enemy; was sentenced by an illegal British Military "Court" to the humiliating punishment of flogging.

We warn the occupation Government not to carry out this punishment, wich is contrary to the laws of soldiers honour. If it is put into effect — every officer of the British occupation army in Eretz-Israel will be liable to be punished in the same way: to get 18 whips.

HAIRGUN HAZVAI HALEUMI (N. M. O.)
b'Eretz-Israel

prison physician protested, but the Director said: "I make the decisions here." Majid got another stroke.

When news of Kimchi's sentence reached him, the usually calm Seligman paced his office like a caged tiger, and kept repeating: "This must not happen!"

Posters in Hebrew and English warning against carrying out the flogging were circulated all over the country. The British made the mistake of underestimating the determination of the "natives" not to tolerate this humiliation. The punishment was carried out on 28 December, 1946. The following day, an officer and three sergeants of the 6th Airborne Division were abducted in various parts of the country, taken to nearby groves, and each given eighteen strokes. Another unit, assigned to similar duty, ran into a British roadblock. Three men were wounded, one of them, Avraham Mizrachi, severely. A search of the car revealed guns and whips. The men were taken to several army camps and over a period of four days were severely beaten and tortured. Although an army medical officer was present when the men were taken prisoner, Mizrachi was left to bleed to death before being taken to a hospital.

Many Irgun members had false identification papers. Yekhi'el Dresner was known as Dov Rosenbaum; it was as Rosenbaum that he was tried, condemned to death and hanged. He was buried under a name not his own; his true identity only emerged after the British left the country. He had three brothers: one in the police, another in African exile, and a third, the youngest, also in the underground. It was essential they did not become identified with Dresner, so he even denied himself the comfort of family visits throughout his ordeal. On 3 January, 1947, the men were transferred to the Jerusalem prison, and Max Kritzman hurried there to see them. What he saw can be imagined from the written record Dresner gave the shaken Kritzman. It is brought here in full:

Before we got to Wilhelmina we ran into an army roadblock, and I ordered the driver to stop and the men to disperse. But it was too late, and he accelerated instead. We dragged the roadblock with us until we hit the second one and the car stalled. A Bren-gun opened fire at us from behind, and we were then surrounded by red berets pointing their weapons at us, whereupon we surrendered. Eli'ezer (Kashani) was wounded in the back and Mordechai (Alkachi), the driver in the shoulder. As we were leaving the car, I was struck from behind and fell into the ditch. As I lay there I heard pistol shots, and saw a soldier pointing his gun at Mordechai and firing. He missed and killed a fellow-soldier. He then struck Mordechai in the head with his gun and threw him into the ditch alongside me. We were told to get up, and I heard more shots. I was sure we'd be killed, but we were taken to an armored car, where I found two of the others inside. A soldier guarded each of us; they ordered us to raise our hands and they emptied our pockets, taking everything we had. Then they began beating us: they punched us in the stomach, and as we doubled up, they'd hit us in the face. When my nose started bleeding like a faucet, my tormentor was jubilant, crying: "I broke his nose!"

We stopped somewhere and were taken out, and told to stand abreast while ten soldiers took up positions in front of us and cocked their rifles. I am proud to say we withstood the test and none of us lowered his head. At that moment an officer came running up and scolded the men, who were apparently serious about shooting us. We were kept with our hands in the air for half an hour, and then loaded onto a lorry. Here they began kicking and stomping on us. They noticed a ring on Mordechai's finger and tried to take it off, and did'nt stop until they broke his finger. We arrived at a camp, where we were taken into a barrack and stripped. They had tied our hands to each other, and what they couldn't tear off, they cut with a razor, slashing us in the process. Now began another beating, with four or five soldiers taking over when the first group tired. We were punched and kicked all over our bodies, genitals not spared. Among the beaters were also two policemen, and I remember the number of one of them: 1617. This one had a large police-club which he used with relish, and with which he broke Eli'ezer's arm and hurt Chaim's back. He struck me on the neck and I almost fainted. This went on until late at night, when an officer entered and ordered a halt to the beatings. We were given blankets and buckets with water, and told to pour it over each other. This did'nt help much, as we were all bleeding, and were soon covered with fresh blood. Wet and shivering, we lay naked on the ground and covered ourselves with the remaining two blankets (that was all they gave us). We thought they would let us sleep, but every fifteen minutes they came back and roused us with kicks and pulling off the blankets. In the morning, we were told to "wash" again. The blanket under us was dyed red with our blood. We were given the rags that had been our clothes and told to dress, but were given no shoes. They made us run the length of the camp to the infirmary, and on the way we were beaten with fists and rifle-butts by every soldier we met. We had to run with our hands in the air, and that is how they kept us for three quarters of an hour until the medical officer arrived. This young lieutenant looked us over, and asked the soldiers if they wanted to have some more fun with us, and that he'd dress our wounds "later" (he was unaware I understood English). We were made to run back to the barrack we came from, where a new group of soldiers came to beat us, but first we were made to wash our blood from the walls and floor. The place looked like a slaughterhouse, and we had to scrape the dried blood with our fingernails while they kept on beating us. Policeman 1617 came in, and ordered us to bow and kiss the floor, and when we refused, received a rain of blows from his club. They had guessed I was the leader, and tied me up more securely. About 9 A.M. they washed us again, and we were each given a pair of trousers. The M.O. applied some plaster tape to a couple of us, and then the police arrived, including the Jewish police officer Karlick. We were hardly interrogated, only asked for our names and addresses. This went on all day, and the soldiers amused themselves with us all that time. Towards evening, only Karlick remained in the next room, and we were taken out one at a time to sign the charge sheet. While this was taking place, a giant of a corporal came in and demanded we do all sorts of demeaning things, and beat us mercilessly when we refused. I told the boys not to keep quiet, as I wanted Karlick to hear us. When I was taken into the next room, I told him he is the only Jew we've seen that day, and that he must get us out of there before they killed us. He promised to do his best. We all refused to sign the charge sheet he read us—something to do with possession of arms—I'm not sure, as I was thoroughly confused and weakened by then. After dark, another company of soldiers arrived, and these treated us well: they gave us food and blankets, and helped us make ourselves as comfortable as possible.

Seligman and Kritzman sent the authorities a memorandum concerning the beatings and torture, and demanded a board of inquiry to look into the matter, but got no response. On 22 January, 1947, the government announced that flogging had been abolished in Palestine. On the 27th, the G.O.C. sent Seligman & Co. a reply, denying the beatings and refusing to appoint a board of inquiry. In order to bring the matter to the public's attention, the Irgun distributed posters describing the event in detail.

The British waited six weeks before bringing the men to trial, and for obvious reasons. The men asked for and received permission from Irgun command to defend themselves politically. Rosenbaum (Dresner) and Chaim Golovsky read prepared statements, and the two others stated they were in agreement with them. The trial was short, the verdict: death sentences for Eli'ezer Kashani, Mordechai Alkachi and Dov Rosenbaum. Chaim Golovsky was given life in prison, since he was under eighteen years of age.

Requests for clemency were immediately submitted, accompanied by letters from the Chief Rabbinate and various municipalities, all over the world, but to no avail. The outgoing G.O.C. confirmed the death sentences, preventing the incoming commander from commuting them. He also made sure the fact would not be made public until after he left the country. Seligman now tried to get a restraining order, while pressure from various public quarters was applied to the condemned men to ask for clemency. They refused. The prison director, present at one of the interviews, told the petitioner: "There is nothing you can do with these boys. They decided they must live as free men, or die."

The request for a restraining order was denied. Seligman and Kritzman asked for leave to appeal to the Privy Council. This too was denied, but the court announced it had decided to stay the executions until after the appeal on behalf of Dov Gruner, which was then pending before the Privy Council, was decided. This was confirmed by the new G.O.C., General McMillan. The fate of the three was thus linked to that of Dov Gruner.

DOV GRUNER

On 23 April, 1946, an army lorry stopped at the Ramat-Gan police station. An army sergeant stepped out of the vehicle and entered the station, telling the duty officer that he had some Arab prisoners caught in a theft attempt at a nearby army camp. He asked for the prisoners to be detained at the police station, and permission was granted. As soon as the Arab prisoners with their British escort entered the building, they shed their disguise and pointed their guns at the police personnel. They blew open the armory door and began loading their booty onto the lorry. The attackers had carried out a classic Trojan Horse tactic. The British policemen were stunned, but a Jewish policeman, thinking the attackers were really Arabs, risked his life and ran to the wireless room, where he radioed a call for help.

Meanwhile, a second unit carried out a diversionary attack on the railway station in southern Tel Aviv. Other units blew up two bridges leading to the police station, cut the telephone wires, and put up signs warning all military personnel to stay away from the station. Some British policemen in the living quarters, overlooked by the attackers, opened fire on the men loading the arms onto the lorry. One man was killed and two wounded, and although the lorry was not fully loaded, the commander of the operation picked up the dead and wounded men and left, not noticing a third man who had been wounded and was entangled in the barbed wire. That was Dov Gruner. When he was approached by the station commander and another policeman, the wounded Gruner tried to lift his pistol, but he passed out. The officer then took aim and emptied his revolver into the prostrate man at point-blank range, smashing his jaw. Miraculously, Gruner did not die. A Jewish doctor who was called gave him morphine and ordered him transferred to a hospital. The ambulance driver was told to take him to the Government hospital in Jaffa, but took him instead to the Hadassa in Tel-Aviv, where he was treated by the celebrated Professor Marcus, chief of surgery and a friend of the underground. Gruner refused to give his name.

After twelve days of devoted care by Dr. Marcus and his staff, Gruner began to make progress, and was able to take fluids, but did not say much: talking was difficult due to his jaw injury, and he did not wish to compromise the people treating him. A male nurse (Asher Segal) would whisper to him during the changing of dressings or while giving him medication, keeping him informed of the latest news. When he learned that Irgun command was going to attempt a rescue operation as soon as he was well enough to be moved, he refused: he was not willing to have any of his comrades risk their lives for him. Furthermore, he felt the hospital staff should not be exposed to risk, and that the British would not allow wounded underground members to be treated in Jewish hospitals if he were abducted. He steadfastly refused to change his mind, and while Irgun command was debating whether to give him a direct order in the matter, the British moved him in an army ambulance to the Government hospital in Jaffa, in spite of Dr. Marcus' objections. In Jaffa, he was subjected to hostile treatment, his condition worsened, and his wounds became infected. When Kritzman threatened to publicize the matter, Gruner was transferred to the Government hospital in Jerusalem, where Kritzman was able to visit him. Gruner, in constant pain but never complaining, was an inspiration to everyone, including Arab patients nearby. Dr. Joseph, an expert in reconstructive surgery was called in on the case, but Gruner was upset because of the expense, and only calmed down after being told Dr. Joseph was donating his services. Drs. Joseph and Shalit performed fourteen operations on Gruner's jaw and palate, and his condition improved slowly. Bathed in cold sweat, he never made a sound, his smiling eyes became the talk of everyone, Arab nurses and British guards included.

Towards the end of November, Gruner was moved to the hospital in the Latrun detention camp, where he was given a trial date in January, 1947. Again, Irgun decided to free Gruner, and elaborate plans were made accordingly. This time, he was not told until two days before the escape. He adamantly refused to go along: escapes were meant to add fighters to the ranks, and he was not in fighting shape. Besides, his wounds would make him easily recognizable to searchers, and the expense of treating him would impose a burden on the Irgun. He was transferred to the Central Prison in Jerusalem, where Kritzman went to consult with him. The lawyer felt a conventional defense could benefit the case, as there were mitigating circumstances: Gruner had served with distinction for five years in the British army, and had excellent reports from his superiors. His severe injuries were also a factor in his favor, but again Gruner refused: he was a soldier of the Irgun, and that is how he would appear before the British, and he was willing to accept the consequences. An ominous turn of events took place: three days before his trial was to open, British servicemen were flogged in retaliation for the flogging of Benyamin Kimchi. This was bound to put the court in a vindictive frame of mind.

The trial was relatively short. Gruner was brought into court in chains and under heavy guard. He was far from recovered, but managed a smile in the direction of Kritzman and the Jewish journalists present. Kritzman announced the defendant had dispensed with his services, since Gruner refused to accept the court's right to try him. The lawyer was granted permission to remain in court during the proceedings. The presiding judge addressed Gruner, telling him the charges against him could result in a death sentence, and advising he retain counsel. Gruner politely declined, adding with a smile: "I will not take part in the trial, but would like to read a statement explaining why I believe you have no right to try me. I will question no witnesses and waive translation of the proceedings into Hebrew." Following testimony by witnesses for the Prosecution, Gruner read his statement:

I do not recognize the right of this court to try me. This court has no legal standing, as it is part of a government which has no legal foundation. You came to Eretz Israel with a mandate given you by the nations of the world, a mandate to make right the worst wrong ever suffered by any nation in the annals of civilization, the wrong of exiling the nation of Israel and turning it into a victim of endless persecution and slaughter all over the world. The obligation you undertook—and that obligation alone—was the legal and moral foundation for your being in this land. But you have abrogated this undertaking, cruelly, brutally and with diabolical malice. You turned your obligation into a piece of paper, which you proceeded to tear to pieces. You may not have said so, but you followed the advice of a certain German chancellor, who said: 'What is an international treaty?—a piece of paper, not worth quarreling over!' I might add, that you have learned a lot from the Germans—or was it the other way around? One thing is clear: you are at one with them in your desire to destroy our nation. You are aware, I am sure, that keeping us from this land is tantamount to a constant attack on the lives of millions of men, women and children, my people. And yet, or perhaps because of this, you have determined to turn this land into a military camp and rob it from a nation that has no other land anywhere in the world but this, given to it by God and history, hallowed with the blood of its sons from generation to generation, and made to bloom with the sweat and blood of its founders. But you arrogantly dismissed the promise made by the Almighty, just as you have trampled the covenant you signed with our people and the nations of the world. There is nothing left of the legal right of your government; all that is left of it is brute force, the bayonet and terror, masquerading as "laws" enacted by the bayonet-wielders, who enforce them in violation of man's basic rights, against the will of the local population, and in contravention of international law. Whenever the government of a country is illegal, when it turns into tyranny and oppression, it is the right of the citizens—nay, their duty—to fight and overturn this regime. This is what Hebrew youth is doing. It will continue to do so until you leave this country and return it to its rightful owner: the nation of Israel. This you must know: there is no force in the world that can break the bond between Israel and its only land. The hand trying to break this bond shall be severed, and the wrath of God will be upon its owner forever.

The judges left for a short consultation, and returned to announce they found the defendant guilty. The presiding judge then asked the defense and prosecution if they had anything to add before sentence was passed. In a surprise move, the prosecutor stated that Gruner had no criminal record, and had served in the British army for five years with distinction. He described the wounds inflicted on him, adding that he will remain an invalid for the rest of his life. He pointed out that Gruner's entire family was wiped out by the Germans, and that only one sister remained.

Following another consultation, the judges returned and put on their caps—meaning a death sentence was about to be pronounced. The presiding judge read from a prepared statement: "The Court has found you Guilty of the charges brought against you, and sentences you to be hanged by the neck until you are dead." Gruner rose to his feet and recited the song "In blood and flames did Judea fall, in blood and flames shall she rise." After they heard a translation into English, the judges rose and left. One of them forgot his cap on the bench.

At this time, Max Seligman was in London, busy with presenting before the Privy Council the application on behalf of Aryeh ben Eli'ezer, concerning his detention in Asmara,

Eritrea. This was an extremely important issue, on which depended the fate of hundreds of deportees in African exile. While Seligman devoted many weeks to this struggle, the burden of defending Dov Gruner fell to his partner Max Kritzman.

Gruner's was a saga, a study in quiet heroism. This was not, unfortunately, how it was reported by the media to the Yishuv. He was labeled a fanatic, wearing the red clothing of death-row like a king his rayment on his coronation day. Irgun circulated a warning to the British that executing a captured soldier is the same as premeditated murder, and that the authorities would bear the consequences if the death sentence was carried out. On 28 January, the prison director visited Gruner in his cell and read him the decision of the G.O.C., General Barker, to the effect that he had confirmed his sentence, which would be carried out the following week, on 28 January, at 08:00 hours. The director recommended he apply for clemency to the High Commissioner. Again Gruner declined. On 26 January, the Irgun kidnaped two officials, a Major Collins in Jerusalem and Chief Justice Ralph Windham of the District Court in Tel Aviv. The British were extremely nervous and threatened a general curfew. The same day, an announcement over the radio notified listeners of the postponement of Gruner's death sentence, to give him time to sign an appeal to the Privy Council. The two British captives were released, and tensions appeared to be subsiding. The pressure on Gruner to appeal for mercy was mounting: Kritzman was called to a meeting with Golda Meir, head of the Political Department of the Jewish Agency. Also present was Chief Rabbi Herzog. They asked Kritzman to appeal to the Privy Council even without Gruner's consent; this he was unable to do, since Gruner officially dispensed with his services. Rabbi Herzog then got in touch with Gruner's sister, Helen Friedman, who lived in the U.S.A., and had her send a power of attorney to lawyer Asher Levitzky in Jerusalem. Pretending he was speaking to him on behalf of Irgun command, Levitzky told Gruner that he should sign the appeal to the Privy Council, which would protest not so much his sentence, as the validity in general of the Emergency Regulations, under which he was tried and sentenced. Gruner asked for time to consider, and the following day informed Levitzky he would sign if Kritzman would add his signature, too. Both the Yishuv and the British heaved a sigh of relief, but it was a short respite. When the two lawyers, accompanied by the prison director came to see Gruner, he reached for the petition and calmly tore it up, adding: "You lied to me!"

The die was now cast: Gruner steadfastly refused to appeal for clemency, and the British could not back down. Evacuation of British families was begun, as were preparations for a military alert over the entire country. Again Gruner was begged to relent: the chief rabbis told him that since he was committing suicide, he would be ostracized. All newspaper editors made an emotional appeal for him to sign. Gruner's sister was coming to see him in Jerusalem. Now Kritzman began various legal maneuvers to prevent the execution. Meanwhile in Britain, P.M. Clement Atlee, Foreign Minister Ernest Bevin, the High Commissioner and other officials were bombarded with appeals to intervene. Ironically, Gruner was handed a letter from the Army Paymaster informing him he was entitled to one hundred twenty Pounds in additional severance pay. Gruner asked the money be transferred to the Irgun for the purchase of arms. On 11 February, Gruner was joined on death row by Yekhi'el Dresner ("Dov Rosenbaum"), Mordechai Alkachi and Eli'ezer Kashani. Gruner's sister arrived on the 15th. They had not seen each other in many years; his disfigured face and red robes frightened her and her eyes misted, but Gruner quickly shifted the subject to the past. They spoke of their family lost in the holocaust. As she was leaving, he asked her not to encourage the appeal. Terribly upset and frustrated, Menachem Begin had the Irgun's clandestine radio broadcast his message:

> From the depths of the underground and the depth of our hearts, we send you, brother Dov, our brotherly greetings.
>
> Many are your enemies. Churchill, ready to sacrifice for so-called British "prestige" millions of men and women (of other nations) wants your blood; the so-called British "socialist" government wants your blood—again, to save it's "prestige". This whole empire with its ministers, commissioners and armies is set against us.

And you, brother Dov, alone and with your only neighbor Death, have for weeks stood up to them. But they could not bend you, these bloodthirsty tyrants, because in you they came up against a man emerging from rivers of Jewish blood, who proved that there is no power on earth that could subdue him, or break his spirit. Truly, brother Dov, if there is meaning to the word "hero", you are the one our children will learn from for generations to come. Take courage, great brother; your fighting family has done everything to extricate you from the hangman's hands. That was its duty to you. This is not a matter of saving life, which is fleeting. Each and every one of us is ready to sacrifice his life for his belief. This is a matter of a sacred human principle that we will not relinquish, no matter what. The life of a prisoner of war is sacred.

Brother Dov—Hebrew youth and the freedom loving world bow their heads before your quiet heroism and your supreme sacrifice.

No stone was left unturned in the efforts to save Gruner. Ironically, the British were equally anxious to get out of the corner into which they had boxed themselves. An uncle was found in the U.S.A., by the name of Frank Gruner. It is doubtful that Gruner or his sister even knew of this uncle's existence. What is certain is that his signature on the appeal to the Privy Council, submitted by two British lawyers, was forged. The British knew this but were fighting for time. Review of the appeal, submitted on 2 March, was immediately postponed to 24 March "awaiting clarification of certain details." Seligman and Kritzman took advantage of the petition before the Privy Council and sent telegrams to the Colonial Secretary, High Commissioner and G.O.C. to put off the executions until after the review. The date was postponed. On 25 March, the Privy Council rejected the petition, on the grounds that an American citizen cannot appeal a sentence handed down in Palestine, and furthermore, there appears to be no direct personal connection between the appellant and Gruner. This meant that a Palestinian citizen, directly concerned with the outcome, *might* succeed in such an appeal. Seligman, who had returned to Palestine in the interim (the C.I.D. tried hard to prevent it), instructed an associate in London, Dr. Sullivan Kaufman, to appeal on behalf of the parents of the three other condemned men. Yet another appeal on Gruner's behalf was submitted by Israel Rokach, Mayor of

Tel-Aviv. This was rejected, and immediately appealed. The British achieved their aim: the public was lulled into believing the sentences were under serious consideration and were likely to be commuted. Even two additional death sentences handed down (Me'ir Feinstein and Daniel Azoulai) did not alter the general mood of optimism.

It was now Passover eve, and all over the country, Jews were welcoming the holiday. Six men were on death row: in Acre, the newly condemned Feinstein and Azoulai, and in Jerusalem, attended by the official prison rabbi, Rabbi Goldmann, the four men celebrated the feast. Only they, and their lawyers, had no illusions. On 13 April, a cable from Dr. Kaufman advised Seligman: "Only Palestine High Commissioner can decide postponement Gruner Execution. Please attend locally." Yet another appeal to the High Commissioner and G.O.C. was made. No response was given. On the same day, 13 April, Feinstein and Azoulai were moved from Acre to Jerusalem; the same convoy of armored cars secretly transferred Gruner and his cellmates back to Acre. The scene was set for the executions.

Word of the transfer reached the Irgun, and Kritzman was roused from his sleep. At dawn, he asked for permission to see the four men in Jerusalem. The reply, that it was too early, confirmed the worst suspicions. A planned rescue attempt from the Jerusalem prison was called off. Another plan, for Gruner to blow himself up with his executioners, also went awry. He was asked to respond whether he was ready to do so, but the message from Irgun was misunderstood by Gruner, and he replied that he was ready to kill himself rather than be hanged. In the event, the grenade was smuggled into the prison, but the men were moved to Acre. Gruner wrote an emotional parting letter to his commander, Menachem Begin, concluding: "I am writing these lines 48 hours before our oppressors are about to carry out their murderous scheme, and at such times, one does not lie. I swear to you that if I had to start over again, I would have chosen the same path . . . Your obedient soldier, Dov."

Officially, the sentences were still under review, and no date was set for the executions. Seligman asked the prison director at Acre whether it was true preparations for the hangings were being made. His reply was negative, that he had received no orders, which in any case had to be transmitted to him three days in advance. To his question, as to why the men had been moved to Acre, the director's response was: "Routine, just routine." The routine was that 24 hours before a hanging was to take place, a sandbag of the condemned man's weight was hung from the gallows. Visiting day was Tuesday, which was also the day set for executions. Gruner's sister asked for permission to visit him, and this was granted immediately. It was Monday, and the men had not been weighed. Tuesday came, and the sentence was not carried out. This meant they had at least another week to live. It was also known that no more than three hangings were to be carried out in one day. What was not known was that, 24 hours before the executions, amendments to the regulations were made, which amendments were not made public until after the men were hanged. These stipulated that no appeals would be entertained on death sentences that had been confirmed by the G.O.C., and that more than three executions may take place on one day, "at the executioner's pleasure."

Gruner's sister Helen Friedman had permission to visit him on 16 April; Kritzman was going to visit the four men the same day, and arranged to pick up Helen Friedman at her hotel in Tel Aviv and give her a ride to Acre. But a pre-dawn visit from the police changed all that: the police officer asked for Helen Friedman's address, and this could mean only one thing—that Gruner had been hanged. His suspicion was confirmed when the police officer told them a curfew was about to be imposed on all highways. The authorities contacted the *Chevra Kadisha* (Burial Society) in Haifa and instructed them to have twelve men ready for pickup. They were taken under guard to Acre and prevented from making any calls. The four men were buried in Safed.

A terrible thought comes to mind: what if? Had Gruner agreed to sign a petition for clemency—could that not have affected the fate of his three cellmates, too? Gruner was senior among the men, his suffering and martyrdom gained him tremendous respect, and his opinion and actions carried a lot of weight. But the British knew they had chewed off more than they could swallow, and were desperately seeking a way to back out of the executions without losing face. Had Gruner relented, the others would have undoubtedly gone along, and all four might have been saved. Yet another question: should not have Begin *ordered* Gruner to sign? In a newspaper interview later that day, Seligman said:

"I could not believe the government would do this. Only after I heard the announcement over the radio did I realize I had been deceived. A few hours before the executions I was told by both Acre and Jerusalem that no date has been fixed and no preparations made for carrying out the sentences on Gruner and the three others. Final appeals were made by me to the High Commissioner, the Chief Rabbi was waiting for an appointment with the Chief Secretary, and Mayor Rokach was waiting to see the G.O.C. To all these applications I received the answer, that they have been given to the G.O.C. for consideration, and that no decision had been made—all this several hours before the hangings."

In London, Dr. Sullivan Kaufman wrote:

This case received world-wide publicity and was widely reported. The American and British Press (particularly the Times and the Jewish Chronicle) covered the case in great detail. The hearing was the subject of several appeals—as one was rejected a fresh one was started. A unique event in British legal history took place: in the middle of the final appeal to the Privy Council, the Military in Palestine took matters into its own hands, and hanged Dov Gruner [and Dresner (Rosenbaum), Alkachi and Kashani] *while their appeal was pending and actually being heard* by the highest court in the land. I wrote a letter of protest to the Times which refused to print it, the editor informing me over the telephone, that the president of the Privy Council mentioned that my letter misrepresented the facts!

Seligman remained preoccupied with the Gruner case for the rest of his life, as the following letters attest.

Mr. Maurice Rosenblatt, 18 February, 1948
c/o "Answer",
25 W. 45th Street,
New York 19, NY,
U.S.A.

Dear Mr. Rosenblatt,

I returned to Palestine only this week, having spent over three months in England enroute. Security conditions here are very grim, although life seems to go on almost normally inside Tel Aviv and the Jewish settlements. But I am glad to be back again. Before I left New York, you asked me to let you have details of the last meeting I had with Dov Gruner a few days before he was removed from Jerusalem Prison to Acre Prison.

As I told you, it was after I had instructed Counsel in London to lodge a petition with Privy Council for leave to appeal against the judgment of the High Court of Palestine rejecting the petition which I had made in the name of Mr. Rokach as Chairman of the Jewish Community of Tel Aviv and Jaffa.

That petition was based on some very strong legal grounds challenging the validity of the Emergency Regulations and of the Military Courts set up thereunder. In short, they seriously threatened the entire military regime under which the civil community was being oppressed. I feared, however, that the Privy Council would hasten to reject the petition on the ground that there was no valid reason why it could not be made by Gruner himself.

I therefore called on Gruner in an effort to obtain his consent to file a petition in his own name. I told him the grounds were strong, and they might succeed if filed in his name. The following conversation ensued:–

Gruner: Is it a petition to a British Court?

Myself: Of course, to the highest court in the British Empire.

Gruner: I refuse to recognize any British Court.

Myself: But it is the Civil Court provided for by the Palestine Order in Council and in accordance with the Mandate. It is a Court to which we all apply.

Gruner: Yes, but it is still a British Court, and I am a Hebrew soldier.

Myself: But you realize that the alternative may be that you will be taken to the gallows?

Gruner: So what. I am not the first and I shall not be the last. But you cannot ask me to break the front.

With that, spoken with a smile, we parted. He was really a great guy.

THE JEWISH CHRONICLE
15 April, 1980
What Happened in Palestine

Sir, – I have read the correspondence in your columns relating to the remarks attributed to Mrs. Thatcher about Mr. Begin and the hanging of the two sergeants as well as the hanging of Dov Gruner. As I was personally involved in the legal proceedings in the Gruner case, it is high time that all the facts were made known which throw a different light on what took place.

Firstly, the decision to hang the sergeants was not made by Mr. Begin but by the high command of the Irgun Zevai Leumi. Dov Gruner, who had previously served in the British Army, was captured while taking part in a raid on the Ramat Gan police station in the hope of obtaining arms. Gruner did not attack anyone but was himself seriously wounded, half of his jaw being smashed. He was in hospital several months before he could be brought to trial before a military court. He refused to take any part in the proceedings as he knew that, although he had not attacked or injured anyone, he would automatically be sentenced to death.

It may be observed that although capital punishment was not permitted in Great Britain, death sentences were frequently passed by the courts in Palestine and were duly carried out in the prisons.

Every effort was made by the Jewish community to persuade the civil and military authorities to commute the sentence. Several days before Gruner was hanged I had a meeting in the King David Hotel with Mr. Fox-Strangways, the political secretary to the High Commissioner, in the course of which I asked him if he could give me any news in regard to the Gruner case, to which he replied, "No, but I do not think that anyone wants to see the poor fellow hanged." This was received by the community as good news, but their relief was very short-lived, for only a few days later Gruner together with three of his comrades was taken out of his cell at night and hanged without any prior warning either to me or to their families.

Repeated warnings had been given to the Foreign Secretary, Mr. Ernest Bevin, that reprisals would be taken against British servicemen if the prisoners were hanged. All these warning were rejected by Mr. Bevin, who could have saved the lives of the two sergeants. However, what is not generally known, Gruner's sentence was carried out while a petition was pending before the Judicial Committee of the Privy Council for leave to appeal against the sentence of the military court, a fact of which both the military and civil authorities were aware. So far as I have been able to ascertain, there was no precedent in English judicial history for a sentence of death to be carried out while legal proceedings on behalf of the accused were pending before the courts.

Max Seligman

THE ACRE PRISON ESCAPE

In April, 1947, Foreign Secretary Ernest Bevin faced heavy fire from the opposition. *Bloody Jews* was a term used daily by British personnel in Palestine. No one could accuse Winston Churchill of stooping that low, but he came close when he thundered in Parliament: "How much longer will we continue to wage this filthy war?! In tiny Palestine we are keeping over one hundred thousand troops—more than in all of India, and it costs us nearly forty million pounds." And in the same vein: "It is wrong to deviate from the path of justice because of threats of the murder of hostages." Violence and counter-violence had come full circle.

The time was ripe now for carrying out an operation that had long been planned, a large-scale military operation with wide political impact: the breaching of the walls of Fortress Acre. Where Napoleon had failed, Irgun planners felt sure of success, by virtue of meticulous attention to detail and brilliant execution of carefully laid plans. Of the ninety Jewish prisoners, forty-one were chosen to be freed. Priority was given to men with combat experience, the remaining number of years left to serve also determined a man's eligibility. A camera provided by the seamen of the *Ben Hecht*[5](detained at the time in Acre) was used to photograph the men for false identification cards which were smuggled into them.

Zero hour was set for 16:00 on Sunday, 4 May 1947. The main force assembled in Netanya, where the men were given British-style haircuts. Four units in military vehicles painted with appropriate insignia advanced on Acre. Unit 1 was to block the Nahariya-Haifa intersection and prevent help from being sent from nearby army camps. A petrol station was to be set on fire to sow confusion. Unit 2 was charged with blowing a hole in the prison wall and directing the escapees to the vehicles awaiting them. This unit, equipped with heavy firepower, was to hold up any assistance from the nearby police station, and to sound the all-clear when the last of the men passed through the wall. Units 3 & 4 were charged with mining the roads leading to the fortress. Other units were assigned to blow up bridges in the area, and to carry out various diversionary actions to keep the military away from Acre.

As soon as the men inside the prison heard the rumble of the trucks outside, they took up their preassigned positions. The wall was breached, and with explosives passed through the opening, the prison gates were blown open and the first lorryload of men got away, only to run into fire from a totally unexpected source: it was a very hot day, and a number of British soldiers went to the beach for a swim. When they heard the explosions, they hurried to the fortress, encountering the army lorry. At first they hesitated, but then they opened fire, and fire was returned. The commander (code-named Samson), dressed as a British army officer, shouted at the British soldiers to hold their fire. This gave the men on the lorry time to disperse in a nearby cornfield. A man sent to warn the other vehicles to stay away was killed. A second lorry arrived, and its men too were able to disperse, thanks to the fire Samson directed at the British from behind his lorry. He continued to fire until he was killed. A third lorry was able to get away. Altogether, thirty-four men escaped, and nine were killed. Four were wounded and returned to Acre, and two were captured later. Because the all-clear signal was not given, five men in cover positions remained behind, and by the time they realized the operation was over, they were unable to catch up with the others. They got away, but three of them were captured by Arabs, and were tortured and severely wounded by their captors, both Arab and British. Two others were captured some distance away.

The daring raid made headlines worldwide, but in Britain, it struck like a thunderbolt. Press and public reaction was unanimous: it's time to leave.

The trial of the five men captured began on 28 May, 1947. The charges: firing at members of H.M. Forces, carrying arms, wearing army uniforms and laying of mines. Two of the men, Amnon Micha'eli and Nachman Zitternbaum were under eighteen years of age and pleaded not guilty. However, all five chose a political line of defense. The three others were Avshalom Haviv, Me'ir Nackar and Ya'acov Weiss. When Haviv rose to deliver an address, he was silenced. The two attorneys, Kritzman and Levitzky, were berated by the presiding judge for rising when the defendants sang *Hatikva*, to which Levitzky replied: "Wherever we may be, we always rise when our national anthem is sung."

Although Haviv, Nackar and Weiss did not take part in the proceedings, it took three weeks for all forty prosecution witnesses to be heard. During the testimony given by a British soldier, Haviv rose and asked permission to question him. The surprised judges, thinking the defendants had changed their line of defense, granted permission. Haviv then turned to the soldier and said: "You swore to tell the truth and nothing but the truth. Could you explain what you meant by telling me, during the identification, that Hitler's gas chambers were child's play compared to what we will do to you in Palestine?" Another soldier was questioned by Weiss about being tortured when they were wounded and bound. All three were then allowed to read their statements (See Appendices).

A United Nations commission, headed by Justice Emil Sandestrom, was at this time conducting hearings in Palestine. An appeal to all sides was made before the committee arrived, asking for a peaceful atmosphere to allow it to do its work. That the British chose to conduct the trial at this time was an indication that they meant to impose severe penalties for the humiliation they suffered in the Acre prison breakout. With the fate of Gruner and his comrades still fresh in everyone's minds, Irgun command decided to take hostages before the men on trial were sentenced. Although it was not easy—the British were on high alert—two soldiers were abducted from a public swimming-pool. The usual procedure again took place: the mayors of Tel-Aviv and neighboring communities were called in to the District Commissioner's office, where they were told collective punishment would be imposed on the entire population unless the kidnaped servicemen were released. When the Hagana mobilized its forces for the purpose of conducting searches, Irgun had no choice but to release the captives. On 16 June, 1947, the U.N. opened its hearings. On the same day, Haviv, Nackar and Weiss were sentenced to hang. The two younger men were given life sentences.

The five men were taken back to Acre; Haviv, Nackar and Weiss were dressed in red and put on death row. Hundreds of policemen guarded the prison now, while the British forces withdrew into even tighter quarters. Petitions for clemency were pouring into government offices daily, from individuals and institutes all over the world. Ya'acov Weiss had been a secret agent during the war: disguised as an SS officer, he daringly rescued several hundred people from certain death. Survivors of Bergen-Belsen signed the petition relating Weiss' bravery, which was addressed to P.M. Atlee; Czech refugees in Palestine alerted Foreign Minister Jan Masaryk and P.M. Eduard Benes; Edith, Weiss' sister addressed an urgent plea to Trygve Lie, Secretary General of the U.N., while in Palestine, Menachem Begin had several meetings with the U.N. commission, who at his behest went to Acre and heard testimony from Irgun inmates concerning the torture of wounded prisoners following the breakout. David Ben Gurion also pleaded for a commutation of the death sentences, reasoning that if carried out, it would interfere with his war on terrorism . . . To all this, the High Commissioner and G.O.C replied that any show of mercy would be interpreted by the terrorists as a sign of weakness. The sentences were confirmed on 8 July. On the 11th, Edith Weiss arrived from the U.S.A., and two sergeants in Army Intelligence, Clifford Marvin and Martin Pace, were abducted in Netanya.

A strict curfew was imposed on Netanya and the vicinity, while British forces unsuccessfully searched for the two sergeants. The Hagana was no luckier in its search. On 28 July, the Government announced the sentences would be carried out the following day, and policemen delivered notices to the families of the condemned men. The curfew imposed on Netanya was lifted—the British had decided that prestige was worth the lives of the two sergeants. On death row, the men wrote last letters.

On 29 July, a call from the Irgun informed the authorities where the hanged sergeants could be found, and that the road and bodies were mined. The British ignored the warning, and a mine exploded while the bodies were being taken down. Max Kritzman, as well as fifty other leaders and mayors, were rounded up and taken to Latrun. Fortunately for Max Seligman, who was also on the list, he was in New York at the time.

Haviv, Nackar and Weiss were the last men to be hanged in

Palestine. The British mandate was coming to an end, and it was generally agreed that the hanging of the two sergeants achieved more than anything else to get the British out of the country.

Max Seligman's defense of underground members extended beyond the borders of Palestine, as illustrated by what became known as The British Officers' Train case[5], as told by Dr. Sullivan Kaufman, Seligman & Co's associate in London who handled their appeals to the Privy Council:

In late 1947, I was approached by the Irgun representative in London to act on behalf of four Irgun members, under sentence of death in Germany. I was asked by the Irgun representative *not* to enquire as to the source of the introduction and I never even asked Max (Seligman), but I think it emanated from him.

I chose Lord Elwyn-Jones as one of the barristers as he had acted for the British Government at Nuremberg. The other barrister, Victor Durand, was a brilliant criminal lawyer and I decided separate representation was required for the two prisoners who were to plead that the evidence against them was inadequate. I also sent to Germany the psychiatrist who had acted for the British Government at Nuremberg, Professor J.D.W. Pearce, who was later Dean of St. Mary's Hospital, London, and an outstanding genius in his field. He assisted Elwyn-Jones in his plea for mitigation of sentence, on the grounds that detention in a German death camp had deranged the young men.

I understand that there was considerable lobbying of Congressmen and the White House in Washington, but no word of this reached me until many years later. Likewise, the case remained completely unreported in the English Press: it may have been the subject of a D-notice (a "request" not to print, which is the British equivalent to censorship).

The Foreign Office gave every facility for our party to visit Germany and obtain evidence at first hand from the prisoners. After the two death sentences were commuted, I kept in touch with the Foreign Office and was eventually able to obtain their release after they had served only one tenth of their commuted sentences. They became useful Israeli citizens.

I think Max deserves credit for what I *guess* (I emphasize *guess*) was his work behind the scenes.

NOTES TO IN THE MILITARY COURTS

1. One of the sixty-nine men was my brother-in-law-to-be, Menachem Moriel (Dardickman). We met when we were both on leave shortly after VE Day, and were dating the two sisters we married in a double ceremony on 18 November, 1946. He died in March, 1989.

2. Jabotinsky had a tacit understanding with the British authorities whereby he was permitted to organize the Jews of Jerusalem for purely defensive action.

3. Without "Palestine" shoulder-patches on my uniform, it was a simple matter for me to go up to the Arab policeman guarding the entrance to the court and ask for directions; I got in easily in spite of the heavy security.

4. Chaim Herzog's younger brother, Ya'akov, was in the Israeli diplomatic service. In 1959, British historian Arnold Toynbee, known for his pro-Arab (and anti-Israel) views stated in a newspaper interview in Montreal that "The nation of Israel is a fossil", best left, in his esteemed opinion, to vanish into history along with the Canaanites and Philistines. Ya'akov Herzog, who was then Ambassador of Israel to Canada, challenged Toynbee to a public debate, which took place at Hillel House on the campus of McGill University in Montreal. The small hall was filled to capacity, and people were crowded in the hall and on the stairs. In my capacity as program director of Radio Station CKVL-FM, I was able to get in to hear the debate and to secure tapes of it. I later released this (after obtaining the debaters' consent) as a two-record set on my Baroque Records label. It was entitled "Fossil or Nation?" The debate itself was conducted in a gentlemanly manner by these two brilliant men. The general feeling was that Herzog made more telling points than did his opponent.

5. The *Ben Hecht* was a refugee ship caught in the British blockade. Its all-American crew was held in Acre Prison for "aiding and abetting illegal immigration into Palestine." The matter was written up in the New York daily *P.M.* April 17, 1947.

. . . The ship and its volunteer crew sailed from Port de Bouc near Marseilles loaded like a transport with 625 refugees and DPs. While still outside (Palestinian) territorial waters, three British destroyers closed in, and they proceeded . . . to Haifa. But still outside the three-mile limit, boarding parties took over the *Hecht*. This weakened the British case against the American crew, since the boarding was outside territorial waters. The refugees were shipped off to Cyprus according to the now well-established routine and the Americans landed in Acre Prison, after carefully being sprayed first with DDT. One of the Americans gave a British soldier a copy of *The Rape of Palestine* by William B. Ziff. He stuck it inside his blouse, remarked: "Guess I'll read this when the officers aren't lookin'.

6. In his book *In My Time*, Lord Elwyn-Jones relates that the two men represented by Victor Durand had their convictions quashed for lack of evidence. The two on whose behalf Elwyn-Jones appeared had pleaded guilty

to attempting to blow up the train, and his speech was in mitigation of their crime. The outcome was that the death penalty in each case was changed to twenty years' imprisonment. He goes on to say: "I understand that the result of the appeals was a great relief to our Foreign Office. The carrying out of the death sentences at that time would have led to serious reprisals. In the event, it was the only Irgun action attempted outside Palestine."

Other Court Cases

JACOB NIRENBERG

Max Seligman was known not only as one of the top criminal lawyers in Palestine, but also as a compassionate and generous man, who gave of his time unstintingly to causes in which he believed. On 10 January, 1942, a man called Jacob Nirenberg shot and killed his father's mistress. He could not afford a lawyer. When the Tel-Aviv Lawyers' Association asked Seligman whether he would defend Nirenberg at no charge, he agreed.

Nirenberg, a 29 year-old worker, shot 40 year-old Shoshana Sternblitz outside her flat at 79 Keren Kayemet Blvd. He had gone there in a desperate attempt to get her to break off relations with his father. Miss Sternblitz had been the father's mistress for the past twenty years. As a result of this liaison, Nirenberg Sr. neglected his family in Poland, who were all wiped out by the Nazis. Nirenberg (son) believed his father could have saved his mother and other members of her family before it was too late, but did nothing, because of his involvement with Miss Sternblitz. He shot her when she refused to stop seeing his father.

Witnesses testified that on the day of the shooting, they met Nirenberg on the stairs of the apartment house. He told them: "I have shot a woman. Call the police!" A neighbor testified that when he heard shouts and a shot, he went to the woman's flat and took a revolver from Nirenberg. Another testified that he found Nirenberg outside, calmly smoking a cigarette, and waited with him for 45 minutes until the police arrived. During this time, Nirenberg repeatedly asked why first aid was not being given to the woman.

Charged with premeditated murder, Nirenberg pleaded not guilty, citing the circumstances that led him to his act. The charge against him was then reduced to manslaughter, and the British judge sentenced him to 15 years in prison. Seligman, assisted by his partner Max Kritzman, appealed the verdict. He pointed out that Nirenberg's was a crime of passion, and he was deserving of lenience. His father's involvement with the victim resulted in the neglect that led to the death of his mother and her entire family at the hands of the Nazis. The suffering caused Nirenberg to become unbalanced. Throughout the trial, the father refused to see his son. The appeal was denied.

Shortly after Nirenberg was sentenced, the following letter appeared in *Haboker:*

FOR A MAN WHO AVENGED HIS MOTHER

The public has been following with interest the trial of Jacob Nirenberg, because it touches on some painful matters that these days are ever more paramount. I am a mother, and like me, I know of many other women who followed this case of a son taking revenge to defend his mother's honor. I would like to propose the establishment of a fund, to which others like me would contribute. It could be administered by Mr. Max Seligman, Nirenberg's unpaid defence attorney, and used to make life easier for him in prison, by means of food parcels and other necessities which would not be provided by his father, who continues to maintain a cruel disregard.

I am sure many like me would wish to express their feelings in this manner.

A mother.

GIRL RETURNED TO JEWISH MOTHER

A British policeman's romance in 1936 with a Jewish girl from Jerusalem named Yocheved Mizrachi resulted in a daughter born out of wedlock. The couple gave up the girl, to be raised in a home run by Danish missionary Lydia Christensen in Ramallah. The policeman paid for the girl's upkeep for a while, then returned to England, promising to send for Yocheved and their daughter. He failed to keep his promise and in time the payments stopped, too. In 1940 Yocheved married another British policeman by the name of King, and the couple wished to have the girl back. Missionary Christensen refused to give her up, stating the girl had been brought up a Christian and spoke only Arabic. She decided to raise the girl at her own expense after the mother no longer showed any interest in her.

In presenting his case, Max Seligman cited verdicts given in similar cases in Britain, where the courts decided in favor of the mothers in question. This impressed British magistrate Copland, who ruled: "A daughter belongs to her mother and to no one else; an institute's claim to have raised her must yield to the mother's wish to have her back."

THE BRITISH ON TRIAL

A group of five British servicemen and police entered the Grand Hotel in Gaza on 12 November 1938, where they attacked and injured several Arabs, including a police officer and sergeant. The prosecution charged that in addition to the injuries, the British servicemen also caused damage to the premises and broke furniture. The premeditated attack, contended the prosecution, was provoked by the murder a few days earlier of two British servicemen by Arabs in Gaza.

When the case came on for trial, Seligman recommended a guilty plea and a request for lenience, since evidence against the group was overwhelming. He described to the court the atmosphere of hostility in which the defendants had to perform their duties, which prevailed since the outbreak of the disturbances in 1936. He cited the excellent record of one of the men, and the youth and inexperience of the others. In addition, he pointed out that although the men were armed, they refrained from using any firearms.

The (British) judge accepted the defense, acquitting one man, and letting the others off with small fines and symbolic restitution for the property damage.

MILITARIZING OF POLICE CHALLENGED

A few years later, another case was tried, which was of great interest to British police personnel. The validity of the High Commissioner's proclamation which declared the Palestine Police a military force and consequently subject to the Army Act and military law was contested before the High Court in Jerusalem on behalf of British constable J. P. Coleman, who had been convicted by a Court Martial constituted of the Inspector General of the Police.

Submitting that the Proclamation was contrary to Article 17 of the Palestine Mandate, Seligman argued that the Government may only organize the defense of the country on a volunteer basis. The constable, he stated, was a servant of the Crown Agents and neither enlisted in H.M. Forces nor consented to be subject to the Army Act.

This was the first time that the court was packed with British policemen and high-ranking officers who were in the audience, instead of in their usual official capacity. The petitioner was convicted of "a disciplinary offense" and was being held by the Superintendent of Lydda Police. Seligman applied to the High Court for an *order nisi* calling upon the Superintendents of Police and of Lydda to show cause why the constable should not be released, and observed that it was not desirable that such an important question should be decided by a single judge.

The *order nisi* was granted by Justice Copland of the High Court, but the Chief Justice, in rejecting the petition, said that it contained nothing legally or constitutionally. The Defence Act of 1940 gave power to require persons to place themselves, their services and their property at the disposal of His Majesty. This act applied to Palestine and formed a good legal basis for the legislation which put the Police Force under Military Law.

The true reason for the petition emerged from Seligman's remark that there existed in Palestine no Legislative Council or other representative body where grievances of members of the Police Force could be publicly discussed as in England. The petition was made in order to air such grievances in open court.

THE DETECTIVE vs. THE MADAM

Detective Michael Latimer of the Criminal Investigation Department was accused in September, 1940 of accepting a bribe from a certain Mrs. Freeman, in exchange for promising to return to her pornographic photographs which were confiscated from her when she entered Palestine from Egypt.

It was only natural that such a piquant case would attract a large audience. Seligman obtained his client's acquittal by convincing the court that the only evidence against the defendant was that given by Mrs. Freeman, who owned a string of brothels in Egypt, where she was known by her *nom de chambre* of "Doris." She was a woman of ill-repute, whose testimony was full of contradictions. His client, on the other hand, had served with distinction for several years as a policeman. He then became a detective and performed his duties to the entire satisfaction of his superiors, so much so that he was now being considered for a promotion.

In addition to the many British police personnel in the audience, there were also many other lawyers present.

ARAB CASES

Jews and Englishmen were not the only ones to benefit from Seligman's services. As one of the leading civil and criminal lawyers in the country, he counted among his clients members of every ethnic group, Arabs included. In these cases, he was assisted by the resident Arabists of his firm, advocates Goiten and Kritzman.

JAFFA WOMAN GETS HER INHERITANCE

Ibrahim and Shoukri Zaboura were Christian Lebanese brothers who came to Palestine in 1900. They bought a piece of land in the Ajami quarter of Jaffa, near the mission, where they built a one-story house in which they lived with their families. When war (1914) broke out, they left the country. Ibrahim went to South Africa and Shoukri to Egypt. In 1920, Shoukri returned and added another story to the house. Brother Ibrahim died in South Africa, leaving a widow, a son and daughter. The son, Issa, went to Ceylon where he was killed in the jungle by lions. Widow and daughter Anna returned to Jaffa, where they lived on rental income they shared with Shoukri's family.

Shoukri died, and so did Ibrahim's widow. Anna and her family moved into the house, but were driven out by Shoukri's heirs in 1935. In a series of lawsuits over the next five years, she sued in District Court, Land Court and the Supreme Court, and lost every case. When in desperation she moved back into the house with her thirteen children, she was convicted of trespassing and spent a few days in jail. Meanwhile, she had accumulated legal debts that exceeded the value of the house, estimated to be worth some LP.750.

She worked as a domestic servant for several British families in Jaffa, and at their suggestion she took her case to Max Seligman. He petitioned the Land Court to amend the records of the property to include Anna as the legal heiress to her father Ibrahim's share.

This extremely complicated case lasted two months. Both sides presented in evidence Turkish deeds. Anna had one showing the property as owned jointly by her father and uncle, while the defendants had a deed showing them as sole owners. Fourteen witnesses were called, including three ancient Arab construction workers aged 103, 92 and the youngest of the trio, a mere 87. They were the crew that had built the house in 1910. The older two testified the house was built and paid for by Shoukri, while the third laborer said it was built by both brothers.

The court ruled for the widow. Shoukri's family appealed, and both sides agreed to arbitration, which upheld the initial verdict. When this too was appealed, the weary court ruled once more in the plaintiff's favour, and further ordered the defendants to pay court costs and Seligman's fee of LP.77.

GENTLEMEN'S AGREEMENT

In 1930, Mouhammad Tilawi, a resident of Jaffa, declared bankruptcy, and made various arrangements with his creditors. One of them, named Sheikh Shahaban, agreed to act as guarantor for Tilawi's debts. As security and by way of compensation if anything went wrong, it was agreed he could purchase Tilawi's house for LP.700, with the proviso that he (Tilawi) may repurchase it within three years at the same low price. Unfortunately, the agreement was done on a handshake, and no written record of it existed.

Years went by, and Sheikh Shahaban added another story to the house, which was now valued at LP.4,000. In 1937, Tilawi demanded, in a lawsuit initiated by his lawyer Abcarious Bey, the right to repurchase his house for LP.700. The court was unable to determine the validity of the plaintiff's claim, since he had nothing in writing, and the case dragged on for three years. After Seligman took over the case, he was able to convince the court of Tilawi's claim and ordered that he may indeed repurchase the house at LP.700, but must pay the Sheikh for the addition, the exact amount to be determined by a court-appointed architect.

AT YOUR OWN PERIL

An Arab worker was murdered near the Jerusalem suburb of Rehaviah on his way to work. He was employed by the Arab contractor Mr. Awwad, who did work for the Jerusalem Electric Company. The victim's family filed suit against the contractor and the Electric Company, claiming he lost his life while performing his duties as their employee. Max Seligman acted as attorney for the defendants, and following the initial arbitration, the magistrate, Ali Effendi Yunis, ruled for the plaintiff. The verdict was appealed and the case went back and forth between several courts for many months.

Finally Seligman prevailed: he was able to convince the court that the murder occurred neither during working hours, nor was it work-related. The (British) judge, in ruling for the defendants, stated that the Government accepted the rule that accidents happening to workers on the way to or after leaving work were not the responsibility of employers. If this were not so, employers would be in constant jeopardy of being sued, and the result might lead to the cessation of all work in the country.

ARBITRATION

Two well publicized industrial disputes were mediated by Max Seligman, who always favored peaceful solutions over litigation. The first concerned the Port of Tel Aviv, which was under the management of a private corporation, *Otsar Mif'alei Yam*. Shareholders were about to vote in the *Histadrut* (Labor Federation) as the managing agency for port operations. This would have meant the exclusion of Revisionist workers.

Acting on behalf of the Revisionist shareholders, Seligman was able to obtain a restraining order halting the vote, and demanded that management of the port be turned over to municipal (and neutral) authority. The court concurred and ordered the parties to be bound by arbitration.

The other case involved the Delfiner Textile Mills, where in October, 1942, a strike resulted from a labor dispute, and spread to the Carmil Dyeing Works, a subsidiary of Delfiner. Seligman was retained by the management after attempts at mediation failed and the case went to court. What made this an unusually interesting case was the involvement of the Wartime Supply Board, in addition to the factory owners and striking employees. This meant the strike was illegal, as it affected the War Effort, and a decision in the matter would affect members of the Manufacturer's Association pledge not to raise wages for the duration of the war. The matter was eventually referred to binding arbitration.

INFLAMMATORY PUBLICATIONS

Miriam Yeivin was brought to trial in April, 1939, charged with the publication of a pamphlet entitled *Al Mishmar Yerushalayim* (Defending Jerusalem), which, contended the prosecution, contained much inflammatory material. A search of the accused's home also yielded a copy of the pamphlet in question. The prosecution called as witnesses workers and the owners of the press who printed it.

In Yeivin's defense, Seligman claimed that the legal interpretation of *publication* implied the delivery of copies of the material to numerous people, and/or the sale thereof, and this the prosecution has not proved. Furthermore, it had not been proven that what she gave the printer is what was printed and delivered to her. Concerning the "inflammatory" contents of the pamphlet, assuming this meant the setting of one segment of the population against another as propounded in the pamphlet, it was common knowledge that these sentiments existed long before it was written. The question of whether to maintain restraint or not was discussed in the pamphlet. One may agree or disagree with this point of view or that, but no one could claim the question cannot be debated.

The court accepted Seligman's definition of *publication*, but the judge insisted the material printed was inflammatory, and voiced his opposition to it. In order to convict a person, he added, the law requires proof beyond any doubt. Lacking this, he was ordering her acquittal. He then said: "When you stated in your pamphlet that terror must be countered with terror, this was tantamount to calling for bombs to be thrown in Palestine. You were fortunate that not enough evidence was found against you, and that *you benefitted from a brilliant defense!*

A month later, the entire directorship of the New Zionist Organization and Beitar along with their printers were charged with disseminating leaflets containing excerpts of articles by Ze'ev Jabotinsky and Colonel Josiah Wedgwood, previously published in a number of dailies. This material was considered by the prosecution to be of a political nature. Following a speech for the defense by Seligman, the court adjourned for ten minutes, returning to dismiss all charges against the accused.

In a similar case, Jacob Lankin of Herzliyah was accused of possessing leaflets in which Jews were called to fight for their own government in Palestine. The accused was brought to trial from Acre prison, where he had been sent (without trial) for a year, under the Emergency Regulations. When the trial began, Seligman rose to announce that following his recommendation, his client pleads guilty to possession of the leaflets, adding that these were found in his home by accident, during an unrelated investigation by the police. The accused does not recall who had given him the leaflets, which he was using for sanitary purposes. The amused judge ordered Lankin released, after posting a bond of LP.50 for one year

COMMUNITY COUNCIL SUES NEWSPAPER

On 14 April 1941, the right-wing daily *Haboker* ran an editorial, in which it stated: 'There is a movement afoot to annex the suburb of Nachlat Yitzchak (which is politically neutral) to the socialist community of Shechunat Borochov, whose management has since its inception been so inept as to burden the community with a huge deficit. The people running the affairs of Shechunat Borochov would like to annex Nachlat Yitzchak, whose coffers are full and free of debt, and use those assets to cover their own debt, and in the bargain to burden Nachlat Yitzchak with taxes and payments not to its benefit.'(Nachlat Yitzchak, as a defensive measure, asked in fact to be annexed to the affluent suburb of Ramat Gan).

The council of Shechunat Borochov sued *Haboker* for libel, and the daily retained Seligman for the defense. In his opening statement to the District Court, Seligman said that the facts given in the editorial were true, and that his client was prepared to prove it. He then pointed out that both sides in the dispute were corporate entities, and that libel in such circumstances had very limited application. Citing precedents, he added that the case in point lacked even the appearance of libel.

Plaintiff's attorney countered by citing precedents from English lawsuits, but was interrupted by the judge, who said that the court was concerned in this instance with a criminal action involving a community and a corporation, not a private business, adding with a smile: "Would you prohibit anyone from stating that the Municipality of Tel Aviv has no debts?" And was this not, he asked further, just another case of left-right polemics?

In his summation, Seligman said there was no libel and therefore no cause to indict *Haboker*. "What would happen to freedom of the press" he wondered, "if every word of public criticism could be used as an excuse for criminal proceedings?"

Following a short recess, the court returned to announce it was dismissing the case without hearing any witnesses, as there appear to be no grounds for a libel suit. The gallery was packed with journalists and public officials, who crowded around Seligman to congratulate him on winning the landmark case.

A GREEDY LAWYER

A young apprentice at a metalworks, 15 year old Ya'acov Tchechovoy, lost the tips of three fingers in an accident after only a few weeks at work. By law, the boy was entitled to compensation, and demand for such was made in court. The prosecution called as witnesses the boy and his father, the *Kupat*

Cholim (Sick Fund) doctor who treated him, the foreman and the secretary of the metalworkers' union. All witnesses were examined at length by Seligman, appearing for the defense. He did not call any witnesses for the defense, asking instead for dismissal of the case on the grounds that it was premature. He went on to explain that the workers' compensation law allows for legal action to be brought only when there is a dispute as to the liability of the employer, or about the amount of compensation to be paid. In this case, the insurance company expressed its willingness to settle, and further offered to obtain other employment for the boy, or to enroll him at the Max Fein Vocational School at its expense. But neither the boy nor his attorney ever made any representations to the metalworks or to the insurance company.

Advocate Bar Shira, acting for the plaintiff, countered by stating he had sent a demand on the boy's behalf "a few days before filing suit." The court sided with Seligman's contention that suit was filed prematurely, that the insurance company could not have possibly responded to the demand before the trial began, and that the attorney's action was taken for the sole purpose of having the defendant pay legal and court costs. There was no real dispute in the case, and attorney Bar Shira's action was uncalled for. The case was dismissed and the plaintiff ordered to pay the legal fees (LP.6) incurred by the defendant, plus court costs. It also appeared that in his haste to file suit, plaintiff's attorney weakened his case for any subsequent claim, since this had to be made within six months of the injury, and this time had elapsed.

A while later I met "Yankaleh" Tchechovoy and we became friends. He casually mentioned the accident that caused the loss of his fingertips, but never referred to the lawsuit, though he knew I was Max Seligman's nephew. He managed to join the British army in spite of his digital impairment, and served in North Africa.

PART III
Bringing the Message

THROUGHOUT HIS LIFE, Seligman traveled extensively, bringing the message of his mission, informing, explaining, and pleading for unity among Jews and an end to the in-fighting, which to him was an extremely painful aspect of political life, in Eretz Israel as well as abroad. He traveled all over the Commonwealth, but most of his efforts were concentrated in Britain, the U.S.A. and Canada. His speeches served to heighten public awareness of the situation in Palestine, thereby exerting some measure of influence on government policies.

THE HOLOCAUST

A Conspiracy of Silence

The worst fears about the Nazis' *Final Solution* were confirmed in 1942 when the full extent of the genocide then underway in Europe became known. Max reacted with as much shock and grief as did any other feeling Jew, but I had the sense, from his remarks and comments, that his anguish had another dimension, something akin to an open wound. His usually ebullient manner became more subdued, and he often seemed lost in thought in those days of shocking awareness.

Those hoping the United States would lead world opinion in a cry of outrage against the extermination of European Jewry, and take decisive action to stop it, were in for a tragic disappointment. The sad truth of the matter was that most Americans, and even more tragically most American Jews, were indifferent or even hostile to any action which could have prevented the continuation of the mass murder. Americans, gentiles and Jews alike, had not forgotten the awful years of the Great Depression, and were concerned with day-to-day matters, and with economic prospects for the time after the war came to an end. The indifference to the plight of their people extended to all levels of American Jewry, including influential persons such as columnist Walter Lippman, who throughout the war never so much as mentioned the Holocaust. Some of the most widely-read newspapers, like the *New York Post* and *New York Times* and the *Washington Post*, although Jewish-owned, consistently played down news about the systematic slaughter of the Jews in Europe. (William Randolph Hearst, whom no one could accuse of being pro-Jewish, was nevertheless sufficiently aroused and lent substantial editorial support to efforts to save the Jews. He admonished his readers that the problem was not a Jewish but a *human* one.)

The conspiracy of silence regarding the Holocaust was matched by most of the widely-circulated magazines and even more significantly, by the mass media of the time: radio and cinema. When at war's end the Allied armies reached the death-camps and the indescribable horrors they found there were shown on newsreels to stunned audiences in movie theaters, the fact that most of the victims were Jewish was studiously avoided.

With Friends Like These, Who Needs Enemies?

Samuel Rosenman, Special Counsel to President Roosevelt, was the man on whom FDR depended for advice on Jewish matters. He and Congressman Sol Bloom were among those who steadfastly maintained that any U.S. Government involvement in saving European Jews would lead to an increase in Anti-Semitism in America. They and their cohorts devoted their energies to *the prevention of saving Jewish lives in Europe*. The President and State Department followed Britain's lead in matters pertaining to the problem of the Jews in Europe. As the tide of war began to turn against the Germans, efforts were made to have the President make a policy speech, perhaps a joint statement with Winston Churchill, warning the Germans that continuing the genocide would bring severe punishment at war's end. This might have given the Nazis pause, and might have halted the slaughter. But Roosevelt was advised against following this course, and what statements he was persuaded to make (against his own and his advisers' wishes) were watered down to the point of mere lip-service.

Hillel Kook, nephew of the first Chief Ashkenazi Rabbi of Palestine at the time, Abraham Isaac Kook, was a high-ranking Revisionist functionary. When he went to America, he changed his name to Peter H. Bergson as he did not want his political activities to reflect in any way on his illustrious namesake. Bergson was instrumental in the creation of the Wartime Refugee Board (WRB). It was a typical move for the Roosevelt administration to cripple the WRB from its inception by understaffing, an inadequate budget, and to hobble its efforts by State Department edicts and directives, which in turn relied for their rationale on lame excuses such as lack of shipping for transporting Jewish refugees, and insufficient facilities for housing them.

The principle underlying all of this was fear of an influx of destitute Jewish immigrants. There was genuine concern that the Nazis might respond to Allied pressure and release perhaps as many as 100,000 Jews, which no country wanted, under any circumstances. Relevant to the foregoing discussion are these items:

- Beginning in 1942, the Allies evacuated some 100,000 non-Jewish refugees, mostly Poles, from Europe. They were settled all over the Middle-East (including, ironically, Palestine) and Africa. Later in the same year, the Russians allowed another 120,000 Poles out of Siberia, where they had been confined since 1939. They went to British-controlled Persia (Iran), where most of the able-bodied men, among them Menachem Begin, went into the Polish Army under General Anders. The rest joined their fellow-countrymen, mostly in East African colonies, where POW camps were emptied in order to accommodate them. The POW's, over 400,000 of them, were shipped to the U.S.
- During 1942–3, the number of non-Jewish refugees allowed into Palestine equaled the number of legally landed Jews.
- By war's end, the U.S. had given refuge to fewer than 2,000 Jewish aliens (at the barbed-wire enclosure of Oswego on Lake Ontario in upstate New York.)
- Inaction by the Allies in matters concerning the desperate plight of European Jews led the Nazis to conclude they were free to continue their extermination program with impunity.

They had no need to concern themselves with consequences, since obviously no one cared about the fate of the Jews.

- The small quota issued by the U.S. for Jewish immigrants was 90% unused, courtesy of State Department directives and bureaucratic manipulations.
- When in 1942 former Republican Presidential candidate Wendell Willkie visited Palestine, he met with the then High Commissioner Sir Harold MacMichael. When he criticized Britain's immigration policy in Palestine, the Englishman blandly replied that as the United States was not allowing even its own quotas to be filled, it was in no position to criticize others in the matter of Jewish immigration. There can be little doubt that President Truman's demand (1946) that Britain allow 100,000 Jewish refugees into Palestine elicited a similar response in ruling circles.

The mass liquidation of the remaining Jews in Europe continued uninterrupted and even picked up speed. Beginning with the summer of 1944, continued requests were made to the military authorities, the State Department, and all governmental agencies concerned, to bomb the rail links, gas chambers and the crematoria at Auschwitz, the main extermination camp. All such requests were dismissed with the excuse that it would constitute a diversion of vital air-power, needed for ending the war. (Requests for aiding Jewish partisans were dismissed with similar excuses, and the statement that all operations were primarily directed at ending the war.) The bombing of Auschwitz was refused in spite of the fact that the Fifteenth Air Force, based in Italy, regularly carried out raids in the immediate vicinity of Auschwitz between July and October of 1944. Bombing the Auschwitz facilities might have saved the remainder of Hungary's Jews from deportation there. Hundreds of thousands of lives might have been spared. Ultimately, it was a group of Jewish women used by the Nazis as munitions workers in Auschwitz who succeeded in smuggling some explosives to the camp underground. These were used in a suicide mission in October when one of the crematoria was blown up.

Max had worked closely with Bergson, their collaboration continuing during the war. I often heard him mention Bergson's name in conversation. In the United States, the Bergsonites, as they were called, were opposed and reviled by the Jewish and Zionist establishments, as were the Revisionists in Palestine. Yet despite their small membership and limited resources, the Bergsonites were more acutely aware of the desperate urgency concerning the Jews in Europe, and accounted for proportionately many more illegal immigrants arriving in Palestine than did their fellow-American Jews and their organizations. The extent to which relations between the two camps deteriorated is illustrated by an outburst from the aging Rabbi Stephen Wise, who called Bergson "As great an enemy (of the Jews) as Hitler!"

After the State of Israel was born, the generosity of American Jews knew no bounds. Fund-raising became a way of life, and what amounts to an industry grew up around it. The money was desperately needed and probably saved the State from going under. What percentage of these funds actually reached Israel is another matter: the fund-raisers had to be paid, and they were paid well. Be this as it may, there was good, solid rationale for the generosity: donors got a lot of "Koved" (honor), and giving no doubt made them feel better about the past. Best of all, it helped Jewish refugees settle in Israel, not in the U.S.

When he spoke in public, Max never used notes. His audiences were spellbound by his eloquence, extraordinary command of the English language, and his ability to sway them emotionally. He spoke in a rich, melodious voice and was a stickler for correct diction and grammar. Nor did he ever make spelling mistakes. Internal dissent pained him in the extreme, and he devoted much of his energies to healing the rift among Revisionists and other Zionist groups.

Following are reports on some speeches and interviews he gave, and the comments they elicited.

THE JEWISH CHRONICLE
March 9, 1945
SEARCHLIGHT ON PALESTINE
Prominent Lawyer's Grave Allegations

Serious disclosures of what is going on in Palestine were made by the well-known Palestine lawyer, Mr. Max Seligman, when he spoke at the Anglo-Palestinian Club on Thursday evening of last week under the chairmanship of Mr. J. Slutsky.

Since his stay in England, said Mr. Seligman, conversations with English Zionists had intensified the feeling which he and most of his friends had that the people in this country were utterly ignorant of what had been going on in Palestine.

Mr. Seligman gave some examples of the way censorship was employed in the Middle East to prevent people here learning the truth. Information had reached him a few days ago from a journalist who had covered the trial in Cairo[1]. This journalist drew his attention to the censored report in the newspapers to the effect that when the two young Jews were arrested they were almost lynched by the Egyptians and their clothes were torn to shreds. The truth was, said the journalist, that far from from lynching the two men, the Egyptian boys had tried to rescue them, while the photographs taken had shown their clothes to be in excellent condition. Again, it had been reported in the press here that a request by the defence for several witnesses to be brought from Palestine had been waived by the accused's own counsel. The truth was that the President of the Court had announced that the Government of Palestine had informed the Court that these witnesses were in prison or concentration camps and would not be produced.

Incarcerated Without Trial

Even before the round-up in connection with the Lord Moyne tragedy, Mr. Seligman revealed, there were hundreds of young men and a large number of young women in concentration camps in Palestine who had been kept there for two, three, four or five years without any trial or investigation of any kind and without any protest whatsoever from the leading Jewish authorities. Many of these poor people—he was not referring to those recently rounded up—were still in those concentration camps, and not a finger had been lifted to help them or to demand an inquiry.

He was invited, said the speaker, to visit these internees and take up some of their cases. He had found, for example, the case of a girl who had been arrested at the age of eighteen merely because she had been the girl friend of a man who was a suspected terrorist. She had been kept together with others in Bethlehem for no less than four years. He had succeeded in getting some of them released, but others were still there.

There was also a lot of beating up and torture of Jewish prisoners going on. There was a so-called "Brown House" to which prisoners were taken and where attempts were made to induce them to make confessions. Jewish men were systematically tortured and done away with, and it did not require much imagination to realise what resentment this must cause in Palestine.

Stern and the Leaders of Irgun

The leaders of the Irgun Zevai Leumi included keen young Jewish nationalists, Palestinians, and young men who had come to Palestine during the past few years, teachers and scholars, all ready to lay down their lives for what they believed to be their cause, just as Trumpeldor had laid down his life for Palestine. Stern was a very devoutly religious Jew, a teacher of no mean ability, and a man who, curiously enough, had never handled a firearm in his life. He led the dissident group who wanted to stop the arrests and the beating up of Jews, and their efforts were directed against people who they believed to be guilty of criminal acts against their organisation and almost entirely against police officials.

The situation in Palestine, he continued, was a little difficult to appreciate unless one had been there. They were always being told of how the desert had been transformed into beautiful agricultural land. But he was talking to them that evening of things about which they were not told.

A Number of Good Englishmen

There were a number of good Englishmen in Palestine, really good men who had been able to withstand the pressure brought upon them by the older members of the British community. There were, he said, a lot of killings of Jews in Palestine which had never been explained or investigated, because the responsible Jewish bodies had not asked for an investigation. These Jewish organisations had not asked for an investigation because the persons concerned had been political opponents of the Jewish Agency and of other responsible Jewish organisations. These official Jewish bodies did not seem to realise that a day might come when they themselves might be the section of the Jewish community which the Government did not like, and that it would be their turn to suffer the very same fate unless this sort of thing was stopped.

Mr. Seligman cited a number of cases, among them that of a barber who was killed, supposedly, he said, while running away from the police. But it turned out the man was deaf! The coroner's inquest acquitted the police.

With all these killings going on, there were, naturally, people who were not going to take it lying down and who felt they must get their revenge, that if their husband, father or son was killed, somebody else must also pay for that killing. This thing was likely to go on forever unless something was done, and nothing would be done unless the rank and file of Zionists in this country insisted upon their leaders announcing all these facts, telling them to the Government, and having them aired in Parliament. He was personally satisfied, said Mr. Seligman, from talks which he had had with Government officials, that the Colonial Office here did not know what was going on in Palestine. If Parliament knew of these things, he did not doubt they would put a stop to them.

It was in that atmosphere that men and women became members of the Stern Group. He was not suggesting for one moment that they were right in doing the things they had done. But it was useless to sit in England in comfort, luxury and ease and merely to condemn these crimes and do nothing more. They must bring to light what was going on. They knew that it had never been the practice of Jews to band together for the sole purpose of committing murder. If they did such things there was something very serious behind it. There was, in fact, all this sort of thing he had described—and much more.

Some Very Good Officials

In his further observations Mr. Seligman said there was a very violent anti-Jewishness on the part of large sections of the Palestine Administration, although there were some very good officials, too. Perhaps the only department where anti-Jewishness was not rife was the Legal Department. There conditions had changed considerably during the past twenty-five years and the bench could be said to be clear of any charge of bribery and corruption.

Today there were no Jewish heads of Government departments, except the newly-appointed head of the Censorship Department. The censorship in Palestine had been a most rigid, unnecessary and oppressive one that had been abused to an extraordinary extent. There had been censorship of the press, postal services and of cables. Telephones were tapped and cables were often held up for a great length of time. Nothing could be published in Palestine before it had passed the Press Censor, and they had had instances where declarations by men such as President Roosevelt or even Mr. Churchill had been censored and not allowed to appear at all. There was once a favourable statement made on Palestine by President Roosevelt which was not allowed to appear. But two days later, an attack on the Zionist movement made by the New York Times was let through in full! Nobody in Palestine could criticise the Administration for these things. If he did he was liable to be arrested and put into a concentration camp—there was no need for a trial.

Referring to the Arabs, Mr. Seligman said they never had any indication from them of any political bias or prejudice or indeed of any political ambitions. These things only cropped up when certain members of the Administration desired it.

If, said Mr. Seligman, they were concerned in the building up of a national home in Palestine, then they must realise this fact—that no national home could be built, any more than any ordinary home, unless the persons who were going to build and live in that home could live in friendship and understanding.

WHAT IS HAPPENING IN PALESTINE?

THE JEWISH STANDARD
March 9, 1945

There was a very large attendance at the Anglo-Palestinian Club on Thursday, March 1, to hear an address on "What is Happening in Palestine," delivered by Mr. Max Seligman of Tel Aviv. Mr. Joel Slutsky presided. The speaker, who is one of Palestine's leading lawyers, said that the people in England were entirely ignorant of many of the things that went on in Palestine. This ignorance was due, firstly, to the very rigorous censorship imposed by the Palestine authorities, and secondly, to a very deliberate policy of suppression by the official Zionist bodies. As a result, people here found it difficult to believe there was so much vicious anti-Jewishness in certain departments of the Palestine Administration. In fact, it was very doubtful whether even the Colonial Office was aware of many matters which would never be tolerated by Parliament if it were brought to their attention.

Just as Jewish misdeeds were magnified here, so also the conduct of an Englishman in Palestine was very naturally unduly magnified, but that was only a reason for an Englishman there to be particularly scrupulous in their treatment of various sections of the community. The vast majority of British officials in the Palestine Administration were violently anti-Jewish. There were a number of men in the Secretariat and District Administration who were fair, but to a great extent they had to be guided by the advice of anti-Jewish officials. The legal and judicial departments were happily free from such prejudice. During the past ten years there had been great improvement in the judicial system. There was, however, a tendency by some judges, when dealing in questions of constitutional importance, to consider the wishes of the Executive. This tendency was, however, but natural in view of the fact that the judges were also colonial officials who might be moved from the judiciary to administrative departments. But it would be a good thing if there was in Palestine that also complete independence from the Executive which is the pride of the English judicial system.

Ex-Fascists

The worst department was probably the Police Department, and the few high minded and impartial English police officers suffered for the acts of the others. There were many police officers who seemed to take particular pleasure in arresting and detaining Jews. Some of these officers had probably been Fascists in England, and in fact one of them admitted to the speaker that he had been such, and that officer occupied a post in the Criminal Investigation Department. Large numbers of young men and women, mostly Revisionists or ex-Revisionists, were in concentration camps where many of them had been detained for several years. Numbers had been detained on the basis of information supplied secretly by an official of the Jewish Agency during the 1936–39 disturbances. There had been numerous allegations of beating up of prisoners and of actual torture in efforts to extract confessions or information. There were serious allegations that the police had deliberately murdered Stern and two men in a house on Diesengoff Street in Tel Aviv. The stories may be untrue, but the allegations were so grave and had spread throughout the country that they deserved a full and open, impartial investigation. Only by proving that these stories were not true was it possible to stop the bitterness and anxiety for revenge on the part of the relatives and friends of the persons concerned. But there had been no demand for such an investigation, and the newspapers were not permitted to publish anything of them. The detention of young men and young girls for years was a shameful thing which should never have been tolerated. The absence of opportunity for investigation or appeal led to all manner of abuses, and people were pulled in merely on information by an interested party. It was very easy to accomplish this if the victim were a Revisionist or an ex-

Beitar member. But the fear of steps being taken against them by the police is so great that persons are afraid to be identified with the New Zionist Movement or to criticise the police or any government department or official. In fact, many lawyers are afraid to take up cases of such persons, and in many instances the speaker had been briefed by other lawyers solely because of this fear. Many lawyers had also been arrested and detained, mainly because of their efforts for these persons, and some of them were still detained.

Campaign of Hate

The speaker also dealt with abuses by the censorship department, and of the monopoly created by the Government for Steel Brothers, which was resented by both the Arabs and the Jews. After replying to numerous questions, the speaker pointed out that no home could be built in Palestine by the Jews unless there was more harmony and understanding, and this was being retarded by the unreasonable campaign of hate against the New Zionists.

GOVERNMENT OF PALESTINE

Much has been written and said about the unsatisfactory conditions in Palestine, but seldom have so many of these allegations been marshalled so impressively as was done by Mr. Max Seligman in an address at the Anglo-Palestinian Club last week. Mr. Seligman is a prominent Palestine lawyer, familiar with the situation there, and it may be asserted circumstantially that nothing but a sense of pressing public duty would have led him thus to stir what he depicts as these very muddy waters so that the underlying evils should be seen and judged in something of their truly repellent state. The same reason commands publicity for his remarks. In their general trend, they are not new. Only recently, for instance, the corruption prevalent in some administrative circles in the country has led to the formation of a society of private citizens to root it out, and it is worth noting that the newly appointed chief of the Palestine censorship, Mr. Edwin Samuel, a son of Viscount Samuel, in a speech the other day was reported in a Palestine newspaper as taking a brave and public-spirited stand beside the organisers of the new body. Such action would surely not have been taken lightly by him. Then again, the answers given by the Colonial Secretary recently to questions about the conduct of the Palestine police provided further disquieting indications.

Readers' letters to the Jewish Chronicle, 16 March, 1945

SEARCHLIGHT ON PALESTINE

I feel that Mr. Max Seligman, the Palestine lawyer, has been of great service to Anglo-Jewry in calling attention to the truth about the Palestine Administration and how it affects the Jews of the Yishuv. This comes as no surprise to me, as some months ago Mr. A. Abrahams, Political Head of the New Zionist Organisation, on his return from a visit to Palestine, spoke to a large London audience on the same subject. At that time there was a great outburst by leaders of the Old Zionist Organisation, who attempted to ridicule and deny these allegations, but it seems that the corroboration which these statements have now received must surely make members of the O.Z.O. wonder whither they are being led and if their leadership is capable of solving this vital problem. Mr. S. Olinsky, "Rookwood", Albert Road, Manchester.

The address delivered by Mr. Max Seligman at the Anglo-Palestinian Club and reported by you will have caused great consternation among your readers, and particularly amongst those who hoped and dreamed that the valiant efforts of the Jewish people during the last decades would fructify into a closer relationship between Great Britain and the Jews. It is astounding that such a state of affairs should have developed as that described by Mr. Seligman, whilst our Zionist leaders throughout the world have gone on perennially preaching the doctrine of the immortal Dr. Pangloss, "that all is well in the best of possible worlds," in order that the flood of Zionist income shall not abate. They at least cannot escape from the implications of Mr. Seligman's indictment, for they cannot plead the ignorance of the man in the street. For our Zionist leaders, with their actual physical contacts and close relationships with matters in Palestine, such a policy of "laissez faire" is a political blunder of the first magnitude. I can only hope that the position of Jewry in Palestine is not so humiliating as that depicted by Mr. Seligman. Mr. L. Levine, 12, Tewksbury Drive, Prestwich, Lancs.

WHAT'S WRONG WITH ENGLISH ZIONISM?

A Visitor's Impressions

Sir,—As an old Zionist, I was pleased to note when visiting this country after an absence in Palestine of over seven years, the great increase in the membership of the Zionist Federation and in the Zionist

Fund collections. It is not so pleasant, however, to note the unreasonableness and intolerance displayed by some Zionist officials and leaders in this country. I have often heard Revisionists described as "Fascists" by other Zionists, but it seems to me that, with Nazi Germany and Fascist Italy practically destroyed, there is no movement outside Spain and possibly Russia with more totalitarian tendencies than the Zionist Organisation. Their leaders appear to be guided by an archaic principle that whoever is not entirely with them must be regarded as being against them. Anyone who disagrees with or dares to criticise them is an enemy who must be villified and attacked without mercy.

Strangely enough, these are people who live in a free England and who have been privileged to witness their Government and even their great Prime Minister being bitterly attacked and criticised even in wartime, and in and out of Parliament. But these critics, men like Shinwell and Aneurin Bevan, have not been outlawed. Members of Parliament freely and violently expressed their opposition to the Government over the decision taken at Yalta regarding Poland, and nobody suggested, or even thought to suggest, that they were not fully entitled to do so.

We are told in effect by the Zionist Organisation here that no Jewish organisation may express views regarding Palestine which differ from theirs. On the other hand, they argue, as they should, that all Jews, and not merely the Yishuv, have an interest in Palestine. We Jews have suffered much from intolerance, and the Zionist Organisation maintains that, therefore, we can be relied upon to show tolerance to the other peoples in Palestine. Nevertheless, the Anglo-Jewish Association is viciously attacked because it dared to advance a programme for Palestine which was not entirely at one with that of the Jewish Agency, although it demanded free Jewish immigration and colonisation, which, after all, are the real essentials for Palestine and the Galut.

I have come across English Zionists who refuse to sit at one table with Revisionists. In the number of pictures which adorn the offices of the Zionist Organisation, there is not included a single photograph of Vladimir Jabotinsky. Could prejudice go further? I have witnessed the Jewish Chronicle being attacked by the Zionist Organisation and for giving space to the views of others, space which is denied in the official publications of the Zionist Organisaton. The Jewish State Party is rebuked since its representative "dared" to attend a conference of the New Zionist Organisation. How they will laugh at this in Palestine! I have seen a great friend of the Jewish people, no less a person than Lord Strabolgi, attacked and even his bona fides assailed because he dared to lead a new movement without first obtaining the blessings and permission of the Jewish Agency, although that movement was calculated to bring additional friends to our cause.

Yet I can remember the days when the Zionist movement in this country was a very small body and Zionists were not prevented from advancing their views as freely as they wished. Today, official Zionist publications contain articles on Zionism and Palestine , but hardly any news of what is going on in that country, certainly not much of the unpleasant news. One Zionist official explained this to me by saying that it was not desirable that members or contributors should know of these things as they might refuse to subscribe further. What a poor excuse! My own impression, the result of conversations with Jews all over England, Scotland and Wales, is that if they were informed they would all too readily join in protesting and in demanding a stop to injustices. They are entitled to know, and ought to know, the truth and the whole truth. Why should they not know that, although a great deal has been accomplished in Palestine, so much more could have been done, and can still be done, if we Jews are given not privileges but only our rights and fair play.

Something is surely wrong in the English Zionist movement. There must be many leading English Zionists who are not so anxious for office or authority that they are not prepared to take into account other points of view deserving of consideration. It is high time that such English Zionists refused to "toe the line" and found some means of getting together with all other bodies interested in developing Jewish Palestine with a view to mobilising every possible effort for our cause. Our real enemies, both in Palestine and elsewhere, only delight in our quarrels and hasten to exploit them to our harm. We cannot have too many friends and allies, however much we may disagree on certain principles. We can urge our own point of view, and they can help us to overcome many of the difficulties which the Yishuv is experiencing. They should not be estranged.

MAX SELIGMAN

Abercorn Place, N.W.8

11 May, 1945
ZIONIST "ISOLATIONISTS"
(Editorial)

Fresh from many years' residence in Palestine, a correspondent in this issue describes the disagreeable impression made upon him by what he calls the "unreasonableness and intolerance" displayed by many "Zionist officials and leaders in this country." His words on this subject deserve the careful attention of all those who have the Zionist cause truly at heart. Unfortunately, there appears to be only too much ground for his strictures. The mentality which rejects any criticism, however well-intentioned and justified, and holds at arm's length those who have the temerity to engage in them, is not Jewish, but reminiscent of the one-party politics which have landed the Germans and Italians in their present desperate plight. It implies in the organisation a perfection given to no body of men in this terrestrial sphere, and, if generally acquiesced in, would establish the conviction in the minds of officials, if it is not already in being, that all who comment on the failings of their organisation are, *ipso facto*, enemies of the movement that organisation was created to further. On such a showing, everyone who has found fault, from time to time, say, with the present Coalition Government, could be denounced as a self-confessed opponent of the country and its war effort. Nobody in his senses, of course, took that crazy view. Yet the Jewish Chronicle, because it has criticised the methods of certain Zionists and Zionist groups, has been subjected from these quarters to an idiotic "smear campaign", in which numskulls have been persuaded that the paper is an enemy of Zionism, despite its tireless, clear, and unvacillating advocacy of the cause over many decades, and never more urgently and persistently than in these recent momentous years. By stupid intolerance of this kind, Zionism has been deprived of much helpful collaboration, for independent and conscientious men of character have inevitably been repelled by it. The sooner the perpetrators of this contemptible folly correct their absurd mental squint, and adopt the democratic attitude which alone can command support in the hour of democracy's greatest victory, the better. After all, the cause is greater than any organisation and infinitely more than the prestige or interests of any individuals.

THEY'RE LIKE HIS OWN CHILDREN

THE NEW YORK POST

June 13, 1947

The 44-year-old Welsh-born lawyer, now in this country on a mission sponsored by the United Zionists-Revisionists of America to raise funds for the families of Palestinian political prisoners, has defended scores of Jewish youths accused of anti-British violence. They have won his heart. He speaks of them as another man would of his children. His voice fills with pride for their reckless—some would say senseless—courage.

"They are a brave and intelligent lot," he says, adding they are not ruffians and that most of them are the Palestinian-born, well-educated sons and daughters of rabbis, merchants and other substantial men of the community.

Nor, in his opinion, are they fanatics. "They are very dispassionate, calm, well-disciplined, well-reasoned. They have thought this thing out. They back up their theories with learned Biblical and historical references."

Why Irgun Was Born: "Terror Begets Terror"

While Seligman, whose respect for the centuries-old principles of English law is deep, holds no brief for violence *per se*, he thinks it natural that these young people should seek relief from oppression by taking up arms, and says, "Terror begets Terror. It is the terror of the British administration which begets the Irgun." For Seligman bluntly characterizes the British regime in the Holy Land as a lawless one. This, he says, is what might happen to you tomorrow if you're a Palestinian citizen:

On the street, in your home, in a store, you might be arrested, without a warrant and for no particular reason, by any policeman or soldier. Then you would be imprisoned in a "filthy, verminous" jail for 48 hours. After that you would probably be transferred to the Latrun detention camp by order of an official who does'nt know who you are, has never seen you and has not studied your case in any detail. There you would be kept for months "on suspicion" and without trial. If, however, there is any evidence against you, you would be tried before a military court staffed by British army officers with no legal training, no qualifications. You could be defended only by special permission of the presiding judge. The court need give no reason for its verdict.

Civil Rights Lacking, Prison Camp Not Unlikely

Whether or not you receive a trial, you could be deported, despite your Palestinian citizenship, to a prison camp in Africa. "All civil rights are gone," Seligman concludes. "The people live under a ruthless military regime."

Such harsh language isn't characteristic of Seligman. He is essentially an easy-going, slow-speaking sort of man who loves to relax. His idea of a fine weekend is one spent with his Canadian-born wife and their two daughters at home in their modern Tel Aviv apartment doing nothing more strenuous than playing bridge, listening to symphony music, smoking English cigarets and drinking straight Scotch. He is quite frank about his little frailties. If, for example, you ask diplomatically whether he takes a little drink once in a while, he laughs and says, "Oh, no, quite often." He admits cheerfully that he left the tough life of a Palestinian collective farm[2] "because I'm not the stuff of which pioneers are made" and that he doesn't care to work more than eight hours a day. But when he hears of another British injustice, anger overwhelms him, and he forgets his desire for a leisurely life and begins a furious legal campaign. A shrewd courtroom fighter, he often scores victories not unlike those of his favorite fictional attorney, Perry Mason.

Has a Way of Turning Defeat Into Victory

And Seligman has a knack of turning initial defeats into triumphs. In 1938, when he was framed on charges of conspiracy to organize "illegal" immigration and convicted on the testimony of a British police officer, the higher courts refused to review the case and he had to serve a four-month prison term. When, however, the government attempted to suspend his license to practice because of the conviction, he took the issue to the Supreme Court and, in the first case of its kind, won a decision against Palestine's Attorney General, who was ordered to pay court costs. The victory was capped four years later when, in behalf of a civil complainant, Seligman prosecuted the police officer whose tesimony had sent him to jail. The officer lost the case, and as a result, was cashiered[3].

More than such personal triumphs Seligman enjoys embarrassing top British administrators on the witness stand. Once, during the trial of alleged "terrorists," he succeeded in the difficult task of getting the court's permission to call the head of the dread CID (Criminal Investigation Department) as a witness. He challenged the CID chief to deny the charge that members of his staff were inciting Arab villagers against Jewish colonists. The CID leader flushed, turned to the judge and asked "the protection of the court"—a British legal device used to avoid answering a query. The judge granted the request, but the net effect was to confirm Seligman's charge.

The lawyer does'nt think that his years-long battle against the English regime in Palestine is evidence of his disloyalty to his British homeland. "I'm not anti-British," he says. "I'm anti-Bevin and pro-Balfour." Seligman has remained a British citizen. And although he left his native Cardiff at the age of 18 after selling his boyhood stamp collection to finance his migration to Palestine, he looks rather British and has British tastes to this day. He wishes with all his heart that his fellow-Englishmen would realize that "Jewish hostility to Britain arose only when Britain repudiated the (Palestine) Mandate" and that "the resistance will end as soon as Britain corrects the error of her ways."

In a letter from Tel Aviv to daughter Aura (11-27-78), Max wrote:

I have to report that we have had two most successful functions. The first was a reception for Terence Prittie which attracted a large audience and at which I presented him with a Certificate of the inscription of his name by my Association in the Golden Book of the Jewish National Fund.

The second was, of course, the Balfour Dinner. Winston Churchill (the M.P.) attracted enormous bookings, so much so that we had to stop taking reservations a week before the date of the function. There were excellent speeches by Haim Herzog and Winston Churchill and I was the recipient of numerous compliments for my chairmanship, and particularly for taking Churchill to task for his interpretation of the Balfour Declaration.

Regarding the peace negotiations . . . I always had some reservations about the progress because I know what kind of a wily Arab is Sadat. It is a good thing for Israel that Begin is in charge of the negotiations for no other Israeli would be capable of standing up to the pressure of both Sadat and Carter.

NOTES TO BRINGING THE MESSAGE

1. The trial of the two Lechi men who shot Lort Moyne. Moyne had been at the head of the Colonial Office and was outspokenly anti-zionist. Resentment against the implementation of the 1939 White Paper policies was mounting, inflamed by a series of incidents. On the British side, there was the claim that allowing Jews into Palestine is not only contrary to official policy, but antagonized "our Arab allies," to which was added the fantastic charge that enemy agents and spies might use the Jewish refugee cover to infiltrate Palestine (this did occur in one or two cases; both Hagana and Irgun had no hesitation in liquidating traitors and spies.) However, the brutality with which the British carried out White Paper policies was an irritating factor, brought to a head by three incidents. In November 1940, the *SS Patria* was in Haifa

Port, its 1771 passengers being processed by the British for deportation to the Indian Ocean island of Mauritius. In order to prevent the deportation, it is believed the Hagana blew up the ship, with the loss of 200 immigrants and 50 policemen and crew members. The survivors were allowed to land. Another boatload was towed into Haifa, and all 1584 refugees transferred to British warships and deported to Mauritius. In December 1941, some 800 refugees from Romania were aboard the *SS Struma*. When it arrived in Constantinople enroute to Palestine, it was held up by the Turkish authorities, who had an agreement with the British. Pleas to allow the refugees in against the quota of legal immigrants fell on deaf ears. The standoff lasted until the end of February, 1942, when the Turks sent the unprovisioned ship back into the Black Sea. The ship, which was barely seaworthy, sank and nearly all aboard perished. The wave of bitter resentment this aroused was focussed on Lord Moyne, who was then Resident British Minister in Cairo. He and his driver were shot in 1944, and the two men who killed them were tried and hanged.

2. This is inaccurate. Seligman worked in his uncle's orange grove when he first came to Palestine in 1921. He never worked on a kibbutz.

3. Gilpin was cashiered for violating the law (fleeing the scene of an accident and other offenses), not because he "lost the case."

Not Allowed to Return to Palestine

by **MAX SELIGMAN**

In September, 1944, I felt in need of a change and some rest. For the past two years I had been working very hard, especially in providing legal aid to members of the underground and to people suspected of belonging to it. I had not been back to England since 1937, and wanted to see the country at war. In order to reach England at that time, one had to travel in an escorted convoy, a service that was provided by the government. This privilege was not extended to the public at large, of course, but was limited to military personnel, government officials, and to very few civilians who had to make urgent business trips. I wrote to the Chief Secretary of the Mandate Government enquiring whether I could travel, as I had a number of clients in England whom I had to see on urgent business that could not be satisfactorily transacted via mail. My friends were mostly of the opinion that I was wasting my time in applying.

To my complete surprise, as well as that of my friends, I received, within a week of writing to the Chief Secretary, a reply instructing me to proceed to the Cairo office of Cooke's Travel Agency. In Cairo I was told to go to Port Sa'eed, where a reduced-price ticket was reserved for me. I shared a cabin with fourteen other people, and was happy to discover among them my friend Judge Rigby, who represented the Crown opposite me in a number of important court cases. There were some fifteen ships in the convoy, and during the entire two-week voyage, we saw not a single enemy vessel or aircraft, making it somewhat boring. We disembarked near Glasgow, and in spite of the approximately 1000 passengers who had to clear customs, it was all done very quickly. Cigarettes were rationed in Britain, and passengers brought in all they could. The quota was 200, but the customs officer waved me on although I told him I had at least 500. Judge Rigby and I boarded the train to Glasgow, where we put up at the Central Hotel. We wanted to continue to London the following day, where I was hoping through friends to obtain lodgings for Judge Rigby. I wanted to send a wire, and was surprised when the desk clerk suggested I telephone. In Palestine it took from two to eight hours to get an intercity connection, whereas in Britain, which was at war and being bombed daily, and where the lines were heavily used by the military and by governments in exile, and further considering the great distance from Glasgow to London, I was amazed and profoundly impressed when I got through in two minutes!

Life in London went on as usual, and in spite of the hardships the people were enduring, they seemed to be in high spirits. Many houses were destroyed by the *Blitz*, especially near the centre of the city, but cafes and restaurants were crowded, in spite of rationing and the poor food. Cinemas and theatres were equally well attended. While I was in London, some missiles struck, one in Hyde Park near my hotel, but caused little damage. Broken glass from the Cumberland Hotel littered the length of Oxford Street near Marble Arch.

There were many air-raid shelters, and the subways were also used for that purpose. During air-raid alerts, most stores remained open and the streets were full of people. The British were proud of their "business as usual" attitude; had they been forced into shelters every time, as in Palestine, this would have caused unbearable economic hardship. I travelled the length of Britain and Wales, but was unable to go to Ireland, where a special permit was required.

In early 1945 I was invited to give a talk at the Anglo-Palestinian Club in London on the subject of "The Truth About Palestine." Official Zionist circles in London were displeased by this, and were even unhappier to read about my talk in the press. My association with terrorists, those rebels against the authority of the official leadership, made me an undesirable person.

During the war there was a strict blackout on news from Palestine, especially in anything that had to do with terrorist activity and the extreme measures taken by the civilian and military authorities against the population there. As a result, the public in Britain knew nothing about the arrests and detentions, of the exiling to Eritrea, about the murder of Ya'ir Stern, or of the brutal treatment of Jewish prisoners and detainees. I gave full details of all this to a profoundly moved capacity audience. My talk was reported verbatim on the first page of the *Jewish Chronicle*. I received hundreds of letters and telephone calls, but a number of Zionist leaders complained that it was a mistake to give all the facts, as this may give them difficulties in their fund-raising efforts: people might use my speech as an excuse for not contributing. My response was that people who gave money were entitled to know the truth, and that to the contrary, donations will increase. The weekly Zionist paper published an uncomplimentary lead article in which I was likened to "a modern Zola."

A few days later I met a high-ranking Palestinian official who told me he had been called to the Colonial Office and asked about the facts given in my speech. He said he was unable to deny them.

In order to return to Palestine, I needed the same permission to join a convoy as I did on my trip to England. Since I originally planned to stay for at least three months, I began preparing for my departure in January of 1945, as travel orders could be given in as quickly as twenty-four hours. I applied to the Passport Office, and was told I'd be notified shortly as to when I could leave. This "short" wait stretched into March, in spite of my repeated enquiries. In letters I received from friends in Palestine, I was told about rumours that my return was being held up by the Palestine Government. I did not believe those rumours until I met an officer who had just arrived from Palestine, who told me he found out, during the course of a conversation with our mutual friend Julius Jacobs, Assistant to the Chief Secretary, that my return to Palestine was indeed forbidden. I then took the matter seriously and approached several British Members of Parliament, including Squadron Leader Fleming (who has since died), and Mr. Lyons, K.C. They discussed the matter, each of them separately, with Mr. Oliver Stanley and with the Duke of Devonshire, the Colonial Secretary and Assistant Secretary. Both were given the same reply: that there is nothing in the files against Mr. Seligman, and that he must wait his turn. I then discovered there were hundreds of Palestinian nationals in Britain who were "waiting their turn" for four years, some even longer. I could not remain here indefinitely, away from my office, and I was terribly worried. Some friends suggested I contact Lord Strabolgi, with whom I had been in touch previously in connection with our efforts on behalf of the Dominion League. We were good friends, but I did not wish to impose on our friendship. Yet when I approached him at the end of April, he admonished me for not seeking his help earlier, and promised to "arrange the matter." He said it was a waste of time talking to Mr. Stanley and the Duke of Devonshire, as these men knew nothing of what went on behind the scenes. He was sure holding up my departure was the work of bureaucrats in the Colonial Office, and that no record of such activity exists. The following morning he called me and said: "Max, it was just as I thought, and I took care of it. Your name has been moved to the top of the list, and you can expect to be leaving in a week or two." Two days later I received a call from the Crown Agency (my clerk erroneously told me the call was from the Colonial Criminal Branch), asking whether I was prepared to leave. When I answered in the affirmative, I was given a week's time to depart from Glasgow. On the return journey I met a number of Palestinian citizens who had waited for years to leave, and who had to depart on twenty-four hours notice.

We left Glasgow on V.E. Day. News that the war had ended caught up with us on the high seas, and the captain invited the passengers to a celebration. Although the war was over, we sailed in complete blackout as far as Malta, where we joined the convoy, which was fully lit. We continued on to Port Sa'eed, and thence by train to Qantara. At the border, I was asked to step into the Passport Control office; they were surprised to see me and thought I would not be able to continue on to Tel-Aviv. After checking further, they apologized for the delay and I boarded the train.

My return to Tel-Aviv caused a sensation, as everyone thought I would be unable to return. I found out later that the day after I left in October, instructions were sent out to all Immigration offices forbidding my return to Palestine. A day before my arrival at Qantara, a new order rescinding the prohibition was sent out. This came as a result of a cable from the Colonial Office in London, and was an unpleasant shock to a number of officials in the C.I.D. who initiated the prohibition against my return. They never found out how I was able to come back, but began treating me with great respect.

Palestine As A Dominion

SIR JOSIAH WEDGWOOD (1872–1943) was a longtime Member of Parliament and an ardent supporter of Zionism. As an artillery officer in WWI, he came in contact with Joseph Trumpeldor, commander of the Mule Corps (part of the Jewish Legion, founded by Ze'ev Jabotinsky) at the Gallipoli front in Turkey. He became interested in the Zionist cause, and was a strong supporter of the Balfour Declaration. He visited Palestine twice; shortly after his first visit in 1926, he published a work which he called *The Seventh Dominion*, in which he advocated a Jewish state on both sides of the Jordan, which would be first a Crown Colony, and eventually acquire Dominion status. The *Seventh Dominion League* was established in 1928, following publication of the book, and was naturally encouraged by the Revisionist movement and its leader, Ze'ev Jabotinsky. But through lack of interest, the movement languished, until in 1936—and in response to the Partition recommendation of the Peel Commission—it was revived by Max Seligman, as the *Crown Colony and Dominion Association*. This time, support and encouragement came not only from prominent politicians in Britain, but also from other Dominions, notably South Africa, which had a large and influential Jewish community, alive to the problems in Palestine and interested in their solution. Even more encouraging, the idea was favorably received in responsible Arab circles: the Arabs did not want a return to the state of affairs that existed before Jews began returning in number to Palestine. Both Moslem and Christian Arabs applied for membership in the Association. Additionally, many British administration officials who voiced their support pointed out that Dominion status would strengthen their position and enhance their work. (An interesting sidelight to the *Crown Colony and Dominion Association* was that the High Court steadfastly refused to allow the registration of the association. The reason given was that under the Law of Societies, [a hangover from Ottoman times], it was unlawful to register any association *whose aim it is to change the regime of the country.*) It took Seligman nearly ten years of lobbying in Palestine and Britain to get the antiquated law revised and the Association duly registered. In the House of Lords, Lord Strabolgi, an outspoken supporter of Zionist aspirations and a personal friend of Seligman's, said he believed that . . . 'the creation of the Jewish Dominion would carry with it the construction of three bridges—a bridge between the British Empire and world Jewry; between Zionist and anti-Zionist (Jews), who would be able to unite within the Dominion, and a bridge between the Arab and Jewish branches of the Semitic race.'

Seligman wrote the following article, which appeared in the February 7th, 1938 issue of the *Jewish Chronicle.*

PALESTINE AS A CROWN COLONY
Another Alternative to Partition
By Max Seligman
(Acting Chairman of the Palestine Crown Colony Association)

The mere suggestion of Partition has demanded a supreme effort to find a more satisfactory solution to the problems in Palestine. The popularity of such an alternative solution, its persuasiveness and success, must depend on its ability to offer something better and more hopeful than does Partition. Will the Crown Colony idea—the proposal to turn Palestine into a British Crown Colony and ultimately into a British Dominion—stand this test?

No kind of future policy can be acceptable to the Jews which does not insist upon the unfettered development of the Jewish National Home in Palestine with all that it implies, more particularly the rights of immigration and settlement. Accordingly, the guarantee of these rights, unimpaired and unrestricted by any kind of political considerations, is a condition precedent to the promotion by Jews of the Crown Colony idea. On the other hand, there is the problem of Arab antagonism to the establishment in Palestine of the Jewish National Home as a State.

We have to probe deeply into the character of these two conflicting claims in order to show that the conversion of Palestine into a Crown Colony would go a long way to reconcile what to the Royal Commission appeared to be hopelessly irreconcilable. To put it briefly, we believe that fear on the part of the Arabs that they will be swamped and squeezed out of the country by sheer force of numbers is not at the root of their hostility to Zionism. It is by now firmly established that Jewish immigration has, in fact, conferred economic and other important benefits upon the Arabs, and that there is every reason to believe that it would continue to do so in the future. But there is a fear, however unjustified, that the Jews may aim at political domination of the country. This fear, be it noted, is entirely irrational in character and, therefore, stands on a different plane from any kind of economic advantage the Jews have to offer in return. It has persisted in the face of our manifestly peaceful intentions in Palestine, of which not even Arab agitators of the basest sort can have the slightest doubt. It is so difficult to uproot just because it is not based upon reasonable grounds. And yet upon the successful allaying of this fear of domination must to a large extent depend the solution of the problem.

Neutral and Friendly Link Needed

What is required is that the whole issue of sovereignty and political domination of Palestine should be withdrawn from the compass of Jewish and Arab aspirations, whether real or imaginary, and that it should be vested in a neutral, but interested and friendly, paramount power, such as the British Crown.

It is in this respect that the Mandate encountered its principal difficulties. Being inherently transient in its conception, and having but dwindling legal and moral support in the authority of its source, the League of Nations, it never offered to Jews and Arabs that kind of common allegiance which was required to unite the two races in a common bond of citizenship. It was easy to encourage apprehension of "Jewish rule" in Palestine in the Arab mind as a very real possibility and as a means to blocking the way to any real effectual understanding. Surely, however, the existence of differences between various sections of a community in culture, creed and economic standards is no reason why, in the political sphere of life, those sections should not be able to meet on a common ground, if only such ground can be prepared. Where the Mandate failed, its place in Palestine must be taken by some government which could make a stronger appeal to the civic sense of the people and which could exercise a neutralising influence upon the conflicting interests of Jews and Arabs.

The Jews cannot and will not abandon their differences of nationality, religion and culture. Again, considerable time must pass before the economic standard of the Jewish and Arab sectors will be equal.

The impact of modern Jewish colonisation in Palestine upon the primitive and backward state of the existing Arab population is bound to result in a certain preponderance of the Jews over the Arabs in many respects, notably in regard to commerce and industry, but not less effectively in regard to education, science, health, and numerous other aspects of life. Political rivalry, however, in the sense that the Jews aim at political domination of the Arabs, is alien to the root idea and all the best traditions of Zionism, and the Jews are not surrendering any of their rights or ambitions in Palestine by leaving the sovereignty and rule in Palestine to a third paramount power, which must, of course, be pledged to the establishment of the Jewish National Home as a free centre for Jewish immigrants and colonisation.

Strategic and Political Advantages

As for the Arabs, the position is more complex. Theirs is a distinct desire for complete national independence, free from any foreign rule. In so far as this desire is not prompted by the purely negative motive of being protected against the danger of Jewish rule, it may be difficult to obtain Arab consent to any kind of foreign sovereignty in Palestine, even if it is the British Crown, with its unique record of colonial administration.

The argument which should influence the Arabs to agree to British rule in Palestine is the same which should persuade the all-too-eager champions of independent Jewish Statehood to curb their ambitions and to take a more realistic view of the matter.

The time has long gone by when small nations could prosper in times of peace and when they had a reasonable chance of holding their ground against aggression in times of war. To-day, the universal trend points to centralisation and combination of power, to alliances and concerted action. Such was the underlying idea of the League of Nations; but there is a striking contrast between the failure of the League, whose primary aim it is to guarantee internationally the integrity of the small nations, and the success of the Commonwealth of the British Empire, which does afford prosperity and peace to its numerous member States. It shows that small nations cannot rely in safety upon international treaties, but that, on the other hand, they serve their interests best by joining as members one powerful group. Today, the real proof of statesmanship for a small nation lies in the kind of alinement which it is able to secure.

As for Palestine, it would surely be the climax of absurdity to expect the Jewish State, as envisaged by the Report, or, for that matter, an

Arab state in a part or in the whole of the country, to be capable of an independent foreign policy of its own. It would be sheer hypocrisy to claim anything like sovereignty for either such Jewish or Arab State, which would be at the tender mercies, in time of war or even of peace, of any foreign power having designs upon it. Nor will the Arab State gain much in strength by entering into a pan-Arabic combination, if ever any such thing were to see political reality. It is pre-eminently from the point of their own national interests that the Arabs must, and will, no doubt, come to realise that they cannot do better than join the British Empire.

Crown Colony's Pliable Constitution

There is, of course, another point which should be remembered by those who object to the Crown Colony idea on the grounds that it withholds from the Jews and Arabs the status of an independent State and reduces their status to that of a mere colony. The conversion of Palestine into a Crown Colony is not meant to be the end, but merely the beginning of a process of development, the final goal of which would only be reached in the course of time by attaining Dominion status. That there is room for such gradual evolution is amply proved by the history of other parts of the Empire. There is nothing rigid about the constitution of a Crown Colony. But the important point is that the attainment of self-government and of all the other incidents implied in the term Dominion are effected by a process of evolution, not by the sudden imposition upon people of a form of government for which these people are not yet mature. The difficulties which will be entailed in this respect by the Partition scheme are very formidable indeed, and are looked upon with serious misgivings even by those who are otherwise in favour of the scheme. Law, custom and institution are all intimately concerned with human development and require natural growth. Nothing good can come of an attempt to translate them into practical life without first giving them time to develop and ripen. Here again, the Partition scheme is at a serious disadvantage as against the Crown Colony system, which can adjust the legal status of the people to its needs and standards for the time being.

It is difficult in the space of an article to cover the whole list of benefits which the conversion of Palestine into a Crown Colony immediately and into a Dominion subsequently would confer upon the country as such. Under the scheme, it would be possible to secure Imperial Preference for Palestine's trade and to open up wider and better prospects for her industrial and agricultural exports. British interest and confidence in the country would be considerably increased, and investments could be expected in a larger measure than in the past. British officials would be brought into a more direct contact with the people, and the responsibility and concern of the local Government would be enlarged. The British Government and its officials would be dealing with a land which was their permanent and imperial concern, and the stepmother attitude would be changed to one of indisputable high British interest.

Converting Mandate Into Sovereignty

The actual conversion of Palestine into a Crown Colony would be comparatively easy. What is required, first of all, is the readiness of the British Government, then a resolution by the League of Nations and the United States of America, and finally, the passing of an Order in Council or Act of Parliament vesting sovereignty in the Crown and giving the country a constitution.

As regards the Arabs, their attitude is of great importance for the success of the scheme. But it is claimed as one of its main assets that it will have unanimous Arab support at least in so far as it obviates Partition. The writer has, in fact, been informed by a number of Arab Christians that the overwhelming majority of Arab Christians favour the scheme, but that they dare not state so publicly for fear of terrorists. The opinion of the Jewish "man-in-the-street" expressed itself very favourably when an association was formed a year ago in Tel Aviv with the object of promoting the Crown Colony idea. Official Zionist circles did not support, although they did not decry, the proposal. A Crown Colony over the whole of Palestine is much more likely to afford a solution to the urgent needs of Jews in the countries of emigration than a State of doubtful security in a tiny territory. There have been numerous applications for membership in the Crown Colony Association from all parts of the country, including supporters of all political parties, and the formation of branch associations in Haifa and Jerusalem has been urged. Later, the promoters circulated among members and their friends a declaration of support, which met with a very remarkable response.

Among the founders of the association there are not only British and colonial Jews, but many Palestinians and other nationals, and considerable support has been coming from Jews of American, German and other origins. The Association has also received messages of encouragement from various important political personalities in Britain.

Following permission for registration of the Association, a strong committee will be established, membership will be canvassed, and branches will be established abroad.

The outbreak of hostilities in 1939 pushed the movement into the background. Towards the end of the war, the Crown Colony and Dominion Association was revived and renamed *The Jewish Dominion of Palestine League*, and as such was inaugurated at a gala dinner in London in December, 1944. The keynote speaker was Lord Strabolgi. Also present were Lady Strabolgi and Lady Wedgwood, widow of Sir Josiah who had fathered the Jewish Dominion concept; and of course Max Seligman. Excerpts from some of the speeches delivered on the occasion follow, as well as a letter of clarification written by Seligman to the *Jerusalem Post*. (See also Letters to the Press, 18 December, 1936)

JEWISH DOMINION OF PALESTINE LEAGUE
Inauguration Dinner
(From the Jewish Standard, 1 December, 1944)

It was a gathering deeply impressed with the solemnity and importance of the occasion which acclaimed Lord Strabolgi when he rose to deliver his address as the President of the Jewish Dominion of Palestine League, at the Inauguration Dinner, last Monday evening. Lord Strabolgi had in the past two years become part and parcel of Jewish history. His work for the Jewish Army Committee, and his staunch support of Jewish rights, had endeared him to Jews far beyond the British Isles, and it seemed only fair that it should be he who should fill the important position of President of the Jewish Dominion League, which may well make history. Beside him sat Lady Strabolgi, who shared in all her husband's activities, and who has in the past few weeks done important work in laying the foundations of the new League.

Lord Strabolgi welcomed the guests, and went on to say that the Jewish Dominion of Palestine League was really a revival of the movement that had been started by a number of prominent M.P.s, among others, the Duke of Devonshire, himself, and the late Lord Wedgwood. That was in 1928. They did not get much encouragement. In 1936, Dr. Seligman, a prominent Jewish lawyer in Palestine, now on a visit to England, had started what was called the Jewish Crown

Colony and Dominion Association, aimed at overcoming the economic and political disadvantages of Palestine's position, and leading up to the creation of a Dominion. That movement received support not only from Jews, but also from prominent Arabs in Palestine; that is, from Arabs who worked and were interested in Palestine, and not in agitating. The present initiative had come from some of the Dominions, and particularly from South Africa, where members of the influential Jewish community were alive to the problems and were interested in that solution. It should be clear that the project had been started long before the murder of Lord Moyne, although the subsequent anxiety certainly strengthened the case for the Jewish Dominion. He was convinced, and the information which he had received confirmed it, that the Arabs themselves did not want to go back to the state of affairs that existed before the Jews came into Palestine, and that many of them would give support to the Jewish Dominion League.

"Speaking as a member of the House of Lords," declared Lord Strabolgi, "We pledged to the policy of a Jewish National Home. That is something which has nothing to do with the violence of a few extremists whose actions shall not be allowed to disturb the course of logical argument and policy. We have been worried about the way things are drifting in Palestine, and we have come to the conclusion that a clear policy must be devised."

Great Focal Point

Speaking of Palestine's strategic interests, Lord Strabolgi said that the British could not abdicate their special position in Palestine. Palestine was the great focal point of the Asiatic airlines, and its very central situation made it the backbone of the British Empire. No one in Parliament or elsewhere would ever dare to suggest that Britain should surrender its interests in the country. There was, of course, an American attitude to the problem. It was a fact that American big business had recently shown an interest in Palestine. Yet both Roosevelt and Dewey had pledged themselves to the policy of a Jewish Commonwealth.

Lord Strabolgi then proceeded to analyse what were the implications of a "Jewish Commonwealth." It was clear that no such Jewish Commonwealth could, in the present state of political development, hope to stand alone. As a branch of the British Commonwealth of Nations it would enjoy the guarantee of that Commonwealth's protection, and would itself contribute to the security of the whole.

Concerning Partition, Lord Strabolgi said, "I hope we shall hear no more about it. The economic needs of the country, apart from political, dictate that the water and electric power of the country could not be separated from the areas of development, and Partition would effectually hold up the growth and progress of the country. Palestine's only line of development was within the historic boundaries of the country."

In conclusion Lord Strabolgi announced that a Fighting Fund of 50,000 Pounds would be raised for furthering the objects of the League. It was planned to hold a monster meeting in Albert Hall at the beginning of the New Year, and a campaign for educating public opinion throughout the country would be initiated. It was hoped, also, in the near future to establish branches of the League throughout the country, in Palestine, and in the Dominions.

Surprised at Transformation

Field Marshal Sir Phillip Chetwode, who followed, said that he spoke as a soldier, and not as a politician. He recalled with pride that he commanded the Army Corps that took Jerusalem in the last war. At that time they believed that nothing else would in future dominate Palestine but the Balfour Declaration. He also recalled that he had under him the first Jewish formation within the British army. They had fought as well as any other army under his command. Later he returned to Palestine after an absence of some years, and was pleasurably surprised to find a great transformation. Large areas that had previously been desert had begun to flourish. The Jewish race had made the desert bloom. He found a great new city on the coast, and industry and enterprise everywhere. Valuable chemicals were being extracted from the Dead Sea, and there was great promise on all sides. "If these people can make this out of a desert," declared Field Marshal Chetwode, with emphasis, "they have the right to the country, and they will continue to do it." There were large parts of the country waiting for development, semi-desert areas like the Negeb, which the Jews could make fruitful. "We English," said the Field Marshal, "cannot afford to have Palestine in the hands of any people except those whom we could trust up to the hilt." Palestine was the artery of the British Empire, and he hoped to God that he would yet see the Jewish people in control of it.

The Millennial Solution

Louis Golding, the well-known novelist, said that the project of the Jewish Dominion League might prove to be the milennial solution of a millennial problem. He told of his own experience and information regarding persons who had come back from Palestine struck with the Jewish achievement. He dwelt particularly on the need for Palestine Jewry and the British officials to understand each other, and told of a British official who had passed through the various stages of anti-Semitism in Palestine, but had resolved to stay on and get to know the Jews. The result was that that same man had changed his whole attitude to the Palestine Jewish situation, and could be regarded as a friend. When he, Mr. Golding, informed him of the formation of the Jewish Dominion League, he immediately declared it to be the only logical step that promised success. He himself would watch with keen interest the development of the idea which was deserving of the widest possible support.

Lord Aylwin, proposing the toast of the guests, said he was deeply impressed with the enthusiasm he sees around him. They had come together in support of a great project that might deter less determined people. But he felt that given the necessary resolve and good will, big things could be achieved.

Major Charles Taylor, M.P., said that the plan for a Jewish Dominion League was one which called for careful study and full examination of all the implications. He, for one, intended to give it most active consideration.

Truth Must be Known

Mr. Max Seligman said that he had only recently come to England on a visit from Palestine. He would go so far as to admit that he had welcomed the brief absence from Palestine with a certain amount of relief. It was quite a novelty to be in a country where one was not followed by agents, not overheard, or listened to or reported. That, in fact, was largely the position in Palestine. He was afraid that the Lord Moyne tragedy had not been seen in England against its true background. Never had Jews banded themselves together to commit murder, and it was his view that Britain must go to the causes of the crime. Things were happening in Palestine which were completely unknown in England. It was essential that the truth should be made known. It was his view that judicial inquiry should be instituted under a non-political personage, preferably under some High Court judge, without any political antecedents. Evidence should be taken. All grievances should be sifted and action should follow on the results.

Mr. Seligman recalled that when he had formed the Crown Colony and Dominion Association in 1936, there was great support forthcoming from Arab circles. He had no doubt that similar support would now be found for the Jewish Dominion League. At the same time he warned that there were essential facts that should not be overlooked by those who hoped to improve the relations between Britain and Jewish Palestine. It should not be forgotten that Palestine was the only free country in the world which Jews were forbidden to enter by statute, or prohibited from acquiring land except in a very insignificant portion of the country. Such a situation could not continue if it was hoped to change the general atmosphere.

Free Immigration Needed

Mr. A. Abrahams, proposing "The Health of the Chairman," said that the Jewish Dominion League should not be regarded as a Movement formed to implore assistance, or merely to express the conventional gratitude of Jews to those who helped. It was a political Movement, whose objects were of equal benefit to Jewry and Britain. It was upon that mutuality that their expectations rested. He wished, at the same time, that non-Jews should understand that it was not their intention to promote Palestine into a Dominion merely for the purpose of adding territory to the British Empire. In common with many non-Jews, he felt that the British Empire was not short of territory, and that there were already enough problems within it, without the additional problem involved by some new annexation. For them, Dominion status implied a voluntary act on the part of a Jewish Palestine, which would of its own accord apply for membership within the British Commonwealth of Nations after achievement of Jewish Statehood. Sir Herbert Williams was quite right in saying that Britain could not itself transform Palestine into a Dominion. The real step would have to come from Palestine Jewry itself. But that could not occur until Palestine policy was so transformed as to permit a completely free Jewish immigration into both sides of the Jordan and removal of all economic and political obstructions to Jewish development. Once that happened, Jewish Palestine would move forward with unprecedented speed, and before very long the country, with a Jewish majority in it, would be in a position to apply for termination of the Mandate and the recognition of Jewish sovereignty. It was at that stage that Jews would be in a position to take the necessary steps for membership in the British Commonwealth of Nations. But he warned that it could not occur unless the intervening stages were appropriate, and were adapted to the aim they had in view—the Jewish Dominion.

Mr. Abrahams concluded with an expression of heartfelt thanks to Lord and Lady Strabolgi for their great help in the formation of the League. It was a work that was based on the recognition that what they were doing served the best interests equally of Britain and Jewry.

To the Editor, The Palestine Post
PALESTINE DOMINION

Sir,—I should be grateful if you would permit me, as Acting Chairman of the Dominion of Palestine Association, to correct one or two misapprehensions which may arise from the comments made by Reflector in your issue of the 1st instant.

The local association and the Palestine Dominion League in London are two distinct bodies. Their aims are similar and they work in close cooperation. It is incorrect to say that the people acting in both organizations are mainly persons of Revisionist tendencies. In the Committee of the Palestine organization there is only one member associated with the Revisionist party. In the Committee of the London organization the persons connected with the Revisionist party form a very small minority.

I do not know of any foundation for the statement that the Revisionist Party is ordinarily regarded as hostile to England. Its leaders have always advocated close cooperation with the Mandatory Power and its founder, the late Vladimir Jabotinsky, was one of the first advocates of the scheme for a "Seventh Dominion."

It is the view of the Association, which, it is felt, is shared by large numbers of all sections of the local communities, that the only practical solution for the Palestine problem is that Palestine should become a British Dominion in which neither Jews nor Arabs should have political privileges, that Britain should be entitled to establish whatever Military bases may be necessary, and that Jewish immigration and colonization should not be artificially restricted.

Yours, etc.
Tel Aviv, October 27, 1944 — Max Seligman

The Grand Master

SELIGMAN AND FREEMASONRY

Freemasonry played an important part in Max Seligman's life. I was aware he was a member of this society, about which I must confess I never knew anything of consequence. It seems to me he spoke more on the subject at home, but in the company of non-members he rarely mentioned it.

The early origins of freemasonry are attributed variously to King Solomon, Euclid, or may be found in ancient Egypt, Mayan Mexico, or the lost continent of Atlantis. Masonic ceremonies may have links to the mysteries of Osiris, the Essenes, Druids, Templars and other sects. The greatest number of Masons are in the English-speaking countries, mostly in America, but Masonic Lodges are to be found in all Western countries and as far away as India and Japan. Many famous men were Masons: the long and impressive list includes Voltaire, Mozart[1], Haydn, Schiller, Goethe, and George Washington, who became Master of a Lodge in Alexandria, Va.[2]. Benjamin Franklin, Lafayette, Napoleon, Mazzini and Garibaldi, were all Masons. In short, they were men of no small stature, these Masons; their ranks included men who shaped the destiny of nations.

"The purpose of all is one, the good of the whole, the fundamental tenet of the brotherhood . . . It is the true social structure, the perfecting of humanity, the new Jerusalem." (Thus the memorable Herr Settembrini in Thomas Mann's *The Magic Mountain.*) The guiding principles of freemasonry are "to act upon the square, keep a tongue of good report, maintain secrecy and practice charity", all this within a framework of a system of morality, veiled in allegory and illustrated by symbols. In simpler terms, it is a fraternity of universal brotherhood, whose first principle is the admission to its ranks of adherents of all faiths, and claiming to be based on those fundamentals of religion held in common by all men. Masonry is secret in that its members are sworn never to reveal anything about its rituals, although the membership, meeting places and progress reports by the directors are not secret.

The *Ancient and Accepted Scottish Rite* traces its origins to the old craft guilds of masons employed in the construction of public buildings such as castles and abbeys in Britain. Records show a Lodge in Edinburgh in 1600. The aristocratic origin of Freemasonry's high officials (none of whom ever laid a brick) conferred upon the movement a certain degree of social importance. A system of degrees of membership was given Masons in ascending rank, up to the thirty-third degree.

Max Seligman became interested in Freemasonry as a youth, attracted by its guiding themes of universal brotherhood and charity, belief in a Supreme Being and the immortality of the soul, the use in every lodge of "a volume of Sacred Law" (the Bible), and perhaps most importantly, "a legend relating to the (re-)building of King Solomon's Temple." There being no lodge in Palestine at the time, Seligman founded the Sharon Lodge in 1935 in Tel Aviv, under the auspices of the Grand Lodge of Scotland.

Fellow-Mason Judge Yehuda Treibisch[3] relates that when the State of Israel was proclaimed, there were in it some twenty unauthorized lodges. He and Seligman decided to found the *Grand Lodge of the State of Israel.* Max travelled to Scotland and convinced the directorship to authorize the establishment of the Grand Lodge. It was consecrated on 23 October 1953, in a ceremony held at the YMCA Hall in Jerusalem, and attended by delegations from Scotland and all English-speaking countries.

In 1959, Seligman and Treibisch were in Edinburgh to attend a convocation at the Grand Lodge. Seligman was received with great honor and was seated upon the dais *(The East).* He was elected Master of Sharon Lodge in 1960 and served in that capacity for two years.

Seligman dreamed of establishing a world center for Masons in Jerusalem, and devoted much time and energy to that end, but was not successful in raising sufficient funds for the project. In 1972, he was made Grand Master of his Lodge, again serving a two-year term. During the inauguration of each new member, Seligman would deliver a speech (a "charge"), which included singing; he had a wonderful voice and loved to sing. He travelled extensively on behalf of the Masons, effectively handing over the reins of his law practice to his partner Max Kritzman. (We met Max and Millie in 1974 when they were in Los Angeles to attend a function at the large Scottish Rite Temple on Wilshire Blvd.)

BROTHER MAX

The following poem, freely translated from the Hebrew, was written in honor of a Masonic occasion, and dedicated to Max Seligman. The author is Avraham Fellman. It is dated 10 January 1975.

In '21 he came here
His hopes were very high
To earn a living
He toiled in an orange grove.

He tired of this labor
And longed for Jerusalem
Where he worked for several firms
And made many friends.

After much deliberation
He began the study of Law
He passed the Bar
The first English advocate.

Liked by the judges
All his cases succeeded
He defended the rebels
With spirit and devotion.

Devoted to the Underground
He did his very best
To help illegal immigrants
But was jailed by the tyrant.

His sentence was shortened
He left the prison singing
Returning to his work
His fame spread far and wide.

His activities far-ranging
Even if poles apart
He labored in all spheres
With Brothers, and others.

He dreamt of a Dominion
That remained, alas, a dream
Instead of this proposal
The State had been proclaimed.

Master of Sharon in '36
He swore me in as Mason
We became good friends
Full of mutual admiration.

He founded Yeshurun Synagogue
(And also the Sharon Lodge)
He sang there as a cantor
His voice thrilling the crowd.

He joined many other Lodges
And breathed life into them
He was chief spokesman
Among founders, his word was law.

He flew to England twice
Adding glory to the Lodge
Representing Britain's Lodges
He gave full time to Freemasonry.

In '60 he became Grand Master
Showing what he could do
And to every Brother's joy
Tel-Aviv Lodge was blessed.

He promoted pilgrimages
And labored without respite
Went to England and Scotland
Paying all his own expenses.

He brought funds from Germany
For the Peace Palace in
  Jerusalem
Enhancing our image
For Brothers and the world.

The Palace of Peace
Remained but a dream
He founded Holyland Lodge
For visiting Brothers.

And King Solomon Lodge in the
  north
And Ein Hakoreh in Nachshon
He met the Masters in
  Washington
And people in high places.

In the hills of Jerusalem
He planted a Freemason grove
He labored on mutual insurance
The Great Lodge affairs he
  directed.

Some two years ago
He turned three-score and ten
In spirit he remains young and
  trusted
In all ways a great Gentleman.

Shortly before Max left for England, a farewell reception was held in his honor on 29 August, 1985, attended by representatives of all the lodges of which he had been a Founding Member. Grand Master Uri Ayalon reviewed the major contributions Max had made during his sixty years of service to the State and fifty years of service to the Masonic Craft. After he was presented with numerous mementos, souvenirs and a specially engraved plaque, Ayalon departed from M.W. Bro. Max Seligman with the triple Masonic Kiss indicating everlasting Brotherhood, Friendship and Good Wishes.

Treibisch met Max for the last time later that year on the eve of the Seligmans' departure for London. He relates that at this point, Max was sadly no longer aware of what went on around him.

NOTES TO THE GRAND MASTER

1. Mozart composed close to twenty Masonic works, mostly vocal, and *The Magic Flute* is rich in Masonic symbolism. In Vienna there is still a *Mozart Grand Lodge*.

2. In the U.S.A., the Shriners ("Ancient Arabic Order of Nobles of the Mystic Shrine") is an offshoot of the Masonic movement. Membership is mostly from the ranks of business and professionals, who place considerable emphasis on impressive titles, colorful, noisy regalia and mass ceremonies. This somewhat juvenile organization concentrates its benevolent efforts (appropriately enough) on helping sick children, through a network of Shriners' hospitals. (Were its founders better aware of the true nature of Islam, particularly as reflected in events of the past decades, they might have opted to leave *Arabic* out of the *Ancient Order of Nobles*.)

3. Yehuda Treibisch went to England to study engineering, returning to Palestine in 1929, when he entered the service of the Government. He met Max Seligman in 1940, when he was employed by the Justice Department. Recommended by fellow-Mason Alec Epstein, Treibisch was initiated into the Sharon Lodge in 1941.

The British Withdrawal

FOLLOWING THE U.N. resolution of 29 November 1947, the country entered a twilight zone of semi-chaos. The British withdrew into barbed-wire enclaves, at first located in various parts of Palestine, and eventually concentrated around the port of Haifa. Such areas were called "Bevingrads." Here they more or less sat out the remainder of the Mandate, until on 14 May, 1948, they lowered the Union Jack and sailed into the sunset. Former Colonial Secretary Leopold Amery summed up British public sentiment when he said: "We left ignominiously, amid carnage and confusion." Meanwhile, however, they were still very much here and in the first Arab attacks on Jews, they plainly sided with the former. There appeared to be no central policy and area commanders were acting on their own. They let it be understood that when (not *if*, mind you, but *when* . . .) things got really hopeless for the Jews, the gallant British would come to their rescue, imposing whatever solutions suited their purposes, and which the beleaguered Jews would be in no position to reject.

During these months, the Yishuv had to defend itself as best it could. The country was still under martial law, and the mere presence of British forces was an inhibiting factor. I was one of the thousands of volunteers who nightly manned the hastily made pillboxes and other defensive positions along the borders, in my case the border with Jaffa on the coast. We could see the British patrols, and armed Arabs moving about unmolested. We were under orders not to fire if the British were anywhere in sight, as this would invite trouble. Arab fire we were to return only sparingly: just enough to remind them we were there. In any event, for every five men we had only one rifle with five rounds, a Sten-gun with twenty rounds, and five grenades. The gallows humor about *those* was that it was better to use them on ourselves than fall into Arab hands. The firing would begin as soon as darkness fell, our attackers cursing and yelling blood-curdling threats with detailed anatomical references, but never

GA/A/99/Rev.7
3 October 1947

GENERAL ASSEMBLY

SESSION *49*

ROLL-CALL FORM

PLENARY MEETING *128* DATE *Nov 29*

COMMITTEE ____ TIME ____

Question at issue *Palestine Partition*

	YES	NO	ABSTAIN		YES	NO	ABSTAIN
AFGHANISTAN		X		LEBANON		X	
ARGENTINA			X	LIBERIA	X		
AUSTRALIA	X			LUXEMBOURG	X		
BELGIUM	X			MEXICO			X
BOLIVIA	X			NETHERLANDS	X		
BRAZIL	X			NEW ZEALAND	X		
BYELORUSSIAN S.S.R.	X			NICARAGUA	X		
CANADA	X			NORWAY	X		
CHILE			X	PAKISTAN		X	
CHINA			X	PANAMA	X		
COLOMBIA			X	PARAGUAY	X		
COSTA RICA	X			PERU	X		
CUBA		X		PHILIPPINES	X		
CZECHOSLOVAKIA	X			POLAND	X		
DENMARK	X			SAUDI ARABIA		X	
DOMINICAN REPUBLIC	X			SIAM			—
ECUADOR	X			SWEDEN	X		
EGYPT		X		SYRIA		X	
EL SALVADOR			X	TURKEY		X	
ETHIOPIA			X	UKRAINIAN S.S.R.	X		
FRANCE	X			UNION OF SOUTH AFRICA	X		
GREECE		X		UNION OF SOVIET SOCIALIST REPUBLICS	X		
GUATEMALA	X			UNITED KINGDOM			X
HAITI	X			U.S.A.	X		
HONDURAS			X	URUGUAY	X		
ICELAND	X			VENEZUELA	X		
INDIA		X		YEMEN		X	
IRAN		X		YUGOSLAVIA			X
IRAQ		X			33	13	10
TOTAL 1st Column:	27			TOTAL:			

Voting record chart of the United Nations General Assembly on the partition of Palestine, November 29, 1947.

coming anywhere near us, just as long as we fired the odd shot in their direction. One night, a British Bren-Gun carrier came rattling along, firing its guns nonstop, the bullets flying in all directions. The boys were just having fun.

The main British force was the 6th Airborne Division, who with their red berets earned the nickname *Kalaniot* (Poppies). These paratroops were used for patrols, roadblocks, searches, etc. Early one morning, in the wee hours, we were asleep at home when we heard noises on the ground floor (we lived on the second). Outside I saw an army jeep; it was a search, and all we could do was wait until they came to our door, which didn't take long. One young Tommy remained outside, and another entered, accompanied by a soldier who looked like a Cypriot. Our baby son was staring at them with wide-eyed curiosity. After checking our identity papers, they started poking around. My old RAF jacket was draped over the back of a chair, and in answer I said yes, I just got "demobbed" a year ago. They apologized for the trouble and left. We discovered our watches and change we had left in the bathroom were gone. All of our neighbors related similar experiences.

Martial law notwithstanding, the Jewish Agency was busy purchasing arms in Europe in preparation for the onslaught everyone knew was coming. This was the period of a brief honeymoon with Russia (anything to embarrass the British), and Hagana buyers were able to get a large supply of Czech-made rifles and some Messerschmidt fighters, courtesy of the Skoda Works. The guns were heavily greased and cleaning them was a monumental chore. The 'planes were nicely crated and ready for assembly. The French Government, sympathetic to the state-in-the- making (again, anything to embarrass the British), allowed free use of its ports, and donated a shipload of munitions, which, along with a full complement of volunteers for the ranks of the Irgun, were loaded aboard the *Altalena*. When it arrived at Tel Aviv on 20 June, 1948, the ship was perceived by Ben Gurion as a challenge to his authority, and he ordered the newly-formed Israel Defense Forces to open fire. Fifteen men were killed and the ship was set ablaze. Menachem Begin, aboard the ship and in command, refused to fire on fellow-Jews.

Also on board was Peter Bergson, who was arrested by Israel's Intelligence Service soon after landing. The incident continues to haunt Israeli politics to this day[1].

Deals were also made with British officers and supply-sergeants for the purchase of tanks, half-tracks and arms. A few Britishers joined the Jews along with their equipment, in one case, a Crommwell tank! Surplus army vehicles were concentrated at various depots, the largest of which was in an olive grove at Atlit, south of Haifa. I believe a simultaneous deal was struck for the sale of the vehicles to the Israelis and the Jordanians. We were told very little, but the depot was divided by barbed wire; the Legionnaires in their checkered headdress and armed to the teeth on one side, we on the other. We studiously avoided each other. I was in charge of a small group of mechanic/drivers, armed only with our tools. We made emergency repairs and got as many vehicles as we could to run, ferrying them in convoys to our base in Jaffa (the Arabs had since fled from there and elsewhere), sometimes making two runs a day. We knew an armed unit was assigned to the area for our protection and would come to our assistance in case of trouble. How we were to summon them remains a mystery, since we had no radio. In the event, the few weeks at Atlit went by without incident, and I could proudly survey "my fleet" of four-wheel-drive trucks and jeeps at our base.

Recently I saw a series of BBC documentaries entitled "End of Empire", and taped as a souvenir the segment on Palestine. To their credit, the British dealt with the subject honestly.

NOTE TO THE BRITISH WITHDRAWAL

1. Ya'akov Meridor and Hillel Kook (Peter Bergson) were held under the (British hand-me-down) Emergency Regulations on suspicion of mutiny, and their whereabouts were unknown. After all efforts to locate the two men failed, Max applied to the High Court, stating that unless the authorities enabled him to meet with his clients, suspicions may arise that they were murdered. He was soon allowed to see the men, and they were released. Meridor later became Minister of Economics in the Likud government.

Epilogue

WHAT MIGHT HAVE BEEN

In order to understand and appreciate a person, it is essential for one to become acquainted with the nature of the society in which the person in question lived and functioned. The majority of pioneers who settled in Palestine from the late 1800's to the emergence of the State of Israel came from Russia and eastern Europe[1]. This was true after statehood as well, with the additional influx of great numbers of people from the Arabic-speaking countries of the Mediterranean basin. English-speaking immigrants (*Anglos*, in Israeli parlance) were always distinctly in the minority, and viewed as outsiders by a majority of the population. A brilliant statesman like Abba Eban, for example, had, in spite of his abilities and great potential, definite limits as to how high he could climb in the Israeli political hierarchy. This was also true in the case of Max Seligman. No one could deny either man's ability or achievements, or those of other *Anglos* like them (and there are quite a few—Moshe Arens and Benyamin Netanyahu are names that come to mind.) Yet there were always limitations and discouragements with which such people had to contend. A lifelong friend of Seligman's, Phil Hyams[2], recently reminisced:

> Max was full of fun, and I believe if he had taken life a bit more seriously, he would have been a very great figure in Israeli history. I have to tell you that his talents were never used to their full extent—his legal talent, how he was able to get along with people. I think they should have accepted the man as he was, and he would have done a good job, like all the work he did. I think the government officials made a terrible mistake by not getting Max involved. But they resented his being in the opposition. If Mapai could overlook that, he would have been a judge, perhaps at the head of the Justice Department, but he was in the wrong party at the wrong time. That was his punishment. He believed in what he believed, he was a very honest man, but was not a political person, and never deviated from the General Zionist path.

In the context of the *milieu* in which Max Seligman lived in Palestine and Israel from 1921 on, it is plain to see how he could not avoid being perceived as an elitist, and being resented as such by a great number of people who did'nt really know him. The Middle East is prone to legends, hyperbole and larger-than-life personalities. The legends grow and persist, especially if the individuals who are their subject encourage this aura. To his credit, it must be said that the only publicity Seligman ever sought was for the causes in whose service he labored. He thus gained notoriety as "The Terrorists' Lawyer", while personally, though richly deserving of a hero's mantle, he remained little known. Human nature as expressed in public opinion is unforgiving, and allows for few winners. Given that even the most adored public figures get carried away by the adulation of the masses, soon become corrupted by power, and lose touch with reality, it is not surprising that the person who could do no wrong, can suddenly do nothing right. Old enemies, ever on the lookout to settle political accounts, mercilessly exploit every opportunity to do harm. Seligman was once considered for the Consulship of Israel in New York (an Ambassadorship in Washington would have been far more appropriate for his talents, mercurial personality and connections, the better to serve the state). But someone with a grudge against him had his name removed from the list of candidates.

Max Seligman was the quintessential moderate: a General Zionist all his life, he disliked extremism and abhorred all violence. He believed in moderation as the best of all solutions for political problems, as exemplified in an article he wrote in 1938, in which he advocated Dominion status for Palestine:

> The argument which should influence the Arabs to agree (to a British Dominion in Palestine) is the same which should persuade the all-too-eager champions of independent Jewish Statehood to curb their ambitions and to take a more realistic view of the matter. The time has long gone by when small nations could prosper in times of peace and when they had a reasonable chance of holding their own against aggression . . . the real proof of statesmanship for a small nation lies in the kind of alinement which it is able to secure.

Above all, Max was a kind and considerate man. For many

years after he came to Palestine, he would send a crate of Jaffa oranges at Christmastime to his old Headmaster at the Wood Street School which he attended as a boy in Cardiff. As for me, I will never forget the generosity, care and consideration he gave me in my youth.

Only a fool could believe all great people are flawless. Seligman represented a group of British investors in Israel. The consortium was accused of under-reporting its income. Max decided to shoulder the responsibility of defending the case on his own. He was set upon by the revenue department with a zeal that bordered on the vindictive, and was severely penalized.

In 1982, when Seligman was eighty, he and Millie were passengers in a car driven by a friend in Tel Aviv. The car was struck from behind, and Max suffered a concussion. Although he claimed to be alright, he apparently suffered some brain damage, as he became very forgetful after the accident. His memory declined steadily, and in addition he was ravaged by arteriosclerosis. Daughter Sheila wrote about his last days:

> We used to go and visit him in the geriatric nursing home, and watched him disintegrate during the six months he was there. You feel so helpless, you can't do a thing, and you can't take him home and look after him either, as he needed watching around the clock. Time meant nothing to him and he would wander (while he could still walk) at all hours. There is absolutely no dignity in that kind of old age, and I wouldn't want it, for sure.

In 1987 he contracted pneumonia, which led to cardiac arrest. He was eighty five when he died in London, with his family at his bedside.

NOTES TO EPILOGUE

1. Although far fewer immigrants came from Germany and central Europe, they exerted a disproportionate cultural influence.
2. In March, 1989, a multi-media facility was dedicated at Ben Gurion University at Sde Boker in the Negev. The newly-opened adjunct to the English as a Foreign Language Department was endowed by Phil Hyams and his son Norman Hyams of London, in memory of their friend Max Seligman.

Tributes

BEGIN ON SELIGMAN

In the preface to Yitzchak Gurion's book *Prakliteihem Shel Lochamei Cherut* (Freedom Fighters' Advocates), Menachem Begin wrote:

Max Seligman's name is inextricably woven with the saga of our War of Independence. More than just a defender of underground fighters, he was a fighter in his own right. He had come to know the British jail from within, when in the fateful 'thirties, he helped Jews come to Eretz Israel without His Majesty's kind permission . . . In the 'forties, the offices of Seligman and Co., with his chief assistant Max Kritzman, were open at all times to every soldier in need. In time, those fleeing the British became the pursuers, and in this they were justified, morally and militarily. But the British, who kept in our little country a giant force of over one hundred thousand soldiers and police, did not stop, until the very end, their efforts to suppress the Hebrew rebellion. Prisons and detention camps were thus filled with our fighters, and there were many military trials, and the gallows were used.

Max Seligman stood by those whose lives were sought by the British. He never feared being linked to the underground. Quite the contrary: he was proud to identify morally with the fighters and their just aims. Some of the greatest sagas of the War for National Liberation are linked with Max Seligman's name. In particular, the work of our friends Seligman and Kritzman shone in their efforts to save Dov Gruner and his comrades, a struggle that tugged at the heartsrings of Jew and gentile the world over. During the period of the Underground, the British courts too became a battleground; when we recall those times we again give thanks to our friend Max.

THE JERUSALEM POST
9 September, 1987
Shamir Saddened by Death of Max Seligman

Prime Minister Shamir expressed his deep sorrow Wednesday night over the death that day in London of attorney Max Seligman, whom he described as "the loyal attorney of the detained underground members during the British Mandate."

A personal friend of Ze'ev Jabotinsky, Seligman was jailed for four months in 1939 for his activities on behalf of Aliya Bet.

Shamir said Seligman "In his own way, using his own methods, without fear or awe, and with total identification, he put himself at the service of the fighting underground movements." Seligman was in direct contact with Ya'ir Stern[1], the commander of the Lechi movement, and I was also in contact with him via emissaries, Shamir said.

"I will never forget," the premier said, "how Seligman brought regards for those exiled in Eritrea from the families and the homeland for which we fought. A place of honour in the pantheon of Israel's freedom fighters is reserved for attorney Max Seligman."

Kritzman on Seligman

He was such a different man. We were together for forty years. I met him on 1 January, 1940. I was his associate, his partner, his close friend. It's a great fortune for a man to find such a teacher, such a partner and such a friend.

No one ever thanked him—perhaps because he never became a *member* of the underground. Perhaps because he never expected thanks for devoting a large part of his life, many long years, to the fighters of Etzel and the underground, and never for gain. His entire life, in the 'forties and until the State came into being, was a saga of defending the freedom fighters, and caring for them in prison and in exile, and looking after their families. This was devotion and sacrifice in the fullest sense.

Max was a superb lawyer, possessed of all those qualities needed to win over people and gain their confidence. A product of British scholarship, he was poised and well versed in courtly conduct. He was charming and possessed of a keen sense of humor. A true *bon vivant*, he appreciated fine food and drink, and women found him irresistible. He could have easily opted for a money-making law practice, but his heart was elsewhere. His partners would berate him for undertaking the defense of penniless underground fighters, who had no institutions or property to finance their court cases. One partner even left for this very reason, to join another, profit-oriented firm.

I was a mere youngster beginning my career, but after I became a junior partner, I asked Max: how was our practice to continue, not to mention prosper and grow, if we spend all our energy and time on underground fighters and their families?

Seligman, not a man given to lofty phrases, but one who tended rather to humor and irony in his manner, assumed a serious mien and replied: "The practice will survive, but the underground fighters and their families are my first priority. I must fight for them, but will not force anyone else to do so." His heart and soul were with them, and there was nothing he wouldn't do for the fighters. This did not mean, however, that he identified politically with their methods, and therein lies a dichotomy: Max was a peaceful, pleasant person. He abhorred all manner of violence and bloodshed. His upbringing and training as well as his personal outlook placed him in the political midstream, and he was a faithful General Zionist, whose path was that of moderation. Yet he devoted himself totally to the reduction of his client's sentences, and to the mobilization of all means for saving those condemned from the hangman's noose.

Max Seligman was above all else a kind, forgiving man. There can be not the slightest doubt that he wholly identified with the desire to establish a Jewish state. He came to Palestine in 1921, when he was 19 years old and aflame with Zionist zeal—in spite of his parents' reservations. He firmly believed, during the first few years, that Britain had a bond of faith with Zionism, and that she would fulfill her promise as given in the Balfour Declaration. When he realized the bitter truth, he felt as though he was personally betrayed. That may have driven him to identify with the underground fighters. He felt for those boys, and for a man like Seligman, that was reason enough to do what he did.

Eventually our offices became the underground and fighters' address, their safety beacon, the link with their families, and occasionally their "bank", whose meager resources funded their defense, and aided their families in need. It got to a point where Seligman once warned some of the Etzel fighters: "In case you are unlucky enough to get caught, don't come right out and say you want a meeting with Seligman or Kritzman. That would be like an admission of guilt . . ."

For many years Seligman defended the underground fighters. He was the central figure in countless trials. Thus he was involved in the trial of Stavsky, Achime'ir and Rosenblatt, accused in the Arlosoroff murder. So he had been in the trial of the twenty Etzel members caught with arms. And so he had been in Dov Gruner's trial, when he flew to London to fight for Gruner's life before the Privy Council, relying on the High Commissioner's word not to order Gruner's hanging until after the discussions in London were concluded—only to be thunderstruck when that promise was cynically broken. And so in tens, perhaps hundreds of struggles to improve conditions for the fighters incarcerated in British prisons and camps.

Max himself served four months in prison when he was found guilty of bribing a British officer to help bring in illegal immigrants. After his release, he bewailed the terrible conditions in prison: "I was given a bed and mattress," he said, "while the fighters slept on the floor, and it hurt me terribly." His personal ordeal strengthened his resolve to help the boys in prison at all costs.

The underground fighters were harassed by the institutes of the Yishuv and by their military arm, the Hagana. This, too, bothered Max Seligman. When an Etzel member in prison pointed to a disfiguring scar on his face and told him it was "Jewish work", Seligman averted his gaze and murmured: "This can't be true, it can't be true . . . this is terrible." It follows that those who stood by the men of Etzel and Lechi could not expect their persecutors, later to become the leaders of the young state, to treat them kindly. Seligman's day was over when the state came into being. Now he had to pay for his deviation. He was never employed by the government or by a Histadrut branch. He who turned his back on the organized Yishuv was not to be forgiven. Once, in the 'fifties, he was being considered as a candidate for the General Consulship in New York, until someone heard of the "plot", and Max's name was quietly removed from the list of candidates. The learned, brilliant Max Seligman, who deflated the arrogance of British judges, now made room for another generation of lawyers, some of whom would ask ironically: "Max who?"

He died a poor man, with members of his family around him, in England. One thing bothers me: that perhaps nature, or God, stopped making this model[2].

When Max Seligman died in London in 1987, his widow Millie asked her sister Lilian Cornfeld in Tel-Aviv to dispose of the belongings which were left in their apartment. Lilian told me that among other things, there were thirty seven (!) medals in a cabinet. For a man who never served in the military, that is quite a collection. Writing in December of 1979 about his childhood friend, Joe Danovitch said:

In 1970 he was awarded a medal by the Israel Ministry of Defence for pre-State services. As Founder and past Grand Master of the Grand Lodge of Freemasons in Israel, he has travelled the world. He was the founder of and presently is the chairman of the Israel, Britain and

Commonwealth Association[3]. He would probably reckon as one of his proudest achievements the propagation for many years of good relations between Israel and Britain, for which he was made Commander of the British Empire by Her Majesty the Queen. He is a Vice-President of the Tel Aviv Commercial and Industrial Club. Still fondly attached to Cardiff, Wales and Britain, he will telephone me on a Sunday morning to ask me the result of the Cardiff City game the Saturday before.

And just now, his latest, and hopefully not his last, honour has just been bestowed on him. Although it has been said that a prophet has no honour in his own town, he has just been made, one of fourteen from a short list of twenty, a Distinguished Citizen of Tel Aviv. This honour was bestowed upon him at a ceremony at the Habimah Theatre by Mayor Lahat in the presence of a capacity gathering. Approaching the age of 77, until 120, he is erect and alert, a gargantuan eater with an enviable absence of fat, an extrovert, a raconteur with a mordant wit, a hedonist with a healthy philosophy that money earned is made to be enjoyed. Max strides on.'

NOTES TO TRIBUTES

1. "Ya'ir" was the code-name used by Avraham Stern.

2. As Max Seligman became increasingly involved with Freemasonry and commercial pursuits (and proportionately less with his law practice), he handed the reins of the law offices to his senior partner, Max Kritzman. In the September, 1972 issue of *The Jewish Herald*, Kritzman was interviewed in connection with his defense of Kozo Okamoto. Okamoto was one of the perpetrators of the massacre at Ben Gurion Airport earlier that year. His accomplices were killed by security forces; Okamoto was tried and given a life sentence. The interviewer's first question to Kritzman was, "Why, Mr. Kritzman? How could you (as a defender of the heroes of the Irgun and Lechi in the days of the British Mandate) accept such a task?" After stating his reasons for accepting the defense of the Japanese killer, the interview went on to deal at length with matters in which he and Seligman had been intimately involved, trying cases before the British Military Courts. It is strange, in view of the rhapsodic eulogy Kritzman delivered on Seligman's death, that during the entire interview, Seligman was never mentioned.

3. Successor to the Jewish Dominion of Palestine League.

Appendices

AVSHALOM HAVIV'S ADDRESS

Officers of the occupation army:

You were unable to prevent the breaching of the Palestinian Bastille, Acre Prison, but you won a "great victory" over a number of helpless prisoners and the three of us. After we ran out of ammunition, your soldiers were able to satisfy their feelings of inferiority and vent their sadism on us. In the best Nazi tradition, they shot wounded men lying on the ground, and prevented their getting medical attention for hours. I too was tortured, threatened with death, had a rope tied around my neck, and was beaten all over my body with rifle butts. When I fell unconscious, I was doused with urine mixed with my blood and sand. I am not complaining about myself, but the world should know what British beasts are doing in our country . . . in Ireland, a small, civilized country, you've imposed your rule using the same tactics of brute force and deceit. There too you set one part of the nation against another, and tried to drown the uprising against you in rivers of blood. You erected gallows and murdered in the streets, bullied people and exiled them, thinking you'd break the spirit of the free Irish, the spirit of resistance that is God's gift to every free man worthy of the name. But you were wrong. Free Ireland has risen.

You have cold-bloodedly shot men taken prisoner. Killing prisoners of war is a crime. Irishmen taking up arms are doing what Englishmen would do if their country were invaded by the Germans . . . those Irishmen executed will join the martyrs who came before them, the martyrs of Poland, Serbia and Belgium. There is nothing on heaven or earth to prevent that.

Not only do you tyrants not know any history; you don't know the human heart. You think you can rule free men against their will with great armies and intrigues. No, no: you are wrong. Intrigues cannot last against the spirit of free men, which can do wonders, and break bayonets. You cannot murder that spirit. You must be wondering: what happened with these Jews, whom you considered cowards, who for generations were the victims of slaughter, and who have now risen against your rule, are fighting your armies, and when in the shadow of death—show contempt? Two things have molded our generation: our land and the holocaust. It is our land that renewed us, gave us muscle and put courage in our hearts and belief in our future. It has given back to us the fighting tradition of past generations—the heroic saga of the Maccabess and Bar Kochba. And the unprecedented holocaust taught us that to remain slaves would doom us all. It has removed all fear from our hearts. It taught us that unless we took our fate into our own hands, we'll perish. If we don't fight—we'll be destroyed. You British tyrants will never understand a free man's spirit, facing death—as did Gruner and his comrades—with a song in their loving and believing hearts. And this, too, you will probably not understand: that I, a young Hebrew man facing the threat of murder, will turn my heart to my God in heaven and give thanks and praise that I have been privileged to suffer for my land and nation, and say with all my being: Blessed be the Lord that has kept us and brought us to this day.

ME'IR NACKAR'S ADDRESS

British officers:

As we face you, we ask ourselves: who are we facing? You call yourselves judges. But we know that you are not judges, you are officers of a foreign army of occupation, that has taken by force the land of another nation and holds it for your own purposes in a grip of cruel subjugation. But that is not the whole answer. Because the question is not addressed to you alone, but to those who sent you, who have made you into the judges of the free people of this country: what is this power? Your Members of Parliament have claimed there is one way to subdue the Hebrew rebellion: to erect gallows in the Holy Land, to murder Hebrew prisoners of war, and you have done it, you have committed one of the basest crimes, you murdered prisoners of war! And what did you gain? Have you frightened anyone? The fire of rebellion is spreading in the land and outside it. And you have brought down on yourselves the contempt of the world by murdering prisoners, something that everywhere has always been considered a crime against humanity. But this crime also has not helped your government, whose bankruptcy is total. You had better draw the conclusions: it is time you left this country, which is ours. Your rulers take offence when they are compared to Nazis. If Hebrew youths in New York draw swastikas on your flag, your newspapers make a fuss about it. But think for a moment: can you really cleanse your flag?

YA'AKOV WEISS' ADDRESS

Officers of the army of occupation:

I cannot begin before mentioning the barbaric treatment of

prisoners that I have seen after falling into your hands. Ashbal, Amrani, Brenner, Moskowitz, Shmuckler and others were shot at close range with dozens of bullets, although they were unarmed and no longer attackers, but prisoners. Your soldiers did not shoot well, apparently, and many of the wounded were brought alive and bleeding into the police courtyard. They were dumped on the ground—not on stretchers—and their blood flowed like water for six hours, while dozens of animals stood around them, hands in their pockets. That is how Ashbal, Amrani, Brenner, Bando and Nissim Levi died. We cannot match your sadism or torture of prisoners, but you will pay for this . . . we do not accept your authority to try us . . . everything you are doing in this country is illegal.

Hear me well, British officers, and tell those who sent you, who are blind to the great warning being written on the wall. Tell them that a new generation has risen in Israel. A life-loving generation, one that values freedom over life, a generation that will wipe out the Nazo-British tyranny and win freedom—even at the cost of life. The nation of Israel lives, and the kingdom of Israel will rise.

YA'AKOV WEISS' LAST LETTER TO HIS SISTER EDITH

Dear Edith:

I'm sorry I was not able to write you sooner. I'm sure you know why. I hope you got the letter I sent with one of the lawyers. You probably know that the English caught me with a machine-gun on May 4th in Acre. We liberated 38 boys, who were prisoners of the English. Unfortunately, we had to pay a high price for them. Nine men were killed, and we were caught after we ran out of ammunition and could no longer defend ourselves. Our trial began three weeks ago (on May 26th) before an English military court. The three of us did not defend ourselves and did not respond to the charges: we do not recognize their authority to judge us, and we demand to be treated as prisoners of war, as we are fighting for our liberty, for our nation's freedom against the oppressor.

What made me take this path? It would be hard to explain, because you're not familiar with the situation. Nevertheless, I'll try. I don't know if you're aware that during the German occupation, I was a member of the underground. We fought the Germans not only for our sake, but for yours, for the Jewish nation. The war we waged was limited, of course, but we did what we could for our people. We thought that the end of the war would bring us—who have suffered more than anyone else—the hoped-for peace. Ever since I came here I wanted to work, not fight, and build a home that you could come to, and in which we could forget the terrible past. Unfortunately, that didn't happen. Why? I thought that with Bergen-Belsen, we were through with the Nazis. But that is not how it happened. Here, I met an even more dangerous form of Nazism. Here, where we hope to ensure our future and that of hundreds of thousands of other people. While the Germans violated and murdered us in Europe, we were hoping for a place on earth where we could live in peace and honour, like other nations, and that could only be here in Eretz Israel. But what is the situation here? The English rule the country. They are driving away hundreds of thousands of our people from our land. They too are murdering and robbing, but more delicately. They do not destroy our bodies, although that too happens occasionally. But they want to destroy our future, the future of our nation. It is no longer a secret. We know there is only one way: to fight, for us, for you—you who are still in the diaspora—and for the future of our children. If we don't fight, we'll perish. If we fight, we'll win, because we have no other choice. We *must* win, or else we'll all perish, and with us, the future of our nation. That is what drove me to take up arms. I felt it was my duty to take part in this war. We are fighting this war for you, for me.

I am sure that, if our late mother were still alive, she would agree with my decision. Remember how proud she was to be Jewish, and how she despised those who bowed to the gentiles in any manner. My dear Edith, I cannot tell you how I felt when I took arms in my hands. I knew this was a war for our liberty and our future. There will no longer be a "dirty Jew", but a fighting Jew, who knows what he is fighting for. I forgot the feeling that any peasant could spit in my face. This is the only way I could wipe the spit. Those times have passed. Blow for blow, spit for spit, that is the only language the English understand. If they don't want to understand now, we'll make them understand. I realized of course that this was dangerous, but there are losses in every war. If we are to reach our destination—a sovereign Hebrew state—we must be prepared for sacrifices. The goal is worth all the sacrifices.

I knew I might lose my life, by a bullet or some other way. Still, I have no regrets; if I had to begin all over again, I would do the same. This knowledge gives me strength to face what is ahead. I think now you know why we refused to defend ourselves in court and why we could not accept the British officers' right to serve as judges in our country.

When I came to this land, I decided that never again would I be insulted for being a Jew. I kept this vow—and will keep it, come what may. I am not alone in this struggle. My comrades will continue until we achieve our goal. I am sure they'll do all they can to help us. A few days ago, two British policemen were kidnaped. Unfortunately, they were found. If they are unable to save us, I know at least that we'll be avenged. There are those who will continue the struggle and the war for independence.

As you can see, we are prepared for anything. Tomorrow morning, they'll announce the sentences. I am almost sure we'll get death. Still, nothing is certain. It's true that political prospects are looking good right now, but we must prepare also for the bad. We knew what we were fighting for and are ready for anything that may come our way. In any case, I'll try—come what may—to be what Mother would have expected of me. I know none of this is easy, for you especially, but if you consider what it is we're fighting for, it will ease your suffering, whatever becomes of me.

Dear Edith, in case we don't meet again—I hope this will not happen—be strong and proud of your Jewishness. Forget the bad things your brother has done. Forgive the pain I'm causing you. Remember me sometimes.

Wear my ring in good health. I wish you happiness. I hope the future compensates you for all you have suffered in the past. Remember always your loving brother. Give a kiss for me to Uncle Eli, Uncle Lajos and Eva. Tell Eva not to forget to be Jewish.

Your loving brother.

SELIGMAN'S LETTERS TO THE PRESS

MAX SELIGMAN INVARIABLY began his day with a perusal of several newspapers. He was an incredibly fast reader who could cover vast expanses of type in a very short time. It goes without saying that he seldom lacked for news items that outraged his deep-rooted sense of fair play. He would express his reaction in a direct and convincing manner. Seligman's responses when read through give the reader the gist of the item or subject matter that prompted his letter. When advancing a topic of his own, he outlines the subject matter concisely.

REPLY TO MRS. MOGANNAM

(The Palestine Post, December 18, 1936)

Sir,—May I be permitted a few observations on the letter from Mrs. Mogannam and the interview appended thereto which were published in your issue of the 13th.

Mrs. Mogannam might attract more sympathy to her cause if, instead of indulging in the platitudes and wild assertions which generally mark the claims of agitators, she would state some facts which are capable of verification.

In the first place, which is the Arab nation to which Mrs. Mogannam so imperiously refers? Is it the Iraqian nation, which does not claim Syria, or the Syrian nation, which does not lay claim to Iraq, or is it the Egyptian nation, which lays claim to neither Iraq nor Syria? Perhaps Mrs. Mogannam will be honest enough to admit that she means only the Arabs who actually reside in Palestine, and some of whom are Syrians or Iraqians or members of other Arab states.

Secondly, it would be interesting to learn why it is considered proper to present the Arab case to the Daily Express or in Hyde Park and undignified to do so to the Royal Commission. Is it because the Royal Commission is composed of persons who are able to differentiate between truth and hot air?

Mrs. Mogannam states that "even a child could understand that we (the Arabs) have the only claim to Palestine. We have been in this country for 1,400 years. Why should an alien race be brought into our country?" Who has been here for 1,400 years? Certainly not Mrs. Mogannam, and I challenge her to prove that 50 Arab families have resided here, not for 1,400 years, but for as little as 250 years. It may be true that different Arab tribes or individuals have been in and out of Palestine for many hundreds of years, but none of them settled here.

If there is one race in the world which cannot be classed as "alien", it is the Jewish race. That fact has been recognized not only by the British Empire, but by the entire civilized world, not excluding Arab nations and leaders. The Jews never ceased to identify themselves and their religion and national aspirations with Palestine, and that their love for the country is true is proved by the fact that they have not hesitated to lay down hundreds of lives and invest tens of millions of Pounds to rebuild the country laid waste by Turkish and Arab negligence and indifference.

And by the way, where were Mrs. Mogannam and her Arab friends when the Turks ruled over Palestine? Did they then claim Palestine as a separate state? Or were they not concerned with the Moslem oppression of the Christians, an oppression which might very easily revive today were it not for the fact that interested parties are setting both against the Jews?

So far as the proposal to convert Palestine into a Crown Colony is concerned, surely the Arabs should welcome it. They allege that their main fear is domination by the Jews. But a Crown Colony would ensure that there would be no such domination. Mrs. Mogannam knows as well as I do that all this talk of fear of Jewish domination is eyewash. It is not the Jews that the agitators want out of Palestine; it is the British. If only the British would leave the country, then a number of Mrs. Mogannam's friends, who would be considered very mediocre material in political life abroad (and I include such countries as Iraq for this purpose), might land some very high and lucrative posts in the government of the country.

At least its conversion to the status of a Crown Colony would ensure peace in Palestine, a condition which has hitherto been denied to it. Would it not be a great thing if Mrs. Mogannam and her friends could forget self and parties and think for once of Palestine and join in a genuine effort for the benefit of the country as a whole rather the aggrandizement of individuals and groups.

Yours faithfully,
Max Seligman

OBJECTIVE APPROACH NEEDED IN CRIMINAL INVESTIGATIONS
(Haboker, 10 July 1949)

Now that the sad Bernadotte affair is over, I beg your indulgence in allowing me to make the following remarks:

It would seem to me Israeli authorities could benefit from the Bernadotte case in order to avoid further failure and much embarrassment. I believe the investigations could have had entirely different results had they been conducted in a more objective and professional manner. The reasons for the failure to capture Bernadotte's killers are similar to those which resulted in failure to apprehend the murderers of the late Chaim Arlosoroff. I am personally acquainted with both cases.

It was weakness on the part of the authorities, who immediately suspected their political rivals of committing these crimes, and concentrated all their efforts in attempting to prove this. In other words, the investigations failed because they were influenced to a large degree by the desire to settle political accounts.

I remember when I was incarcerated in the Central Prison in Jerusalem in 1939, one of my first experiences there was meeting two

Arabs who freely admitted to all the other prisoners that they killed Arlosoroff, never knowing who their victim was. They described the tragedy in detail, as well as the manner in which they were duped into withdrawing their confessions. It was obvious to anyone who came into contact with them that they were the guilty parties. Were it not for some peoples' decision to try to fix the blame on the Revisionists, these killers could have been convicted of the crime. This view was confirmed in conversations I had on the matter with British police officers.

A very similar situation prevailed in the Bernadotte case, as became clear during the trial of Messrs. Friedman-Yellin and Shmuelevitz before the Military Court in Acre, where I appeared for the defendants. At that time the authorities, whether rightly or wrongly, held certain views about the Lechi movement. When news of Bernadotte's death became known, it was decided to fix the blame for it on Lechi, and all efforts were made in this direction. Lechi was outlawed, its camps liquidated, warehouses confiscated, and all officers and men and anyone known as or suspected of being a sympathiser of the movement were arrested. Normal police investigational routine was waived in this instance.

No appropriate search was made at the scene of the crime in order to discover leads. No witnesses were questioned as required, no attempt was made to find the vehicle used in the crime, and no identification line-up was made. Instead, a long military court procedure resulted in a clear vindication of the Lechi movement, showing it and its leaders had nothing whatever to do with Bernadotte's murder.

I wish to point out that the tendency to use such incidents as an excuse for settling political accounts has another potentially dangerous aspect: it is liable to encourage criminals to commit crimes for which innocent people will be blamed, while they go unpunished.

The lesson to be learned from these tragic events is that in future, investigations of crimes must be approached in an unbiased and purely juridical manner, in order to ensure their success and avoid false accusations.

Your truly,
Max Seligman

IRGUN AND STERN FIGHTERS
(The Jewish Chronicle, January 14, 1972)

Sir,—Gerald Kaufman appears to lose no opportunity to exploit your columns to vent his hate of Menachem Begin and the Irgun Zevai Leumi (Etzel) and the Stern Group (Lechi).

It might be inquired where Mr. Kaufman was when these two groups were fighting for the establishment of an independent Jewish state and for free Jewish immigration into Palestine and what part, if any, he played in that struggle.

Mr. Kaufman would be well advised to check his facts with circles outside Mapam. He implies that the activities of Etzel and Lechi were condemned by the Yishuv, which is quite untrue. They were condemned by the "leaders", but the Yishuv at large never concealed its sympathy. Had it been otherwise, Etzel and Lechi could not have survived for very long.

It was my proud privilege to be the legal adviser to the leaders of both groups and to many hundreds of the brave men and women who fought in their ranks, and I can testify to the cooperation and assistance which was extended by many (non-left) leaders of the Yishuv to these groups, including the Mayors of Tel Aviv, Ramat Gan, Petach Tikva and Netanya, as well as by prominent physicians who took great risks in giving medical help to those who were wounded in their battles with British troops or police.

Mr. Kaufman may be surprised to learn that many of the Etzel and Lechi troops were the sons and daughters of some of the most respected Jewish families in the Yishuv, that they all risked their lives and liberty voluntarily and did not have the benefits of uniforms, wages, decorations or even financial support for their dependents.

Why does Mr. Kaufman repeat the lie about the battle of Deir Yassin? He must surely know that the Government of Israel has long since published the truth of this episode, which only reflects credit on Etzel. Mr. Kaufman should be told that the Jewish State has demonstrated its pride in the courageous and glorious exploits of Etzel and Lechi and in their leaders by naming numerous settlements, streets, buildings and institutions all over Israel in their names. Moreover, all the surviving members of both groups have received decorations from the Government of Israel in recognition of the services which Mr. Kaufman now sees fit to condemn.

By the way, I am not aware that any British soldier, apart from the two sergeants, was hanged by Etzel or Lechi despite the tremendous provocation they suffered when British troops took Dov Gruner and three other heroes out of their prison cells secretly in the middle of the night and hanged them while a petition on their behalf was actually pending before the Judicial Committee of the Privy Council—a most shameful blot on British judicial history.

MAX SELIGMAN
24 Rambam Street, Tel Aviv

(The Light, December, 1973)

25 YEARS AGO IN THE TWILIGHT OF THE BRITISH PALESTINE MANDATE

Two Blots on British Judicial History

By Max Seligman*

Voices have recently been raised in England by certain politicians criticising the Government of Israel for its treatment of hostile elements in Israel. Quite apart from the fact that such criticism is unjustified by the facts, it is timely to recall some unpleasant aspects of the behaviour of the British Government in Palestine twenty-five years ago, from which it is not difficult for any unbiased person to make comparisons with the manner in which the Israel Government is behaving, comparisons which do not rebound to the credit of the British authorities. By way of illustration, I mention two matters in which I was personally involved as Counsel for the Jewish resistance movements.

In the years 1945 to 1948, under the orders of the British Government, *thousands* of Jewish men and women suspected of terrorist activities or sympathy were held for years in camps and prisons in Palestine without any trial or any charges or any right of appeal. Several hundred of them were deported to Eritrea, which for Palestinian citizens was foreign territory.

The right to deport Palestinian Jews to such territory was tested in a Habeas Corpus petition lodged by the undersigned in 1945 in the High Court in Jerusalem on behalf of Arie Ben Eliezer, who later became a most respected Deputy Speaker of Israel's Parliament, against the General Officer Commanding the Army in Palestine, representing the Commander in Chief, Middle East, and the Inspector General of Police in Palestine. That petition was rejected on the flimsy ground that the Court could not issue an order directed against an Eritrean authority, namely the British Military Governor who had made the detention order at the request of the British Authorities in Palestine. Thereupon, the matter was taken to the Judicial Committee of the Privy Council in London, where a petition for leave to appeal against that decision was heard by Lord Justices Thankerton and Du Parc. It was strenuously resisted by Counsel appearing on behalf of the Foreign Office.

At that time, the Foreign Office had assumed control of Palestine

*The author, a prominent Israeli attorney, was Counsel for the Jewish resistance movement, defending Dov Gruner, who was tried by the British Mandate Authorities and hanged.

matters, as the writer was informed by Mr. Creech-Jones, the then Colonial Secretary, at a meeting which I had with him in London. Mr. Creech-Jones told me that he was then helpless to assist in any matters relating to Palestine. Their Lordships, on the 11th April, 1946, in rejecting the arguments adduced on behalf of the Foreign Office, said that they could not conceive that the British Government would enter into an arrangement with a foreign government to detain a British subject and that they would subsequently be unable to demand the return of that subject. Therefore, they had no hesitation in granting leave to appeal. An Order-in-Council granting such leave was accordingly promulgated by the Privy Council on the 18th April, 1946.

Bergen-Belsen 'Salubrious' Says British Judge

When the appeal came on for hearing, there were some very strange developments. Firstly, Lord Justices Thankerton and Du Parc were not included as members of the Court. Secondly, before entering the Court, information reached the writer that the Attorney General had refused to appear, a most unusual course, the reason for which, according to rumour, was that he knew that some approach had been made to the Court behind the scenes. Another lawyer appeared in his stead to oppose the appeal. After a hearing lasting several days, during which it appeared that the Court could have no possible alternative other than to allow the appeal, a decision was given on the spot, after a deliberation in the presence of Counsel lasting only a few minutes, rejecting the appeal for the same flimsy reason as that which was given by the Court in Jerusalem.

In the course of the hearing, Mr. Patrick Devlin (later Lord Devlin), who appeared with me to conduct the appeal, asked the Court to consider what the position would be if Mr. Ernest Bevin (the Foreign Minister at the time) had entered into an arrangement with Herr Hitler to take a number of British Jews and put them into the concentration camp at Bergen-Belsen. Would Bevin be unable at a later date to demand their release? To this the President of the Court, Lord Wright, made the shocking observation that he had recently paid a visit to Bergen-Belsen and that he "found it a most salubrious place." This, be it noted, was less than one year after the end of the Second World War and the discovery that six million Jews had been murdered at Bergen-Belsen and other camps! When I rose to protest bitterly against Lord Wright's remarks, I was persuaded to refrain from doing so on the ground that it might annoy the President and influence the Court to rule against us. Fortunately, before the Privy Council announced its decision, Mr. Ben Eliezer made a spectacular escape from

Eritrea together with a number of other detainees and returned to Palestine after the failure of all efforts to recapture him by the British authorities in the various countries through which he had to travel on his perilous way back to Palestine.

How Dov Gruner Was Hanged

In the same year, 1946, a member of the Jewish resistance forces named Dov Gruner, who had fought as a volunteer in the British Army during World War Two, was captured in the course of a raid upon a police post in Ramat Gan, a suburb of Tel Aviv, and was sentenced to death by a Military Court in Jerusalem. Early in 1947 a petition for leave to appeal against that sentence, which also challenged the powers of Military Courts to try such cases, was submitted to the Judicial Committee of the Privy Council in London. The fact that the petition had been lodged was brought to the knowledge of the authorities in Palestine. Nevertheless, while that petition was pending, the security forces in Palestine, with the connivance and approval of the Government in London, and without giving any notice or any warning either to his family or to his legal advisers, one night took Gruner out of his cell and hanged him.

There was no known precedent in British judicial history for carrying out a death sentence while legal proceedings relating thereto were pending before the Courts, and the only possible reason for doing so was to attempt to strike terror into the ranks of the Irgun Zvai Leumi and the Stern Group, in which attempt, as history has demonstrated, the authorities not only failed miserably but actually spurred the resistance movements on to even greater efforts which contributed substantially to the termination of the British Mandate and the establishment of the State of Israel.

The Deir Yassin Incident

7th December, 1977

The Editor
The Daily Telegraph,
135 Fleet Street, LONDON.

Sir,

From Sir Ian Gilmour's letter (Dec.1) it is obvious that he has unquestionably accepted all the false propaganda of the P.L.O.

1. As for Deir Yassin, he ignores the fact that there was a battle which resulted also in heavy casualties to the forces of the Irgun Zvai Leumi. These were not caused by peashooters or water pistols.

2. He appears to be unaware of the Arab slaughter of the entire Jewish community in Hebron in 1929, nor of the murder of an entire convoy of doctors and nurses on their way to the Hospital on Mount Scopus, nor of the repeated murderous attacks on unarmed and helpless Jewish women and children.

3. As for the allegation that the Arab refugees were driven out of Palestine by the Israelis, perhaps Sir Ian would be frank enough to change his mind on perusing the following published Arab statements, viz:–

(a) On September 6, 1948, Emil Ghory, Secretary of the Palestine Arab Higher Committee, told the Beirut Daily Telegraph:

> "I do not want to impugn anyone but only to help the refugees . . . The fact that there are those refugees is the direct consequence of the action of the Arab states in opposing partition and the Jewish State. The Arab states agreed upon this policy unanimously."

(b) The Jordanian daily, Falastin, wrote on February 19, 1949:

> "The Arab states encouraged the Palestine Arabs to leave their homes temporarily in order to be out of the way of the Arab invasion armies . . ."

(c) Another Jordanian newspaper, Al-Urdan, wrote on April 9, 1953:

> "For the flight . . . it is our leaders who are responsible . . . they instilled fear and terror into the hearts of the Arabs of Palestine until they fled, leaving their homes and property to the enemy."

(d) A refugee told another Jordanian Daily, A-Difaa, on September 6, 1954:

> "The Arab governments told us: 'Get out so that we can get in.' So we got out, but they did not get in."

(e) Again in Falastin, on May 30, 1955:

> "We, the refugees, have the right to address the members of the Arab League Council and declare...we left our homeland on the strength of false promises by crooked leaders in the Arab states . . ."

Yours truly,
MAX SELIGMAN, C.B.E.

Sir,—I am shocked that Ben Azai, with whose views I am usually in agreement, should be a party to the canard that Deir Yassin was a shameful and unjustifiable act of terrorism. His observations in this connection are worthy of the likes of Mayhew. He relies upon a verdict by Dov Joseph, but Joseph was throughout an avowed enemy of the Irgun Zvai Leumi.

Ben Azai is apparently ignorant of the fact that the daily massacre by residents of Deir Yassin of helpless Jews travelling on the road to or from Jerusalem was the cause of the attack. Nor does he explain how a large number of casualties were inflicted upon the Irgun troops by innocent and unarmed inhabitants of Deir Yassin.

It would be only fair if Ben Azai were now to rely not only on the prejudiced views of Dov Joseph, but on the very reasoned findings of the Foreign Ministry of the Israeli Government.

Tel Aviv MAX SELIGMAN

The Jerusalem Post, July 4, 1978
THE ARLOSOROFF MURDER

Sir,—I would like to add the following information to the excellent article by Ian Black, "Murder on the Beach" (June 16).

In July 1939, I was an inmate of the Central Prison in Jerusalem after having been convicted on charges of conspiracy to organise "illegal" immigration into Palestine. Naturally, I immediately became the free legal adviser of many of the other inmates, all of whom contended they were absolutely innocent.

I met Abdul Majid and Issa Abras, who frankly admitted to me that they were the murderers of Chaim Arlosoroff. They told me that they had no idea of the identity of their victim and had not thought of killing anyone, but were merely intending to rob him. They complained that Arlosoroff shined a torch light at them when they asked *kama hasha'a?*" (What time is it?) and that Majid fired his revolver in a thoughtless reflex action. They were frightened and ran away immediately and sat on a bench in Rothschild Boulevard for a few hours before proceeding to Jaffa.

They told me that they had agreed to admit their guilt after having been assured by one of the defence lawyers that they would not risk the death sentence because the killing was unpremeditated and they were in any event undergoing a life sentence for another murder. They said that they had withdrawn their admission of guilt after a police officer visited them in the prison and warned them that they might otherwise be sentenced to death.

After my release from prison, I addressed a public meeting in Tel Aviv on prison conditions and in the course thereof, I related all the facts stated above. A C.I.D. officer (Sergeant Stewart) was present during the lecture and took notes of all I said. After the meeting, he told me that all I had stated was correct.

By the way, it was common knowledge that, in her first statement to the police, Mrs. Sima Arlosoroff stated that the murderers were Arabs and that statement subsequently disappeared mysteriously from the police file.

I would add that both Yehuda Arazi and Behor Shitrit, who participated in the police investigation of the crime, told me that they knew that Stavsky was innocent. Shitrit, who publicly kissed Stavsky immediately on his acquittal by the Court of Appeals, told me that he intended to reveal the truth. Unfortunately, he died before he could do so.

Tel Aviv MAX SELIGMAN

The Editor,
Daily Telegraph August 17th, 1982
London.

Sir,

All the reports by Hugh Davies from Jerusalem have been slanted against Israel, but his article on Mr. Begin in your issue of the 13th August is insulting and replete with allegations which are false.

Mr. Begin did not desert from the Polish army but was honourably discharged. He was appointed to succeed David Raziel as leader of the Irgun Zvai Leumi when Raziel was killed in Iraq while he was on voluntary service with the British Army.

As for the attack on the King David Hotel, I can personally testify to the fact that warnings were given in good time. There was no denial of the fact that there were warnings, but the Chief Secretary stated that he would not accept orders from the Irgun and discouraged officials from leaving the Hotel.

Not three but four members of the Irgun and the Stern Group were hanged in the middle of the night without any warning to them or to their families, or to me as the lawyer acting on their behalf. The threat to hang two soldiers in revenge was made in the event that the sentences of death would not be commuted. There was no demand for their (the British soldiers) release. Ernest Bevin refused to consider the pleas on their behalf, knowing full well that his refusal would result in the hanging of the two sergeants. It was generally rumoured that in this matter he was advised by Christopher Mayhew. Moreover, the hanging of the four (Jewish) prisoners was carried out while a petition on my instructions was pending before the Judicial Committee of the Privy Council for leave to appeal against the judgment of the Military Court. There was no precedent for this in British judicial history.

Yours truly,
MAX SELIGMAN

MAX KRITZMAN

Max Kritzman was born in Chicago in 1915. His parents were active in the Jewish community there, and their home was both religious and Zionist. In 1921, when Max was six years old, the Kritzmans came to Palestine, settling in Rehovoth. Kritzman's father first tried his hand at agriculture, later moving to Tel-Aviv. The boy was enrolled in the *Tachkemoni* national-religious school, and after graduation attended teacher's seminary.

Two of Max Kritzman's teachers at *Tachkemoni* left their mark on the young man: The late Rabbi Mordechai Raziel (father of David Raziel, commander in chief of the Irgun) inculcated in him the national spirit, and Moshe Zilberg, who later became a Supreme Court justice and theoritician in Israel. His classmates included some of the main leaders-to-be of the underground: David Raziel, Aryeh ben Eliezer, Benyamin Ziv'oni, and others.

When he was thirteen, Kritzman joined Beitar and passed the leaders course. He attended the Hebrew University in Jerusalem, under Professor Joseph Klausner, and studied law in London. To supplement his income, he gave Hebrew lessons, and in 1940 passed the Bar. When war broke out, Kritzman took advantage of his American passport and left England for the United States, but once enroute, changed his destination to Palestine, where he joined the law firm of Max Seligman & Co.

While on a speaking tour in the U.S.A., Seligman met with Congressman Emanuel Celler. Following their meeting, Seligman wrote Celler in an effort to obtain his partner's release from administrative detention in Palestine.

August 29th, 1947

The Honorable Emanuel Celler,
17th Floor, 1450 Broadway,
NEW YORK CITY.

Dear Mr. Celler,

I am very grateful for your kindness in agreeing to make representations in connection with the detention in Palestine of Mr. Max Kritzman.

Mr. Kritzman is an American citizen. He was born in Chicago and received his law education in Palestine and London, being a member of both the English and Palestine Bars. He is married. At least one of his brothers served in the United States Army during the last World War. He has been employed in my law firm (M. Seligman & Co., Tel Aviv and Haifa) for the past six years. During that period, he has been particularly engaged in the criminal section of my practice. In the course thereof he has had to defend or assist in the defence of numerous men and women alleged to be members of the Irgun Zvai Leumi or in efforts to effect the release of many persons arrested merely on suspicion and kept in detention camps.

In March 1944 Kritzman became involved in an argument with a British Police (C.I.D.) officer. The argument took place in the Tel Aviv Law Courts, when Kritzman told the officer that, if British Police Officers murdered Jews in cold blood, they must naturally expect reprisals. A few days later, Kritzman was arrested, and after being kept for two days in a filthy lock-up in Jaffa, he was transferred to the Detention Camp at Latrun under an order by the Military Commander for his detention for a period of one year. Representations by the American Consul and other parties were met with the reply that he was held on information which could not be revealed. As Kritzman informed me at the time of his argument with the C.I.D. officer, I was able to challenge the C.I.D. authorities regarding the nature of the information on the basis of which he was arrested. As a result, he was released within a few days.

In October, 1944, following upon the assassination of Lord Moyne in Cairo, a large number of Jews were arrested in Palestine and taken to the Latrun Detention Camp. Kritzman was included. I was in London at the time, and a cable was sent to me informing me of the fact. The C.I.D. held up the cable for nearly four weeks. When it reached me, I immediately contacted a number of members of the House of Commons and the House of Lords, and they all very kindly intervened with various departments of the Government in London. It was obvious that Kritzman was being treated in this way only because of the professional assistance which he had very properly rendered as a lawyer, and leading lawyers in England, who were also Members of Parliament, deeply resented the fact. Questions were asked in Parliament and lengthy correspondence ensued between the Colonial Office and the Palestine Administration. The matter dragged on for about three months, and Kritzman was then released as a result of particular pressure being brought to bear by Lord Strabolgi, who threatened to introduce a motion for debate in the House of Lords.

Since he was released in the early part of 1945, Kritzman has suffered no further molestation at the hands of the Palestine Police authorities, and he has continued to render legal assistance to members of the underground movements.

At the beginning of this month, as you are aware, the Mayors of Tel Aviv and other Jewish towns together with a large number of other persons were arrested—allegedly as being implicated in the resistance movement and/or the hanging of the two British sergeants—and have been detained ever since in the Latrun Detention Camp. Kritzman was included among these, and my office has telephoned and cabled me to take such steps as are possible over here to procure his release.

He is not charged with any offense. He is unable to appeal to any court of law or other tribunal and has no opportunity to establish his innocence of any charge which the police may allege to have on their files but which cannot be revealed. He is not a member of any underground organization. So far as I am aware, he is the only American citizen included among those who were arrested and are now being held in the Detention Camp at Latrun. His enforced absence from my office, particularly at present when I am away from Palestine on a public mission, is only calculated to cause him and my practice very considerable financial harm.

I trust that your efforts in the matter will be attended with speedy success, and I tender grateful thanks in anticipation.

Yours sincerely,
MAX SELIGMAN

Sources And Bibliography

ENCYLOPAEDIA BRITANNICA (New York, Funk & Wagnalls, 1954)

ENCYCLOPAEDIA HEBRAICA (Jerusalem, Encyclopaedia Publishing Co., 1957)

ENCYCLOPAEDIA JUDAICA (Jerusalem, Keter Publishing House, 1972)

GURION, YITZCHAK: PRAKLITEIHEM SHEL LOCHAMEI HERUT (Tel Aviv, Jabotinsky Institute, 1973)

NIV, DAVID: MA'ARCHOT HA'IRGUN HATZEVA'I HALE'UMI (Tel Aviv, Hadar Publishing Co., 1984)

O'BRIEN, CONOR CRUISE: THE SIEGE (New York, Simon & Schuster, 1986)

PUBLIC RECORDS OFFICE, LONDON

SELIGMAN, MAX (1902-1987): "ILLEGAL" IMMIGRATION; ARTICLES & LETTERS in various dailies and publications (see under Newspapers & Periodicals)

TUCHMAN, BARBARA: BIBLE AND SWORD (New York, N.Y. University, 1956)

WYMAN, DAVID: THE ABANDONMENT OF THE JEWS (New York, Pantheon Books, 1984)

NEWSPAPERS & PERIODICALS:

ANSWER (New York) 4/16/47

L'AURORE (Tel Aviv?) 7/20/39

LA BOURSE EGYPTIENNE (Cairo) 7/26/38

CAJEX (Toronto) 5/3/47

THE DAILY TELEGRAPH (London) 8/17/82

DAVAR (Tel Aviv) 10/19/38, 7/11/39

THE DAY (New York) 5/23/47

HA'ARETZ (Tel Aviv) 11/7/36, 1938: 6/14–15–20, 10/2–18, 11/3–9, 1939: 3/20, 4/14–17–18, 5/31, 9/8/40, 1941: 2/17, 9/10, 12/22, 1942: 6/8, 11/29, 12/25, 4/27/82

HABOKER (Tel Aviv) 9/15/38, 6/5/39, 1940: 11/6–14, 1941: 1/31, 9/14–17, 11/18, 12/25, 1942: 1/11, 2/22, 6/16, 11/12–22–25,

12/6–25–27, 1943: 1/1–8–10, 2/3–23, 3/14–29, 4/4–18, 9/6/44, 1947: 11/6–11, 7/10/49

HASHA'A (Tel Aviv) 10/14/40

HASHACHAR (Tel Aviv) 10/15/40

HAMASHKIF (Tel Aviv) 1939: 3/30, 11/12, 1947: 4/17, 11/11

HATZOFEH (Tel Aviv) 2/8/42

HAYOM (Tel Aviv) 3/14/39

HERUT (Tel Aviv) 4/15/64

ITON MEYUCHAD (Tel Aviv) 10/10/41, 2/8/44

ISRAEL, BRITAIN AND THE COMMONWEALTH ASSOCIATION (Newsletter, 11/87)

IVRI ANOCHI [Onouchi] (London?) 10/25, 12/1/25, 5/1/26

THE JERUSALEM POST (Jerusalem) 7/4/78, 6/19/80, 9/9/87

THE JEWISH CHRONICLE (London) 12/25, 1926: 3/12, 6/28, 2/7/38, 8/18/39, 4/5/40, 1945: 2/2, 3/9–16, 5/11/45, 1/14/72

THE JEWISH STANDARD (London) 1/26/43, 12/11/44, 3/9/45

LE JOURNAL D'ORIENT (Cairo) 10/25/38

MA'ARIV (Tel Aviv) 11/17/78, 1987: 9/10–11

THE MANCHESTER GUARDIAN (Manchester) 2/8/39

THE NEW YORK POST (New York) 6/13/47

P.M. (New York) 4/17/47

THE PALESTINE POST (Jerusalem) 12/14/36, 1938: 3/11, 10/4, 1942: 2/2, 12/10, 1943: 1/10, 3/2–14, 4/18, 5/23, 1944: 9/5, 10/27

THE PALESTINE WEEKLY (Jerusalem) 6/11/26

REUTERS NEWS SERVICE (International) 1938: 2/2–7, 6/6/39

SOUTH WALES ECHO (Cardiff) 2/2/38

LA TRIBUNE JUIVE (Jerusalem?) 10/18/38

THE WESTERN MAIL (Cardiff) 5/14/30

YEDIOT ACHRONOT (Tel Aviv) 9/22/44

Chronology Of Events

1798 – Napoleon conquers Egypt, advances north to Acre.
1838 – First British Vice-Consul appointed to Jerusalem.
1840 – Beirut bombarded by British Navy.
1864 – Palestine Exploration Fund begins survey of Jerusalem and vicinity.
1869 – Opening of the Suez Canal.
1876 – Suez Canal acquired by Britain.
1878 – The Cyprus Convention. Britain gains control over island.
1896 – Theodor Herzl publishes *Der Judenstaat*.
1897 – First Zionist Congress at Basle, Switzerland.
1898 – Herzl meets Kaiser Wilhelm II in Palestine.
1902 – Prime Minister Joseph Chamberlain proposes settling Jews in the Sinai.
1903 – Pogrom in Kishinev, the worst to date. The Uganda Scheme for settling Jews in East Africa.
1904 – Aliens Bill passed, designed to keep Jewish refugees out of England. Herzl dies.
1914 – World War I begins.
1917 – The Balfour Declaration.
1918 – War ends. Anglo-French Joint Declaration.
1919 – Arab attacks on Jews in Palestine.
1920 – League of Nations Mandate over Palestine given to Britain. Ratified at San Remo Conference.
1921 – Seligman comes to Palestine. Arab riots and temporary suspension of Jewish immigration. Second wave of Arab attacks on Jews. White paper creating Trans-Jordan.
1922 – Colonial Secretary Churchill separates over 70% of Palestine, designating it Trans-Jordan.
1925 – Seligman marries Mildred Kert in Montreal, 18 June. Joins Potash Co. as secretary.
1926 – Daughter Aura born in Jerusalem, 11 November.

1928 – Sir Josiah Wedgwood publishes *The Seventh Dominion*. League bearing same name founded.
1929 – The Hebron and Safed massacres. Wall Street crash.
1930 – Seligman passes Bar in Jerusalem.
1931 – Seligman sent as delegate to Zionist Congress in Basle. *Hagana Le'umit* (National Defense), forerunner of the Irgun founded, commanded by Avraham Tehomi (code name: Gideon).
1932 – Second daughter Sheila born in Jerusalem, 11 July.
1933 – Seligman opens offices in Tel Aviv and Haifa. Hitler becomes Chancellor of Germany.
1934 – First shipload of illegal immigrants arrives in Palestine.
1935 – Seligman founds Sharon Masonic Lodge in Tel Aviv.
1936 – "Arab Rebellion" begins 19 April. Hagana retaliates with punitive actions against known Arab offenders. Seligman establishes Crown Colony and Dominion Association.
1937 – Peel Commission recommends Partition. Irgun goes on the offensive, under the command of Robert Bitker.
1938 – "Peace in Our Time"—Neville Chamberlain capitulates to Hitler; Germany occupies Sudetenland. First Irgun member Shlomo Ben Yosef hanged.
1939 – Germany occupies Czechoslovakia. White Paper scraps Partition, openly favors Arab rule in Palestine. Seligman begins serving four month sentence 7 July. War begins 3 September. Seligman volunteers for active duty. Released on 7 November, wins against prohibition to practice law.
1940 – Irgun suspends offensive operations for duration of war.
1941 – Ya'akov Meridor assumes command of Irgun following death of David Raziel.
1942 – Worst rumors about Holocaust confirmed.
1944 – Avraham Stern (code name (Ya'ir) assumes command of Irgun. Breaks with Irgun to form Lechi (Fighters for the Freedom of Israel).
1945 – War in Europe ends. Under Menachem Begin's com-

mand, Irgun declares revolt against British occupation.

1946 – Civil disobedience (Tenu'at Hameri Ha'Ivri) in which Hagana cooperates with Irgun. Black Sabbath (29 June). C.I.D. headquarters in King David Hotel (Jerusalem) blown up 22 July. President Truman demands Britain admit 100,000 refugees into Palestine.

1947 – Britain admits failure of Mandate. SS *Exodus* returned to Europe with 4,500 refugees aboard. Irgun and Hagana join forces in battle against Arab attackers. Sergeants Marvin and Pace hanged by Irgun. U.N. General Assembly votes for creation of Jewish State 29 November. British announce withdrawal date. Arab attacks tolerated by British.

1948 – Arab attack on convoy of doctors and nurses enroute to hospital on Mt. Scopus. Irgun attack on Deir Yassin. State of Israel proclaimed 14 May, recognized by U.S.A. and U.S.S.R. Mandate terminated. Seven Arab armies attack Israel. First cease-fire 11–17 June. U.N. mediator Folke Bernadotte assassinated.

1949 – Britain (reluctantly) grants recognition to Israel. Second cease-fire, followed by armistice agreements with neighboring Arab states; others (Confrontation States) remain "at war" to the present. Jerusalem declared Eternal Capital of Israel.

1950 – Beginning of Operation Magic Carpet—the transfer of Jewish populations of Arab countries to Israel.

1951 – King Abdullah assassinated at el-Aqsa mosque in Jerusalem.

1953 – Seligman founds Grand Masonic Lodge of the State of Israel.

1954 – Gamal Abdel Nasser seizes power in Egypt.

1956 – Nasser nationalizes Suez Canal. Israel attacks, occupies Sinai.

1957 – I.D.F. withdraws from Sinai, replaced by U.N.E.F.

1960 – Seligman elected Master of Sharon Lodge (1960–62).

1964 – P.L.O. founded in Cairo

1967 – Six Day War, 5–11 June. Israeli occupation of all areas west of the Jordan River, held by Jordan since 1949, and of the Gaza Strip, formerly held by Egypt, and of the Golan Heights, formerly held by Syria.

1970 – Hijacking and blowing up of airliners by P.L.O. King Hussein ousts P.L.O. from Jordan. Anwar Sadat succeeds Nasser on latter's death. Seligman awarded medal by Ministry of Defense for pre-State services.

1972 – 11 Israeli athletes murdered by P.L.O. at Munich Olympics. Seligman elected Grand Master of Masonic Lodge.

1973 – The Yom Kippur War, 6–25 October.

1974 – Pistol-packing Arafat addresses U.N. General Assembly. U.N. loses what little credibility it had left.

1977 – Begin forms Likud government, invites Sadat to come to Jerusalem. Sadat addresses Knesset 20 November. Seligman made Commander of British Empire by H.M. Queen Elizabeth II.

1979 – Peace treaty signed between Egypt and Israel. Seligman named Distinguished Citizen of Tel Aviv. U.S. Embassy taken over by mob in Tehran. All American staffers taken hostage.

1980 – Anti-Israel violence on West Bank.

1981 – Sadat assassinated. Israeli warplanes destroy Iraqi nuclear reactor.

1982 – Ariel Sharon Minister of Defense. Israel invades Lebanon; P.L.O. ousted from southern Lebanon and Beirut. Premier Bashir Gemayel assassinated. Christian militiamen massacre Palestinians at Sabra and Chattila.

1983 – I.D.F. pulls back to south Lebanon. Begin retires, succeeded by Yitzchak Shamir.

1985 – Seligman leaves for London.

1987 – Max Seligman dies in London 9 September, aged 85.

1989 – English Department at Ben Gurion University dedicated (in March) in memory of Max Seligman.

Glossary

NOTE: Letters following word indicate plural form and origin (e.g., A = Arabic, T = Turkish, etc.)

ABBA (H) – Daddy, father

ALEPH (H) – First letter of Hebrew alphabet

ALIYAH (-OT, H) – Lit. *Ascent*; the act of settling in Eretz Israel

ALLIANCE (F) – *ALLIANCE ISRAELITE*; an educational and social body founded in France and funded mainly by Baron Edmond de Rothschild. Its schools disseminated French culture and were located mostly in the former French colonies of North Africa, but also all over the Middle East. *Alliance* alumni are fluent in French.

ASHKENAZI (-IM, H) – Jews of European descent, as distinct from *SEPHARDIM (q.v.)*, Jews of oriental and Spanish/Portuguese descent.

ASIREI ZION (H) – *Prisoners of Zion*; political prisoners in British jails.

BEDOUIN (A) – Nomadic tribesmen originating in the Arab Peninsula.

BEVINGRAD – (As in Lenin*grad*, Stalin*grad*); nickname for a series of heavily-fortified enclaves in various parts of Palestine, into which the British withdrew during the last months of the Mandate.

BEITAR (H) – a. Bar Kochba's last srtronghold (fell 135C.E.) in the Jewish rebellion against Rome. b. H. acronym of *Brit (q.v.) Yosef Trumpeldor*, a youth movement (begun 1923) founded on the ideologies of Jabotinsky and Trumpeldor, devoted to Zionist education, Hebrew and self-defense, and encouraging Aliyah. Beitar in Palestine was part of the Revisionist *(q.v.)* movement.

BNEI BENYAMIN (H) – *Sons of Benjamin*; a cultural, defense and agricultural assistance association, active from 1921 to WWII, named after Baron Rothschild and Theodor Herzl, whose Hebrew name was Benyamin.

BRIT (H) – Covenant, Alliance.

CHALUTZ (-IM, H) – Pioneer(s), people who settled the land in the "early days."

CHALUTZ ETHIC – The ideology of hard work and self-denial.

CHAZAN (-IM, H) – Cantor.

CHEVRA KADISHA (Aram.) – Lit. *The Holy Brotherhood*; the community-sponsored burial association entrusted with the care and disposal of the dead according to Jewish custom. All deceased persons in Israel are prepared for and buried by the Chevra Kadisha.

C.I.D. – Criminal Investigation Department of the Palestine Police, often likened to the Gestapo.

CINEMA BALASH (A) – A free show.

DRUZE (-IM, A) – Religious extremist sect residing principally in Lebanon, whose faith combines in it elements of Islam, Judaism and Christianity. Druze soldiers served with the IDF, primarily as scouts.

DUNAM (-IM, H) – A land measure unit, about one quarter acre.

EMEK (AMAKIM, H) – *Valley*; the name became synonymous with the Valley of Jezreel, Israel's breadbasket.

ERETZ (ARATZOT, H) – Land, country.

ERETZ YISRA'EL (H) – Land of Israel.

FALAFEL (A) – Israel's national snack: balls of chickpea mash, highly seasoned and deep-fried, eaten with *Tahini* in a *Pita (q.v.)*

GALUT (GALUYOT, H) – The diaspora, exile.

GALILEE (fr.H. GALIL) – Lit. Region, but used to denote the northern part of Israel, divided into Lower and Upper Galilee.

GALILEE, Lake of – Lake Tiberias *(Yam Kinneret.)*

GAZOZ (fr. F. *eau gaseuse*) – Generic term for effervescent soft drinks.

GHAFFIR (T) – Jewish or Arab auxiliary policeman (see NOTER).

HAGANA (H) – *Defense*; the underground military arm of the *Yishuv (q.v.)*, an outgrowth of the earlier *Hashomer (q.v.)*, the first Jewish defensive organization in Palestine. Hagana units were the nucleus of the IDF.

HASHOMER (H) – *The Guard*; turn-of-the-century defense organization for agricultural settlements, forerunner of Hagana.

HAVLAGA (H) – Restraint, as practiced by the Yishuv leadership in the face of provocation, a policy bitterly opposed by the Revisionists (*q.v.*).

HATIKVA (H) – *The Hope*; Hebrew national anthem, adopted by the State of Israel. The words are by poet Naftali Herz Imber, the melody freely adapted from Bedrich Smetana's *The Moldau*.

HERUT (H) – Liberty, the name of the political party which succeeded the *Irgun* tradition, following the underground organization's incorporation into the IDF.

HISTADRUT (H) – Lit. The *Organization*; the first and largest (to this day) labor federation, which controls vital services, such as health insurance, retirement benefits, credit union, etc.

I.D.F. – Israel Defense Force (H. Z'VAH HAGANA LEYISRA'EL, ZAHAL)

IRGUN (IRGUN Z'VA'I LE'UMI, H) – *National Military Organization*; founded 1931 by dissident members of Hagana and Revisionists. Also known as *ETZEL* (acronym), *IZL*, *MA'AMAD* (Class, as in middle-class), *HAFIRMA* (The Firm).

All units of the *Irgun* and its splinter *Lechi (q.v.)* were absorbed into the IDF.

ITONUT (H) – The Press.

KEREN (H) – Fund; *Keren Kayemet Leyisra'el* and *Keren Hayessod* were the two main Zionist development funds, responsible for supporting most agricultural settlements in Palestine from the beginning of the century.

KFAR (-IM, H) – Village.

KIBBUTZ (-IM, H) – Lit. *Gathering*; the name given to communal settlements, whose members share all assets and own no personal property.

KIRYA (KRAYOT, H) – Town.

KISLEV (H) – Name of month corresponding to November-December.

KNESSET (H) – Lit. *Meeting*; Israel's parliament.

KOL NIDREI (H. & Aramaic) – The ceremonial prayer recited three times on *Yom Kippur (q.v.)*

KUPAT CHOLIM (H) – The *Histadrut (q.v.)* and other labor union sick fund, health and social services body.

LAG BE'OMER (H) – Thirty-third day of Omer (harvest); a holiday in May commemorating Bar-Kochba's victory over the Romans, celebrated with bonfires.

LECHI (H. acronym for *Lochamei Cherut Yisra'el)* – Fighters For The Freedom Of Israel, founded in 1940 by Avraham Stern (Code named Ya'ir); known also as *The Stern Group* or *Stern Gang*. Stern was shot in cold blood by officers of the CID *(q.v.)*. Lechi units were absorbed into the IDF.

MAPAI – (H. acronym for *Mifleget Po'alei Eretz Yisra'el);* the main labor party in Palestine.

MARONITE – The main Christian sect in Lebanon. Traditionally, the Lebanese government was headed by a Maronite.

MENORAH (-OT, H) – Candelabrum, a powerful symbol in Jewish tradition.

MIZRACHI (H) – Oriental. *Mizrachi Party*: turn-of-the-century movement founded in Poland, advocating renewal in Eretz Israel according to religious principles.

MUFTI (A) – Moslem religious headman.

MUKHTAR (A) – Village headman, a term also used by early Jewish settlers.

NESSIUT (H) – Lit. *Directorship*.

NO*TER* (-IM, H) – Lit. *Watchman*; auxiliary policemen first recruited by the British during the 1936 riots.

OTTOMAN (T) – Pertaining to Turkey.

PALMACH – H. acronym for *Plugot Machatz* (assault units); Hagana's commando force, further developed in Wingate's *S.N.S. (q.v.)*. Unlike the all-volunteer Hagana, Palmach members were full-time soldiers.

PARABELLUM (Lat.) – *Prepare for War*, brand name of a German-made 9mm. automatic machine pistol, popular since WWI.

PEKIDUT (H) – Bureaucracy.

PESACH (-IM, H) – Passover.

PITA (A) – Flat, round bread (Pocket-bread.)

POGROM (Rus.) – Anti-Jewish riots by incited peasant mobs.

PURIM (H) – Minor holiday in February celebrating the demise of the wicked Haman in the time of Esther and Mordechai, celebrated with masquerades.

REVISIONIST – Right-wing party founded by Jabotinsky.

ROSH HASHANA (H) – Jewish New Year, a high holiday in September.

SAISON (F) – Name given to a period in 1944/5 during which

Hagana cooperated with the British in the persecution of Irgun and Lechi members.

SABRA (A) – The cactus pear; native Israelis are called *Tzabarim (H)* "because they are thorny on the outside and sweet inside."

SHABBAT (-OT, H) – Sabbath.

SEDER (SDARIM, H) – Lit. *Order*; the ceremonial meal of Passover.

SEPHARDI (-IM, H) – Lit. *From Spain*; Jews of Spanish and Portuguese descent, but also those from M.E. countries *(Yotz'ei edot hamizrach)*, as distinct from Ashkenazi (q.v.) Jews.

SHAMASH (-IM, H) – Sexton.

SHECHEM (H) – The Arab town of Nablus.

SHOFAR (-OT, H) – The ram's horn, blown during high holiday services.

S.N.S. – Special Night Squads; commando units recruited from the ranks of Palmach and trained by Capt. Orde Wingate.

SUKKOT (H) – The Feast of Tabernacles.

TAHINI (A) – Sesame-seed sauce mixed with lemon juice, used in many dishes and on *falafel (q.v.)*.

TALMUD TORAH (H) – Lit. *Learning the Torah (q.v.)*;a school devoted exclusively to Jewish religious studies.

TEFILIN (H) – Phylacteries.

TEL (TILIM, H) – A raised place, hill (*Tel* Aviv = Hill of Spring.)

TORAH (-OT, H) – Lit. *Law*; the Pentateuch, knowledge.

TZADIK (-IM, H) – A very pious person, given to charity and good deeds.

UNDERGROUND – (H. *Machteret*); the collective name given to all organizations whose activities were deemed illegal by the British.

VA'AD LE'UMI (-OT, H) – Lit. *National Commitee*; the organization representing the *Yishuv (q.v.)* in its internal dealings and vis-a-vis the British.

WHITEHALL – The seat of the British Government in London.

YEKEH (-IM, Y) A Jew of German descent, a term often used derisively to indicate a naive person, a newcomer.

YEMENITE – Jews from Yemen in the Arab peninsula. In the early days of the *Yishuv (q.v.)*, Yemenite Jews lived in the poorer areas of town and worked at menial jobs.

YESSOD (-OT, H) – Lit. *Foundation*; (See Keren Hayessod).

YIDDISH (H. *Idit)* – A medieval German dialect of the Rhine basin, adopted by European Jews, Hebrew being the Sacred Tongue reserved for study and prayer. Wherever used, Yiddish absorbed much of the local idiom.

YISHUV (-IM, H) – Lit. *Settlement*; the collective name for the Jewish population in Palestine.

YOM KIPPUR (-IM, H) – The Day of Atonement. A day of fasting and prayer, it is the holiest day in the Jewish calendar.

YOM TOV (H.pl: Yamim tovim; Y: Yontev) – Lit. *Good Day*; holiday.

ZECHUTENU (fr. Zechut [Zechuyot], H) – *Our Right*; name of Revisionist movement devoted to protecting the Yishuv's rights under the British Mandate.

Index

Note: The frequently occurring references to Max Seligman and Max Kritzman have not been included in the index. For the sake of economy, place and other names such as Hagana, Herzl, Irgun, etc. have also been omitted from the index.